BILLION DOLLAR
BRAND CLUB

BILLION DOLLAR BRAND CLUB

How Dollar Shave Club, Warby Parker, and Other Disruptors Are Remaking What We Buy

LAWRENCE INGRASSIA

HENRY HOLT AND COMPANY

NEW YORK

Henry Holt and Company
Publishers since 1866
120 Broadway
New York, New York 10271
www.henryholt.com

Library of Congress Cataloging-in-Publication Data

Names: Ingrassia, Lawrence, author.
Title: Billion dollar brand club : how Dollar Shave Club, Warby Parker, and other
 disruptors are remaking what we buy / Lawrence Ingrassia.
Description: First edition. | New York : Henry Holt and Company, 2020. |
 Includes index.
Identifiers: LCCN 2019029390 | ISBN 9781250313065 (hardback) |
 ISBN 9781250313058 (ebook)
Subjects: LCSH: New business enterprises—United States. |
 Branding (Marketing)—United States. | Disruptive technologies—
 United States.
Classification: LCC HD62.5 .I545 2020 | DDC 658.8/27—dc23
LC record available at https://lccn.loc.gov/2019029390

International edition ISBN: 9781250759252

Our books may be purchased in bulk for promotional, educational, or business
use. Please contact your local bookseller or the Macmillan Corporate and
Premium Sales Department at (800) 221-7945, extension 5442, or by e-mail at
MacmillanSpecialMarkets@macmillan.com.

First Edition 2020

Designed by Meryl Sussman Levavi

Printed in the United States of America

1 3 5 7 9 10 8 6 4 2

For Vicki, always.
You are my everything.

Contents

1. Our Blades Are F**king Great   1

2. The Pied Pipers of Disruption   23

3. Making It in the World Bazaar   44

4. Survival of the Fittest   58

5. From Mad Men to Math Men   70

6. The Algorithm Is Always Right   84

7. Eyes on the Customers   97

8. Delivering the Goods   114

9. The Mattress Wars   132

10. Breaking the Sound Barrier   152

11. Flying High, Then Crashing to Earth   166

12. Back to the Future?   182

13. Building a Digital Brand Factory   200

14. The Brand Is Dead, Long Live the Brand   217

Notes   223

Acknowledgments   243

Index   247

BILLION DOLLAR
BRAND CLUB

1

Our Blades Are F**king Great

At 6:15 in the morning on Tuesday, March 6, 2012, Michael Dubin woke up and immediately checked his computer. He was puzzled by what he saw—actually, by what he *didn't* see. Before going to bed, he had posted a video about his start-up, a company that virtually no one had ever heard of.

His venture's website wasn't working that morning. Even though everything had been fine the night before, the site had crashed, and all he saw now was a blank screen. So, he quickly hopped in the shower before heading to sort things out at the cramped office he shared at a start-up incubator with a bunch of other entrepreneurs striving to get off the ground.

Dubin was thirty-three years old. He was at this point an unsuccessful—well, failed—entrepreneur. A few years earlier, after the financial market meltdown, he had gotten laid off from a digital marketing job at Time Inc.'s *Sports Illustrated Kids* and had applied to Columbia, New York University, UCLA, and a few other business schools to get an MBA. He was turned down by all of them. Frustrated, he'd moved to Los Angeles, where he stayed rent-free at a cousin's apartment initially, while deciding what he wanted to do.

Tall and charming, with an easy smile and a winning personality, Dubin had studied improv on and off for eight years at Upright Citizens Brigade in New York City while dabbling in entrepreneurial ventures. As a side project, he started a social media network for travelers in 2006, not long after Mark Zuckerberg started Facebook. It never went anywhere. "My basement has a corner of what I call the failed business corner," his mother would later tell a journalist. "And we have a number of things that we have bought and he made me invest in that he thought would be very successful businesses, which obviously they weren't."

After leaving Time Inc., he used his marketing skills to do some consulting work for friends who had a Christmas holiday decoration business. Then he worked at a digital marketing firm in Los Angeles, developing and placing promotional videos online for corporations such as Ford. After less than a year, he departed after a disagreement with his boss over the company's strategy.

His friends wondered if he'd ever find anything he was both good at and liked.

Now Dubin was working on his most ambitious idea yet. In the eyes of many friends, it was grandiose. Or perhaps *quixotic* would be a better word to describe it. His start-up was Dollar Shave Club, a David taking on a Goliath known as Gillette. Dubin had already spent more than a year on it, but rather predictably, the business had gotten off to a slow start.

What happened on the morning of March 6 would change that, thanks to his start-up's one-minute, thirty-three-second video. As he headed from the converted garage where he was living to his nearby office in Santa Monica, California, the good news was that the video was going viral—a whole lot of people had been watching it. The bad news was that so many people were trying to watch it that the website server was crashing or, when it did work, was sluggish.

The tech company managing the Dollar Shave Club website had put an expert to work trying to fix the problem—then a second, then a third, with little success. At 10:30 that morning, the head of the tech firm sent an unnerving email to Dubin and his colleagues: "We have been working for three hours already to keep it working stable. And we need more work here." Hours later, the website was still crashing. One of Dubin's colleagues shot off an angry email to the tech firm: "Can you please come to our office right now? . . . it's 2 p.m. guys. It's 2 p.m. and dollar shave club is still down . . . this is unacceptable."

Dubin was in a panic. A week earlier, he had told the tech guys he thought his video was going to generate a lot of traffic and had urged them to be ready. Now this. With the website working intermittently, few people could watch the video, and it was also hard for them to place orders. It was a disaster in the making. After all his false starts, this was his big chance.

What he didn't know at the time—what no one knew—was that the humorous video, painstakingly written and rewritten over months and then shot in a single day at a total cost of just $4,500, would humble one of the most dominant and storied consumer companies in the annals of American business.

Against all odds, Dollar Shave Club would go on to succeed wildly, taking a big chunk of its giant rival's market share and forcing it to cut prices for the first time in memory. More than that, Dubin, in the process, helped announce a disruptive business model for twenty-first-century entrepreneurs to take on previously unassailable consumer brands.

In most ways, Michael Dubin, the founder of Dollar Shave Club, could hardly be more different from King C. Gillette, the founder of Gillette, his century-old rival. But each man was emblematic of the capitalist zeitgeist of his era—the changing nature of innovation, the way consumer brands were produced, how and where they were sold, and even how wealth was created.

Like a lot of entrepreneurs of his epoch, King Gillette was an inventor. The turn of the twentieth century was a time when America's industrial prowess was emerging and combining with marketing to feed the nascent middle class's growing appetite for consumer goods. Make a product better and you could become rich. Levi Strauss had amply demonstrated this decades earlier. In the 1870s, his company started making denim trousers using an innovation suggested by a customer: it strengthened them with copper rivets in places where the fabric was most prone to ripping.

King Gillette wasn't the first to come up with the idea of a safety razor to replace the straight razor that needed sharpening with a leather strop. But after several years of tinkering, he invented a way to dramatically improve it. On December 3, 1901, he submitted a patent application (later approved) with elaborate drawings showing a razor handle with a thin, disposable double-edge steel blade—"two cutting edges, so that the life of a blade may thus be doubled"—designed to provide a close shave while protecting the face from cuts. There was no need ever to sharpen it because the consumer could throw the blade away and easily replace it—which meant another sale for Gillette every time he did.

In 1903, when the Gillette razor went into production, the company sold all of 51 razors and 168 blades. But the next year, as word of how good it was spread, 90,000 razors and 15 million blades were sold. Gillette's razor became one of the most enduring and iconic products in the history of brands.

Michael Dubin is not an inventor; he has no patents to his name. But like King Gillette, he seized on a transformational idea: technology has the potential to change the world of physical goods and the way brands are created. Dubin recognized that technology and globalization were leveling the playing field in every imaginable way. You didn't need to start with a big advertising budget to get the attention of consumers and take on an established rival. You didn't need an expensive manufacturing plant. You didn't need to spend millions of dollars on research and development. And you didn't need a retailer to carry your product.

By targeting a corporate giant's weakness (high prices or inconvenience or a stodgy image), a clever start-up with the right strategy, the right message, and the right product value could create a new brand virtually overnight. Indeed, the terms of competition were being upended, enabling new entrants to gobble up territory. All this was happening at a time when growing legions of consumers in their twenties and thirties were up for grabs. Unlike their parents, they weren't yet attached to long-favored brands. They lived digital lives, and were accustomed to—happy to!—buy things online. All this was happening just as buying anything and everything online was becoming easier and easier, and delivery of what you bought was becoming faster and faster.

Michael Dubin was one of the entrepreneurs at the vanguard of this revolution, though that wasn't exactly what he was thinking when he first got the idea of selling razors and blades on the internet.

* * *

Out of work, Dubin was looking for his next opportunity when he attended a friend's holiday party in Beverly Hills in December 2010. At the party, he started schmoozing with Mark Levine, his friend's father. Levine, who was fifty-six, had an odd assortment of consumer products he'd purchased in bulk a while back that he was having a hard time unloading, including cake slicers and off-brand razors and blades (some 250,000 twin-blade cartridges in all). All were sitting in a nearby warehouse running up unpaid storage fees, a fact he didn't bother to mention to Dubin when they met.

"Oh, you're the internet guy," he said to Dubin. "Can you help me sell them?"

"Not the cake slicers. But maybe the razors," Dubin replied.

The conversation got Dubin thinking. He hated purchasing razors at a store. Gillette's top-of-the-line blade cartridges, which cost $5, were obscenely expensive. Adding aggravation, the blades were rarely stocked on store shelves—their small size made them easy to steal, so many retailers stocked them behind the counter or kept them in a locked case. They were like contraband: to buy them, you had to ask for them. What a hassle. Dubin knew a lot of guys who felt the same.

A few weeks after they met, Dubin agreed to go into business with Levine, investing $25,000 (most of his life savings at the time), figuring he could sell Levine's stash of blades online. By pricing the blades at just $1 each, he calculated, he could pocket a very nice profit and maybe even start building a business. Dollar Shave Club was born.

By the middle of 2011, Dubin had launched a beta website and for several months sold the blades—though he had to pay $800 in overdue storage fees just to get access to them.

The response by customers was . . . well, underwhelming. Dubin did sell some blades, but most people would come once, buy a supply, and then disappear. So, he decided to test a monthly subscription model, to keep customers coming back. This was critical because the customer acquisition cost (CAC in marketing jargon), that is, the amount you spend on marketing and advertising to bring in a customer, needs to be offset by how much that customer spends buying your product over time.

About a thousand people signed up, which gave Dubin confidence that he could sell razor blades online. Still, to have any chance of succeeding, he knew he needed to get the attention of a much larger pool of potential customers—young guys like him who didn't have the money to spend on expensive blades and who weren't as tied to Gillette as older men.

Dubin had little money for advertising, so he started thinking about making a video to post online. He wrote a script and called Lucia Aniello, a friend from improv acting circles in New York, who was now a director in Los Angeles.

At 7:30 on a Saturday morning in October 2011, Dubin and a couple of friends he asked to play parts gathered in a warehouse on a drab industrial strip in Gardena, near Los Angeles International Airport, where the boxes of unsold blades were stored. They were finished by 4:00 that afternoon.

The video, as with improv, seems informal when you're watching it, even casual. But that was all for effect. Every scene, every line, had been written and rewritten to communicate a specific message: price, quality, convenience. And the video had to be irreverent and make viewers laugh, so they would share it with their friends. The script initially ran about four pages, but Aniello helped cut it in half. They didn't want wasted words that might give viewers a reason to stop watching.

"Razors are an oddly emotional business," says Dubin, who plays the starring role in the video. "I wanted people to say to each other,

'Remember how we were talking about razors being so expensive to buy? This video is hilarious.'"

One challenge, he knew, was that potential customers would wonder about the quality of the blades. Every guy wants a cheap shave, but no one wants nicks and cuts all over his face. Rather than skirt the question, he decided to hit it head-on with humor. The video starts with Dubin on camera introducing himself and the company: "What is DollarShaveClub.com? Well, for a dollar a month we send high-quality razors right to your door. Yeah! A dollar!"

Next, just fifteen seconds into the video, Dubin poses the question he knew viewers would be asking: "Are the blades any good? No," he says, pausing briefly before delivering the punch line: "Our blades are f**king great!" To punctuate the point, he gestures to a fluorescent orange poster with those words in white letters. All this is delivered deadpan, with a straight face.

The line was suggested by Aniello, as they tried to come up with something that would grab the viewer. "I remember Mike's face when I first said that line. There was a half a second of concern, and then whatever angel [was] sitting on his shoulder—or devil, maybe—said, *Go for it*," Aniello would recall to a reporter.

Dubin also takes potshots at Gillette throughout the video (though never by name), to make sure no one misses the point of how expensive its products are. "Do you like spending twenty dollars a month on brand-name razors? Nineteen go to Roger Federer," he says, alluding to Gillette's well-paid pitchman. "And do you think your razor needs a vibrating handle, a flashlight, a back scratcher, and ten blades? Your handsome-ass grandfather had one blade, and polio." He concludes, "Stop forgetting to buy your blades every month and start deciding where you're going to stack all those dollar bills I'm saving you."

The video ends with a simple and memorable slogan: "Shave time. Shave money."

Dubin was confident he had nailed it with the video, but he still needed funding if the company was to have a chance. Even at the video's low cost, the venture was running short of cash. So, he got a friend to arrange a meeting with Michael Jones, the cofounder of Science Inc., a

Santa Monica venture capital incubator firm. Jones had been a successful entrepreneur himself, most recently as chief executive of Myspace,
before deciding to use his knowledge to help early-stage start-ups. If
Jones liked an idea, Science would provide seed money in return for
a small stake, as well as advice and shared office space (really just a
desk and internet connections). Jones also used his Rolodex to recruit
managers, whom entrepreneurs like Dubin often needed to help with
different aspects of running a business.

Jones wasn't especially enthusiastic when he got Dubin's call in the
fall of 2011. *Razor blades?* "I was skeptical," he recalls. "My partners
were, too. Razors are a hard market to crack. There is a big, dominant
competitor. And Michael didn't actually make anything. He bought the
blades from someone else."

The meeting didn't go well initially, as Jones grilled Dubin on the
particulars. Yes, the blades would be cheaper than Gillette's, and the
subscription model sounded intriguing, but the Dollar Shave Club web-
page looked amateurish. "I have a lot of knowledge about how consumers interact with buttons and colors on a web page, and what I saw
was pretty bad," he says.

Jones was about to say "thanks, but no thanks," but then Dubin
said he had filmed a marketing video. It was short. Could he at least
show it to him?

"When I saw the video," Jones recalls, "it hit me. You could crack
YouTube and really connect with the consumer. By the end, I told him,
'I get it.' It was fantastic."

Soon after, Science agreed to invest $100,000 in Dollar Shave Club.
Tom Dare, Science's chief financial officer, wrote Dubin a check, which
Dubin excitedly raced to a nearby bank to deposit. Only when he got
there did he realize that the check had been mistakenly written for only
$100, causing some embarrassment and laughter when Dubin promptly
"came back from the bank looking flushed," recalls Dare, who issued
a new check.

But $100,000 was only enough money to start hiring a small team
and improve the website. The next step was to try to raise enough additional funding to finance ongoing operations and pay for a new supply

of blades. Peter Pham, a cofounder of Science with Jones, proceeded to take Dubin on a series of trips to meet venture capitalists in Silicon Valley.

The initial reaction of everyone there was, again, skepticism: *Razor blades?*

Pham has raised money for dozens of start-ups. Dollar Shave Club was among the hardest to sell to investors. This was in the very early days of digitally native brands that were bypassing retailers and selling directly to consumers on the internet. The men's clothing company Bonobos was about five years old, and Warby Parker, the eyeglass start-up, had launched in 2010. But there wasn't much else.

Starting in January 2012, Pham contacted about seventy venture capital firms, and he and Dubin went to San Francisco a dozen times, often booking Airbnb rooms rather than staying in hotels, to save money. One problem they encountered: When Silicon Valley venture capital firms thought of disruption, they thought of companies like Facebook and Google, Twitter and YouTube, Instagram and Snapchat. They rarely thought of physical products such as clothing or eyeglasses or razors. Those are commodity products, often dominated by big multinational companies. "Dollar Shave Club wasn't tech. Or wasn't considered tech at the time, and these were tech investors," Pham recalls.

Even when they managed to schedule meetings, most of the investors they spoke with didn't get it. "Venture capitalists are rich. They couldn't figure out why people would need to save money on razors," Pham says. "They don't understand that there is a massive population of people who can't show up to work with facial hair, people in the military or companies that frown on guys with beards, who couldn't afford thirty dollars a month to shave with Gillette razors."

And many couldn't fathom the idea of taking on Gillette, Pham continues. "They asked, 'What if Gillette does this, starts its own online subscription service and lowers prices?' I said, 'They're not going to do that because they can't get out of their own fucking way. They can't cut prices, because there's the pressure of delivering earnings for the next quarter. And they don't want to go online and screw up their relations with retailers.'"

Most VC investors flat-out said no. But a few, like Mike Jones, were amused and intrigued when they saw the funny video Dubin had shot. One investor agreed to ante up $250,000. But, reflecting the feeling that this was a real long shot, most firms put up what were, for them, paltry sums: $50,000, or even $25,000. After nearly seven weeks of pleading and cajoling, Pham and Dubin managed to raise $950,000, falling just shy of their goal of $1 million but garnering enough to relaunch Dollar Shave Club.

Even as Dubin was starting to work with Pham to raise money, he was searching for an answer to another problem: a source of better razors and blades. The initial batch his partner Mark Levine had purchased and stored in the warehouse were old-fashioned twin-blade razors, which were unlikely to be good enough to attract repeat customers. If a purchaser tried the blades and didn't like them, there was a big risk he would cancel his subscription and never come back. Dubin needed to find a quality manufacturer to supply state-of-the-art four-blade and six-blade razors he could put Dollar Shave Club's name on.

Levine knew someone who had connections to foreign manufacturers and offered to make introductions. One option was Kai, a Japanese razor company. Another was Dorco, a Korean manufacturer with a U.S. subsidiary in San Diego. That was a lot closer to Los Angeles, so Dubin headed down the coast to meet with Ken Hill, a razor industry veteran who had been president of Dorco's U.S. business for about a year.

As a favor to an old friend, Hill agreed to meet Dubin. Like the Silicon Valley venture capitalists, he wasn't exactly wowed by Dubin or his pitch. "He showed up in white pants and sneakers. He looked like he had just rolled out of bed," Hill recalls. "I've been in this business for a long time. I don't see how this subscription idea could possibly work." But what the heck, he figured. "Okay, Michael, sure, good luck. We'll sell you as many blades as you want—as long as you pay for the product in full, up front."

Dollar Shave Club finally had all the pieces in place.

The amount of VC funding he had for his start-up was too small to get much notice in the media. Hoping for some buzz, Dubin decided to hold off announcing the news, so it would coincide with the debut of the video. He also hired a public relations firm that gave a handful of tech media outlets a sneak preview of the video. For the release date, he chose March 6, which was the start of the annual South by Southwest digital media conference in Austin, Texas. If people there liked the video, it could create an echo-chamber effect online and draw attention elsewhere.

It worked. The morning the video was posted, Twitter exploded with hundreds of you-gotta-see-this comments.

> I don't shave often, but if I have to, I will use #dollarshaveclub, just for their wicked video.

> Awesome!! Finally don't have to chop off an arm and a leg just to get a shave.

> Watch this! Freakin' brilliant video by start-up @ DollarShaveClub.

> That Dollar Shave Club commercial is awesome.

But inside Dollar Shave Club and Science, there was anxiety. TulaCo, the small Santa Monica company hired a few weeks earlier to manage the website, was under siege. Steve Lackenby, TulaCo's cofounder, had cautioned Dubin that Dollar Shave Club's site was built on a clunky platform without enough computer servers to support much traffic. TulaCo had tweaked some things to improve its performance, so Lackenby wasn't worried going into that morning. "For ninety-nine out of a hundred companies, it would have been fine. You go live with the website, and it's crickets," he says, joking about the sound you hear in the background when things are quiet. He had dealt with many entrepreneurs who were wildly optimistic about the attention they would get. "You may tell me that you think you're going to get hundreds of thousands of people to come to your website, but I'm saying to myself, 'Good luck with that.'"

Lackenby could hardly have been more wrong. With high traffic crashing the website, the TulaCo team worked frantically throughout the night before finally managing to stabilize the site so it could handle the huge volume of viewers.

Within forty-eight hours of the video's launch, Dollar Shave Club had twelve thousand subscribers, exceeding expectations so much that Dubin and his small team of a half dozen employees worked into the evening pasting on shipment labels by hand because they didn't yet have any automated equipment. The company briefly ran out of blades to ship and sent emails to customers begging them to be patient.

* * *

Across the country, at Gillette's headquarters in Boston, the reaction was a collective yawn. Okay, Dubin's video was humorous. But the blades themselves?

"Their blades are not fucking great. It's just not true," a former Gillette senior executive recalls thinking at the time. "Our customers love our product, and they're not going to switch to this piece of junk. In a head-to-head test with our blades, they got slaughtered." Another former executive says, dismissively, "Even the handles of Dollar Shave Club's razors are clunky!"

Gillette researchers, in fact, had already tested the blades that Dollar Shave Club was selling. Gillette maintains a sophisticated R&D laboratory that employs hundreds of scientists—metallurgists, dermatologists, chemists, ergonomics experts. The company spends millions of dollars a year checking the quality of its own blades (how sharp they are, how long they last before starting to dull, when they become prone to cause abrasions) and the quality of rivals' blades as well.

As Gillette knew from its surveillance of everything to do with blades and razors, Dollar Shave Club didn't make its blades. It just put its name on them after buying them from Dorco.

Founded in 1955 as a knife maker, Dorco began making razors and blades in 1962. It didn't have to compete with Gillette back then because its home market in South Korea was largely closed to imports until the late 1980s. Dorco is the top-selling brand only in South Korea, with about 40 percent of the volume by units sold, and is outgunned by Gillette in the rest of Asia and the world.

Dorco had begun selling blades in the United States several decades before its relationship with Dollar Shave Club. But most of its sales weren't under its own name. Instead, it had largely been confined to selling inexpensive "white label" store brands, blades made on contract for retailers such as Kmart, 7-Eleven, and Aldi. Indeed, before Dollar Shave Club came along, Dorco's market share in the United States was a minuscule 1 percent.

"Gillette knew more about Dorco blades than Michael Dubin did," says Mike Norton, a former Gillette executive. "Our side-by-side tests would prove to you that you could take any Gillette razor, and it would be better than Dollar Shave Club." That includes the Gillette Mach3, he claims, referring to a model introduced way back in 1998.

Thanks to this obsessive attention to quality and detail, few companies have dominated any consumer product so much or for so long as Gillette. After successfully storming the market in the early twentieth century with its groundbreaking double-edge disposable blades, Gillette entrenched itself as the razor and blade of choice thanks in part to the U.S. government. During World War I, the military ordered 3.5 million razors and 36 million blades for troops. When the Doughboys returned home with their Gillette razors in hand, most naturally bought Gillette blades that fit them.

Gillette wasn't good just at innovative and efficient manufacturing; its marketing was brilliant as well. It was among the first consumer brands to recognize the potential of sports marketing. In 1939, sales soared after it bought the radio broadcast advertising rights to the World Series, which it continued to sponsor for decades. It cemented this strategy a few years later, when it began sponsoring the *Cavalcade of Sports*. What was perhaps its most famous slogan, "The best a man can get," was launched during the 1989 Super Bowl.

Competitors came along now and then, but they barely dented Gillette's business. England's Wilkinson Sword Co. stole a march on Gillette in the early 1960s with stainless steel blades that resisted corrosion and stayed sharp longer. Then, in the mid-1970s, Bic pioneered the disposable razor. But Gillette scientists created most of the innovations in shaving—the company has thousands of patents—and any small losses in market share were quickly recovered.

Little wonder that Gillette's market share for decades had hovered around a virtually monopolistic 70 percent—unheard of for a consumer product. The company was impregnable, selling $4 billion in razors and blades worldwide every year and traditionally enjoying rich profit margins of around 50 to 60 percent—which prompted the consumer product giant Procter & Gamble to buy Gillette in 2005 for about $55 billion.

The reaction to Dollar Shave Club's video was much the same at Schick, long the distant number two in the U.S. market. Brad Harrison, then head of Schick marketing, recalls, "When the video came out, my team and I joked that we should start a drinking game and swallow a shot every time someone forwards it to us. Friends, family members—everybody I knew was forwarding it to me. There must have been at least fifty."

Dubin's pitch was very funny, they all agreed. "We went online and bought a batch of every type of blade they were selling," Harrison says. "Sent it to our lab. Tested them ourselves. We said, 'Whew, it's a pretty crappy product. It won't stick. They'll get a lot of people to try it because of the video but will never get repeat customers.' Okay, 'sucks' is probably too harsh. But it isn't on par with anything that Schick or Gillette makes. This will pass."

* * *

David Pakman had a very different reaction. "I live on Twitter, and was sitting at my desk in my office in New York when I saw all these messages about this video going viral."

Pakman is a partner at Venrock Associates, a venture capital firm. In his small, twenty-second-floor corner office overlooking Fifth Avenue in Midtown Manhattan, he stopped everything he was doing and watched the video not once but a half dozen times, even though he was frustrated by how slow Dollar Shave Club's site was. "I remember clicking through and laughing out loud and thinking, 'This guy is hysterical and brilliant.'"

Like the people at Gillette, Pakman wondered how good the blades were, so he placed an order online. Even he agreed, when he finally got them and tested them at home, that Gillette's were better. "I tried Dollar Shave Club's blades and thought they were pretty good, but not great."

But here's the thing, he thought: Pretty good actually might be more than good enough for most guys, especially considering that Dollar Shave Club's blades cost about half the price of Gillette's. (Dubin's company charged $4 for five of its old-fashioned, lowest-quality two-blade cartridges, or just 80 cents each, but its better blades actually cost more than a dollar each. Despite the company's name, it charged $6 for four four-blade cartridges and $9 for four six-blade cartridges.) And you didn't have to go to a store and wait for a clerk to get them from a locked cabinet behind the counter. Dollar Shave Club would mail blades to you every month.

Price and convenience, plus clever marketing that appealed to young men—Pakman had a hunch that Dubin was on to something.

Pakman had once been an internet entrepreneur himself, working for several music download services starting in the late 1990s. On his office wall hung framed stories from *Fortune* and *USA Today* about a company he ran called eMusic, a leading online retailer of independent music before Apple came along with iTunes.

But the Dollar Shave Club video caught his attention not just because it was funny but because it came along when he was looking for companies that would help test an idea he had: "I have a specific investment thesis. The best opportunities exist where there is an underlying innovation that is slow to be appreciated by incumbents. If the disruption is big enough, the start-up can ride the wave, because it takes a while for the incumbent to realize it faces a big challenge and to adapt to the threat."

Granted, Dollar Shave Club didn't have an innovative product, but it did have an innovative idea. Pakman grasped that Gillette was vulnerable despite its being the dominant player—or, actually, it was vulnerable precisely *because* it was such a dominant player and had been for so long. Its strength could also be its weakness: It was so successful that it couldn't fully comprehend the disruption that could be caused by a start-up with a "good enough" product using the internet to level the playing field and change the rules of the game.

Gillette may offer the best shave, Pakman thought to himself, but Dollar Shave Club was offering the best *value*. And that wouldn't occur to Gillette because it was overconfident, even arrogant—and because reacting too soon or too much could lower profits. And then Gillette's senior executives would have a lot of explaining to do with their bosses at Procter & Gamble, who needed earnings to keep growing to justify the tens of billions they had spent buying Gillette.

Pakman's instinct was right. A few Gillette insiders also wondered if this guy Dubin might be on to something. "I could probably recite every line of that video," says David Sylvia, a Gillette executive at the time. "Some of us were certainly watching it in our own cubicles and offices." For most executives, however, protecting the razor-and-blade piggy bank was paramount. At meetings to discuss this new, tiny competitor with the funny video, a price cut (or any other serious response to crush Dollar Shave Club early on) never came up. "We'll just ride them out," another Gillette executive recalls as the thrust of the conversations. "We're going to ignore them. They're not well funded."

This would soon change, thanks to Pakman. Within days of seeing the video, he reached out to Dubin and Peter Pham at Science Inc. After visiting with Dubin for several days in June, Pakman was even more convinced that the idea could be a winner, and he wanted to invest money—which Dollar Shave Club needed, to spend more on marketing and take advantage of the early attention. Pakman liked the subscription model, and the early retention rate was strong. And he liked Dubin's vision of building a lifestyle brand with clever marketing to Millennials.

His biggest worry wasn't about competing with Gillette. Rather, he was concerned that Dollar Shave Club's big-name initial seed investors, including Silicon Valley VC firms Kleiner Perkins and Battery Ventures, would decide to invest *more* and elbow his firm aside.

After all, Dollar Shave Club was doing better than even Jones or Pham had dared dream possible; three months after the video was posted on YouTube, it had been viewed 4.75 million times. "We predicted a half million dollars in revenue by the end of 2012. We hit that after one quarter," Pham says. Sales for all of 2012 would end up at $4 million.

To Pakman's surprise, however, some of the initial VC investors didn't want to put in more money. Undeterred, Pakman got Venrock to invest, and four VC firms in the original financing ponied up more money—some after being cajoled by Peter Pham—for an additional $9.8 million in funding in November 2012. Among these were Science and Forerunner Ventures, which had been the biggest investor in the initial round. Kirsten Green, its founder, who had a background in retailing and sensed that e-commerce offered a new way to create brands, also had taken a seat on Dollar Shave Club's board; Pakman, who would later lead another round of VC funding, became a director, too. The overall investment would eventually total about $163 million over a half dozen rounds, which funded more marketing and more hiring. Raising money got easier as Dollar Shave Club's sales grew, but still, Pham notes, "The number of nos we got was in the hundreds over time." Some of the early VC investors, in fact, even bailed out in early 2014, unloading their initial investment to Venrock. "Would you buy our shares? We don't have the conviction in this company long term," Pakman recalls them saying.

One potential investor that turned Pham down was Gillette. He had approached Dubin's rival, figuring an alliance might be good for both. "They have a venture arm that makes investments. At one point, I called Gillette's head of corporate development about making an investment. He said they weren't interested," he says. "They were overconfident. Their attitude was 'Why do we need that? We own the market.'"

Dollar Shave Club's relationship with Dorco also had a tense moment early on. Dorco was happy with the new business it was getting; it now needed to invest more of its own money and ramp up production to meet the fast-growing orders from Dubin's customers. So, in the fall of 2012, at the suggestion of Ken Hill, its U.S. head, it asked for—well, insisted on—getting shares in Dollar Shave Club.

"We had a lot of leverage. Michael didn't have a lot of options. He had seeded his initial customer base with razors he bought from us, and to go with anyone else at that point would have been hard for him," Hill recalls. Dorco's owners left the negotiations to Hill, as they thought the stock would never amount to much. He won't say what percentage ownership Dorco got, except that it was between 5 percent and 8 percent. The price? Zero. As part of the deal, Dorco signed a long-term agreement to supply razors and blades to Dollar Shave Club until 2019.

Dubin had little choice but to acquiesce and give a piece of his company to Dorco. "Let's just say that I understood the importance of the supply chain and wanted to make that deal," he says.

While Gillette and Schick still weren't paying much attention to Dollar Shave Club's early success, others were. Jeffrey Raider, one of the four cofounders of Warby Parker, the online eyeglass company, helped start a copycat competitor, Harry's; in 2013, it started selling razors and blades made by a German manufacturer, which Harry's would eventually buy, pursuing a different strategy from Dollar Shave Club's supplier relationship with Dorco.

The razor wars were heating up. To fuel its advantage as the first direct-to-consumer razor brand, Dollar Shave Club plowed much of its revenue, along with millions of dollars raised from subsequent investment rounds, into marketing. In 2013, it became one of the first consumer-product companies to recognize the power of social media advertising and hired the start-up digital marketing firm Ampush, in San Francisco, which specialized in Facebook analytics, to demograph-ically target likely Dollar Shave Club customers, a tactic that would soon be used by virtually all other digitally native brands.

By 2015, Dollar Shave Club, while best known for its viral video and its Facebook marketing, was ratcheting up its spending on TV commercials to the tune of millions of dollars a month, to steal even more business from Gillette. None of its later ads would come close to the cult success of the first video, which to date has more than

26 million views on YouTube. But most kept to Dubin's formula of cheeky, jaunty humor, hitting hard on the high price of other blades (i.e., Gillette's) and how frustrating it is to buy them in a store. One commercial showed a stern store clerk dressed like a security guard first grilling and then Tasering a customer who said he wanted to "grab" a few blades from a locked case. Many of the ads featured Dubin making a cameo appearance, a visual reminder that—yeah!—this was the company with the "Our blades are f**king great!" video.

Dollar Shave Club's annual sales for 2015 hit $153 million, up from just $20 million two years earlier. And in 2016, only a few years after it arrived on the scene, the company would control about 8 percent of the razor-and-blade market as measured in dollars in the United States. (Dubin claimed double that percentage in unit volume, because its blades cost less.) Gillette's market share had plummeted in the same period, to about 54 percent from 67 percent.

Some chest thumping was in order. As a way of signaling that it was no longer a tiny wannabe, Dollar Shave Club spent a couple million dollars for a thirty-second commercial during the 2016 Super Bowl. Many board members worried that it would be a waste of money, but Dubin persisted, arguing that "in the advertising world, the Super Bowl is the big boys' game, and we're going to be taken much more seriously."

Even as Gillette's market share kept declining, its response was tepid. It tried to counter with its own Facebook video ad, which was mocked widely as a lame response to Dollar Shave Club's. In 2014, it introduced the me-too "Our Shave Club," but to avoid angering stores that sold Gillette blades, it required customers to initially subscribe through a "preferred retailer" rather than directly from Gillette. "We never wanted to have to be called into Walmart and told, 'Wait a minute, you're selling razors direct to the consumer? You sell through us, or we're going to take your razors out of here.' The risk-reward wasn't big enough," explains Mike Norton, the former Gillette executive, echoing Peter Pham's prediction from back in 2012 about the dilemma Gillette would face in responding to Dubin's threat.

Still, Gillette stubbornly refused to reduce prices. In one ad, the company lamely, laughably, asserted that its blades were up to 50 percent cheaper than the "other shave club." How could that possibly be? Well, the claim was based on using a Gillette blade for a month, versus a week for its rival.

So, Dollar Shave Club kept hammering at "shave tech you don't need," denigrating the bells and whistles of Gillette's razors and the high cost of its rival's blades. One ad simply showed side-by-side photos of packages of four three-blade cartridges with only the words "OURS $6.00. THEIRS $18.00." The company also included pithy, humorous messages on the packages delivered by mail to its subscribers: "'I like shaving with a dull razor.' *No one, ever*. CHANGE YOUR BLADE EVERY WEEK."

Meanwhile, Gillette executives blandly, and cluelessly, kept repeating their traditional "But our blades are better!" mantra. "Gillette's product is significantly consumer preferred over any and all shave club competition, winning on closeness, smoothness, comfort, and eighteen other attributes tested, including importantly, overall better shaves," Jon R. Moeller, the chief financial officer for Procter & Gamble, told Wall Street investors in October 2015.

It didn't matter to Dollar Shave Club's legion of more than 2.5 million subscribers that just about everyone—including independent testers such as *Consumer Reports*—agreed that Gillette provided a superior shave.

Frustrated, Gillette filed a lawsuit against Dollar Shave Club in December 2015, alleging patent infringement, a sign in Pakman's eyes that it was getting worried. The patent in question was for the protective coating applied to the edge of the blades so they wouldn't corrode and thus would stay sharp longer; the litigation was subsequently settled without any terms disclosed. To Pakman, each move by Gillette came out of the standard playbook of how an entrenched giant reacts. "We count on this behavior when we invest. It is eminently predictable."

Former Gillette executives acknowledge that the company was living in a cocoon. Dubin, who knew nothing about the razor-and-blade business a couple of years earlier, kept outmaneuvering and outmarketing executives who had been in the business for decades. They were focusing on incremental improvements, but the quality of all blades, including Dorco's, had improved so much that minor improvements no longer made a noticeable difference to most shavers—especially given that Gillette had pushed the price of cartridges to five dollars each, which several of its executives, looking back, refer to as the "pain point" that opened the door for Dollar Shave Club. "To what extent is highest quality really important to each consumer? Would I rather have a much cheaper brand that also is a sharp razor? Not everybody is after the best product," says David Sylvia, the former Gillette executive.

As Dollar Shave Club's sales reached an annual rate of $240 million in 2016, Dubin began talking with suitors. Colgate-Palmolive, which had become an investor, was one. So was Schick. But Unilever, a rival of Procter & Gamble in detergent and many other consumer products, topped everyone, offering $1 billion in cash in July 2016. At that point, Dollar Shave Club was on its way to having more than three million subscribers. In keeping with Dubin's vision, and to keep growing for its new owner, the company has expanded into other grooming products: hair gel, toothbrushes and toothpaste, shampoo, face cleanser, cologne, lip balm, even a "tool kit" that includes tweezers and nail clippers. It's added so many new products that its marketing material has included the line "Dollar Maybe We Should Change Our Name Club."

Some people wondered if Unilever overpaid. But in May 2019, Harry's, which had a lower market share than Dollar Shave Club, announced that it was being acquired for $1.37 billion by Edgewell Personal Care Co., the parent of Schick and Wilkinson Sword razor brands. Although the purchase price was higher than Dollar Shave Club's, the backers of Harry's overall made a lower rate of return because the sales price was 3.7 times the total investment in the company of $375 million, while Dollar Shave Club fetched more than six times what its investors had put into it. Early backers of both companies made many multiples of their original investment.

Various rounds of VC investment had reduced Dubin's stake, but he still owned about 9 to 10 percent of the company, worth $90 million to $100 million, with the potential for additional payouts depending on the growth of the company over the next few years. Science, for its early bet, made tens of millions of dollars in profits. (It declined to be more specific.) Forerunner Ventures and Venrock, among the earliest major investors, were big winners as well. Dorco also made tens of millions of dollars on the stake it extracted from Dubin. In addition, thanks to its production for Dollar Shave Club, Dorco's earnings have soared as its share of the worldwide market has more than tripled to around 16 percent in unit volume, compared with less than 5 percent before Dubin came along. Mark Levine, Dubin's cofounder, who had bowed out of an active role early on, also walked away with several million dollars for the small stake he retained.

In the spring of 2017, Gillette finally had no choice but to hit what former executive Mike Norton calls the "nuclear button": it cut prices by an average of 12 percent, in a stinging admission that its business was being eroded. Trying to win back customers, it took out full-page ads in the *New York Times* and the *Wall Street Journal*: "YOU SAID YOU WANTED THE BEST SHAVE AT LOWER PRICES. DONE." On its website, instead of marketing bravado, it made an honest, and humbling, admission: "You told us our blades can be too expensive and we listened."

Just a few years earlier, for a few million dollars or perhaps a little more, Gillette could have bought a significant stake in the fledgling Dollar Shave Club. Now the price reduction it was swallowing would cost Gillette more than $100 million *a year* in lost revenue, and that was on top of the hundreds of millions of dollars in annual sales it had already lost as its market share dwindled and customers turned to Dollar Shave Club's razors.

Michael Dubin smiled when he saw the ad.

2

The Pied Pipers of Disruption

Usually the pitches from entrepreneurs arrive electronically. Occasionally, they arrive in the mail. At times, they even arrive hand-delivered by a particularly eager young person hoping to stand out by conveying an I'll-do-anything-to-succeed passion.

Their destination: 1161 Mission Street, Suite 300, in San Francisco. It's in a building that also houses WeWork offices, but it's not the typical glass-enclosed, chicken-coop-like warren crammed with a few desks and computers occupied by many WeWork tenants who can't afford anything bigger or fancier. This office, with a separate entrance from the striving or struggling start-ups, has an airy feel, with stylish modern office furniture, subdued wall art, and a spacious, well-appointed conference room.

It's the office of Forerunner Ventures, Kirsten Green's venture capital firm.

The pitches, however they arrive, never stop coming. Each year, there are 2,500, give or take. July 2018 was a typical month: 198 business proposals, including 67 wanting to launch new online brands (cosmetics, shoes, toiletries, clothing, you name it), another 64 pitching "platforms" (mostly for selling goods on mobile devices), 16 new retail concepts, and 18 e-commerce marketplaces. Green and her team of a half dozen colleagues sift through all of them. About 1 in 10, perhaps 200 to 250 a year, get invited to present their ideas to Green in person. Like pilgrims heading to Mecca, the entrepreneurs trek to Forerunner's office just south of downtown San Francisco's Tenderloin district, passing or stepping over homeless people on the way.

In the hour or so they are allotted to persuade Forerunner that they are worthy of an investment, the would-be entrepreneurs are grilled by Green or one of her partners about everything from the competitive landscape for their product to its financial potential to their strategic vision.

Don't bother coming if you aren't thinking big. Forerunner's brashly stated mission: "We partner with those who challenge industry norms. Those who upend entire categories." Other venture capital firms, notably Lerer Hippeau, in New York's Silicon Alley, have stakes in many digital-first consumer brands, including some of the same start-ups as Forerunner. But Forerunner stands out for investing almost exclusively in e-commerce, a bet-the-ranch strategy that has made Green a celebrity in this corner of the VC world and beyond.

Fashionable and photogenic, with a megawatt smile, Green no doubt is the only venture capitalist ever named to both *Time* magazine's 100 Most Influential People list and *Vanity Fair*'s International Best-Dressed List—in the same year, 2017. (For her *Vanity Fair* photo, she wore a black-and-white, floor-length Chloé dress and held a red Chanel clutch purse.)

Becoming one of the Pied Pipers of the direct-to-consumer brand world didn't happen overnight for Green. A decade earlier, she was virtually unknown. After getting a business degree in college in 1993, she initially toiled for several years at a big accounting firm—"I mean, who ever aspires to be an auditor?" she told an interviewer—where she once found herself in a Safeway grocery freezer counting inventory.

Then she worked for nearly a decade in relative anonymity as a Wall Street analyst following the retail industry, before quitting because she sensed that e-commerce would transform the retail world. It was at that point that she began consulting and dabbling in investing in start-ups.

Without a track record in the venture capital world, she was a supplicant searching for deals. The pitches from entrepreneurs started to come to her, slowly, only in 2012 and 2013, after word circulated that she was the biggest early investor in Dollar Shave Club and also had put money into other new online brands such as Bonobos and Warby Parker.

Then came the summer of 2016, when Green's name entered the VC stratosphere. In a matter of weeks, two companies in which she was an early investor became *unicorns*, the term for start-ups worth at least a billion dollars: In addition to Dollar Shave Club's $1 billion sale to Unilever, the online discount retailer Jet.com was bought by Walmart for $3.3 billion. "For a long time, we took our address off our website because people would come and knock on our door with pitches," Green says.

By then, an investment by Forerunner in a start-up had become an imprimatur among the cognoscenti in Silicon Valley. Liz Reifsnyder, one of the early employees of Dollar Shave Club, recalls meeting with the founder of Ritual, a direct-to-consumer women's vitamin start-up, to discuss a senior job in 2016, before it had officially launched. "I said, 'I don't know if you're raising money, but if you are, you should really talk to Kirsten Green. This is right in her wheelhouse,'" Reifsnyder says. Told that Forerunner had already agreed to become a lead investor, Reifsnyder didn't hesitate. "I was like, 'Basically, I'm on board. I'm in.'"

Like many revolutions, the direct-to-consumer brand revolution was slow to take off and caught the old guard by surprise. It was led by a loose but, over time, intertwined band of entrepreneurs and investors from new or lesser-known VC firms like Forerunner, who sensed an opportunity that more prominent investors overlooked. It was aided by research on how data could be used to target online shoppers, and by the lessons gleaned from the failures, and occasional successes, of first-generation digital retailers. A burgeoning infrastructure, underpinned by inexpensive plug-and-play technology, made it possible for just about anyone to launch a new product with a remarkably small amount of money. Few online shoppers have ever heard of Shopify, but it was a game changer. Founded in 2004, Shopify created an e-commerce software platform that takes care of everything a start-up needs to do to create an online store—build a website, take orders, receive payments, track inventory, and manage shipping—all at an initial cost as low as $29 a month, less than the cost of a single cash register at a brick-and-mortar store.

Little of this was immediately obvious, at least not to most venture capitalists, who pride themselves on peering into the future. In the not-too-distant past, if an entrepreneur had wanted to pitch an idea for a new consumer product (outside of a tech gadget), the reaction at just about any VC firm would have ranged from "Huh?" to "You're kidding" to "Go away." The price of creating a new consumer brand was steep, and the odds of succeeding were slim.

"Twenty-five years ago, if you had an idea for a radically better toothpaste, there was nothing you could do with the idea," notes Randall Rothenberg, chief executive of the Interactive Advertising Bureau. "If by some stretch you knew where to get the ingredients, that was of little use because you could only buy a ton, not small batches. Let's say you knew somebody who made toothpaste. They wouldn't take you as a customer because you weren't a large-scale producer. If you could get someone to make your toothpaste, no retailer would carry it; you couldn't drive consumer demand because demand was driven by national media advertising. You were out of luck."

In contrast, the glow of an existing brand established over many decades yielded immense dividends. With the help of Madison Avenue ad agencies, once brands had won customers, most kept coming back—and back, and back. As a result, dominant brands often enjoyed fat profit margins. Customers might grumble about the high prices, but they often had little real choice in product categories dominated by a few companies.

This model of creating and sustaining brands had endured for many decades because of a symbiotic relationship among those making brand-name goods, those advertising them, and those selling them.

Everyone in this orderly universe benefited, in no small part because this model created significant barriers to entry.

Little wonder that dozens of brands that were either number one or number two in the first half of the twentieth century were also number one or number two toward the end of the twentieth century, Rothenberg notes. "The idea that you could lose sixteen points of market share in six years, like Gillette had"—to Dollar Shave Club, mostly, but to Harry's as well—"that's unbelievable."

If most VC firms didn't recognize how technology had the potential to lower the barriers of entry and disrupt this orderly world, Kirsten Green had an advantage. She, like most of the people at the forefront of the revolution, was an outsider who didn't know that it couldn't be done.

While working as an analyst at Montgomery Securities, Green had studied the mall boom and had tracked the growth it had spurred among traditional chains and specialty retail boutiques catering to teenagers in particular. "I watched a ton of companies get built on the back of the mall. Really a big impetus was the unlocking of teen spending," she says. "A bunch of teens would show up at the mall with twenty dollars in their back pocket, and that added up to a lot of money. And the whole thing worked in tandem really well, with teens being the tailwind, malls being the tailwind enabler."

But she believed that the rise of e-commerce would change this landscape. Technology was supplying the new tailwind for selling goods of all sorts, and Amazon and eBay were in the early stages of rewriting the rules. "Clearly," Green thought, "a shift is going to happen away from stores." She was hardly the only person to feel this way, but she did something about it. If there was going to be a revolution, why sit it out?

After leaving her job as a Wall Street retail analyst at the end of 2002, Green used her knowledge of retailing and consumer brands to do consulting projects for private equity firms. But she realized that what she really wanted to be was an investor. While she continued consulting, she scouted for start-ups with promising new models for creating brands and selling to consumers.

When she found an idea that intrigued her, she would scramble to raise money, putting together syndicates of former colleagues or wealthy "angel" investors she had gotten to know, with each contributing $25,000 or so, which added up to enough to make investments.

In 2007, Green started looking into a relatively new start-up called Nau, which she found especially interesting. It brought together many of the ideas about the new world of retailing that she had been pondering. Founded by former executives of Patagonia and Nike, Nau sought to create a brand of casual but trendy clothes you could wear to work during the day and then to a concert or a bar or dinner in the evening. And they were produced in an eco-friendly way, to connect with Millennial customers, another nascent trend that she had an inkling would go mainstream. "They said people's lives are merging. The idea that you go to work nine to five and then come home—that's changing," she notes.

Just as intriguing to Green, Nau was rethinking how to use technology to sell its clothing. Its model wasn't digital-only, but it was digital-centric. Nau clothing would be carried not by other retailers but only at its own boutique shops (of typically two thousand square feet or less), which were more like showrooms that artfully displayed only a handful of items in different sizes and colors.

Nau's shops had another novel feature for their time: touchscreen computer terminals. Customers were encouraged to use them to surf Nau's website, and shoppers who placed an order online while in the store got a 10 percent discount. "We didn't call it a store; we called it a 'webfront,'" explains Ian Yolles, who was a cofounder and vice president of marketing at Nau. "We even trademarked the name."

After researching Nau, Green contacted Yolles. "She was interested in the fact that we were structurally a consumer-direct business in an industry that was entirely driven from a wholesale model," he recalls. Convinced that Nau was on to something and was ahead of its time, Green persuaded a prominent hedge fund, Tudor Investment, to invest $10 million in the company, and she got a seat on Nau's board of directors as Tudor's representative.

But Nau, it turned out, was too much ahead of its time. The cost of building the elegant, easy-to-navigate website was high because there was less off-the-shelf technology back then. While Nau built a very loyal following in the five cities where it had "webfront" stores, that's all it could afford with the initial capital it had raised. It didn't have enough money for a television advertising campaign, and there was no social media back then to get the word out widely enough to increase online sales. Facebook was in its infancy, and Instagram had yet to arrive. Running low on cash, Nau sought to raise additional funds. But it was the spring of 2008, when the financial markets were starting to buckle, not long before the financial crisis that fall. Unable to get additional financing, Nau was acquired by a distressed-asset buyer for a small amount, not even enough to fully cover its debts, and its investors got nothing. The company managed to stay in business, but as a tiny brand without the ambitious vision of its founders. In Yolles's view, and Green's, their grand plans for Nau might have succeeded if it had been founded a few years later, when it could have used the tools available to the next generation of digital-first brands.

Green, along with the founders, was devastated. "There were a lot of heartbroken people," she says.

Yolles remembers consoling Green, but what he recalls most is that she remained confident in her view of the inevitable change coming in creating new brands and in retailing. "She believed in what she had spotted. That professional trauma didn't derail her fundamental belief in her central investment thesis," he says.

Despite the Nau debacle, Green was undeterred. "I had gotten it instilled early in me that the way to make money was to think differently than other people, to have a point of view that other people didn't have and try to be a contrarian," she says.

In the months after Nau's failure, one of Green's contacts in the retail world connected her with the online menswear start-up Bonobos. Still enthusiastic about the idea of using technology to build new brands, Green made a personal investment in Bonobos in 2008 to become one of its early backers and an adviser as well. "I pitched at least fifty venture capitalists and went zero for fifty," recalls Andy Dunn, one of the company's cofounders. "She saw around the bend in retailing before others did. It's not surprising that the person who saw it wasn't a venture capitalist but a student of retailing like Kirsten."

Even as she continued consulting, Green kept looking for new brands to invest in. "For a lot of years, it was like, 'Hey there's this one person in San Francisco who doesn't have any money but she's really interested in this stuff,'" she says. "In 2010, no one gave a shit about a direct-to-consumer brand. Nobody even knew what it was." Among those she would eventually find, thanks to her network of retailing and consumer brand connections, would be one that was far from Silicon Valley.

* * *

In the fall of 2008, four graduate students attending the Wharton business school at the University of Pennsylvania were talking when one of them, David Gilboa, lamented losing a $700 pair of eyeglasses when he left them in the seat pocket on an airplane. (In another version of the story, one of the other students, Jeffrey Raider, said he had broken a $500 pair of glasses and didn't like having to pay so much for a new pair. Maybe they were both careless with their eyeglasses.)

"Hey, glasses don't cost much to make," Neil Blumenthal, another member of this group, recalls saying. "I know because I've been to the factories." For several years, Blumenthal had run a nonprofit called VisionSpring that provided eye exams and low-cost prescription glasses in developing countries. "Here we were producing glasses for people living on less than four dollars a day, and literally ten feet away on that same production line were some of the biggest names in fashion that you would find on Fifth Avenue. So, there's a disconnect."

Blumenthal had learned that the eyeglass business was dominated by a few big players, led by Luxottica, an Italian multinational that owns or produces on license many popular brands (including Giorgio Armani, Ray-Ban, Chanel, Ralph Lauren, Prada, and Versace) and operates retail chains such as LensCrafters, Pearle Vision, and Sunglass Hut.

The four students knew that new vertical retailers (e.g., Zappos

.com in shoes and Diapers.com), following Amazon's early success in books, were successfully selling products online. These companies were basically New Age retailers selling other companies' goods on the internet, rather than a new brand they had created. Still, "what it demonstrated to us was that all categories could be sold online, even ones that you would think would be very difficult to sell without being physically present for the shopper," Blumenthal says.

So, the Wharton students started researching how to make their idea into a business. "The problem we wanted to solve was walking into an optical shop, getting excited about a pair of glasses, and walking out feeling you had gotten ripped off. The way to solve that is through cutting out the middleman," Blumenthal says, explaining the group's thinking. "If we designed the frames we loved and sold them direct to consumers, we would have high margins but effectively sell them at wholesale prices. That was the whole idea and the magic of the internet." They agreed to put in $25,000 each initially, with another $5,000, if needed, to fund the start-up.

Wharton gave them an ideal place to work on their concept. They enrolled in a class whose sole requirement was to develop a business plan. At the very least, they would get credit toward their degrees, and they could tap their professors for advice.

Initially, they planned to charge $45 for a pair of glasses, including frames and prescription lenses. They visited a professor and bounced that price off him. "He looked at us and slid our PowerPoint back at us and said, 'No, it's not going to work. Listen, guys, one-tenth the price is just outside the realm of believability,'" Blumenthal says.

Chastened and deflated, they conducted an online survey, asking people how likely they would be to buy a pair of glasses online at various price points starting at $50 and increasing to $500. Sure enough, the professor was right. The willingness to buy increased up to $100, and then declined. So, they decided on a $95 price. "That was a pivotal moment," Blumenthal recalls. "If we had priced [the glasses] at $45, first of all, nobody would have believed the quality would be good. And we would have had no gross profit margin to run the business and market to people."

As they did more research with potential customers, an even trick-ier issue emerged: Many classmates and friends liked their idea for quality, low-priced glasses but confessed that they would be reluc-tant to buy a pair sight unseen, as it were. David R. Bell, a Wharton professor at the time specializing in digital marketing (who would become an enthusiastic adviser), remembers the four Warby Parker cofounders coming into his office and telling him of their plan. His response was "It's sort of an absurd idea. How could you possibly do that? I mean, I don't wear glasses, but when you do get glasses, don't you want to try on a lot? I mean, how are you going to get over that?"

Initially, they tried to solve this by adding a Virtual Try-On feature to the website they were developing. A customer could upload a photo of her face and then superimpose various frames over the photo. But the technology at the time wasn't very good. The images were diffi-cult to scale properly, and the frames often appeared distorted. They decided to keep the feature on their website for the time being, but the shortcomings prompted them to consider an alternative.

"That sent us back to the drawing board, where we came up with the idea for the Home Try-On," Blumenthal explains. Warby Parker would ship five different frames to each customer at home, and she had five days to try them on before sending them back and ordering the frame she liked best (or not ordering at all, if she decided she really didn't like any).

But that would mean free shipping, in both directions, so customers wouldn't be discouraged from giving the frames a try. To keep the cost from eating into their tight profit margins, the Warby Parker founders had to figure out how to keep the package weight below one pound, above which the U.S. Postal Service's rate rose sharply. "So, we had our Apollo Thirteen moment—you know in the movie, where they dump out everything to get the weight down," Blumenthal says, recalling how he and his colleagues cut fractions of an ounce here and there by elim-inating the heavy-duty cardboard box, getting rid of metal snaps, and adding lighter plastic to protect the frames.

At one point, they entered their business idea (then called One-Vision) in Wharton's "Start-up Challenge" competition. They made it to the semifinals but weren't selected as one of the eight finalists. A disappointed Jeffrey Raider said to his colleagues, "Guys, I don't know. I'm not sure this is a good idea." But Blumenthal responded, "We are going to make this happen, and we are going to prove to these naysayers that they are wrong."

In mid-February 2010, Warby Parker's website went live. Because they didn't have much money for advertising, the founders hired a PR firm that persuaded GQ and Vogue to run stories about their new cheap-but-fashionable eyeglasses. With limited inventory, Warby Parker quickly sold out of its most popular frames. To finance the company's growth, they obtained some small bank loans before raising $550,000 in funding, most of which came from friends and family. One of Warby Parker's early backers was a newly created venture capital firm in New York, Lerer Hippeau, whose $8.5 million investment fund was tiny by VC standards.

"I bought their pitch about eyeglasses being a fucked-up industry," says Ben Lerer, a managing partner at Lerer Hippeau. "They showed you don't need innovation around what you sell. You can succeed with innovation around the way you sell it. Leverage the traditional supply chain and sell direct to the consumer. Take your savings from the wholesale channel and pass it on to the consumer."

Another early investor in Warby Parker was the founders' Wharton professor David Bell, who had overcome his initial skepticism about selling glasses online. A tall, disheveled New Zealander, Bell had come to the United States as a graduate student in the 1990s and gotten a PhD at Stanford University, where he wrote his dissertation on retail pricing strategy. In 1998 he joined the Wharton faculty, where much of his research focused on analyzing sales data, with a special interest in the growing world of e-commerce. "What excited me from a conceptual point of view was the contrast between physical and digital retail worlds. Physical stores had a predefined trading area. With digital retailers, you can start selling stuff to the entire nation," he explains.

Like Kirsten Green, Bell understood that e-commerce had set in motion a structural shift in the world of retailing and brands. Especially attractive, he believed, were categories whose leading brands combined high price, little meaningful innovation, and a bad customer experience.

Bell's academic work was buttressed by what he discovered as an adviser to (and investor in) Diapers.com, cofounded in 2005 by a Wharton graduate. The company didn't make its own diapers but sold existing brands such as Pampers and Huggies. What it offered was a price slightly lower than that offered by most retailers and, more important, a good customer experience—convenience for the harried parents of babies and infants.

Even before Facebook became a social media behemoth, Diapers .com found that its most effective marketing was social marketing—in its case, digital word of mouth—which would become a key building block of direct-to-consumer brands. Word of mouth is hardly new, but the data analyzed by Bell showed that the internet could supercharge its effects. About 10 percent of Diapers.com customers came through referrals from other buyers, a rate several times higher than that for shoppers who bought a product in a store. Moreover, the company's top one hundred customers generated through their extended family and friends about fifteen thousand other customers. Bell saw that by tapping into and even fostering a sense of community among consumers, the internet could turn a company's most ardent customers into a powerful adjunct to its sales force.

Another insight: online sellers could increase sales rapidly by using data to identify and target their most likely potential customers. In the case of Diapers.com, that meant specific geographical areas where clusters of potential customers lived. The company focused its online advertising on zip codes in different parts of the country that were demographically similar.

"The large urban centers always predominate initially, in terms of sales: New York, Boston, San Francisco, Philadelphia, Los Angeles, Chicago," Bell said in a marketing podcast for Wharton based on his research. "But in order for those businesses to really survive and, in fact, to thrive, they must also pick up customers in what are some of the more remote places, sort of the 'tail' locations. Those 'tail' locations tend to be geographically far apart, but similar in some other sociode-mographic dimensions. So, there's a community somewhere, located in Texas, that actually is not that different from one that's somewhere in Nebraska, and identifying them becomes very important."

By today's standards, this targeting may seem rudimentary, but it helped create a data-driven road map for new digitally native brands. Selling online provided reams and reams of data about the preferences, wants, interests, gender, age, and location of every customer. Each click could be tracked, stored, and analyzed. You could "chat" with custom-ers and pick their brains in order to quickly make changes to improve a product or to introduce new products. The new brands actually knew their customers better than the big brands that had been selling to them forever, because the established brands didn't—couldn't—know the identity of individual customers who went into a store and grabbed a product off a shelf. This amounted to a significant change in the way brands were created, Bell concluded.

Bell drew on his previous consulting for Diapers.com and Bonobos for his work with Warby Parker on segmenting and targeting potential consumer groups.

As Warby Parker took off, he began teaching a new course, called Digital Marketing and E-Commerce, which quickly became one of Wharton's most popular; in fact, all three classes he taught each year were oversubscribed. With Bell as one of the movement's intellectual gurus, Wharton emerged as a center for digitally native brands. Stu-dents began dropping by Bell's office seeking advice on their ideas for start-ups—the school's graduates have launched online brands for underwear, sneakers, outdoor gear, tampons, and strollers, among others. Many openly pitched their companies as "the Warby Parker of . . ." and unabashedly mimicked its playbook: good value, an improved customer experience, heavy use of technology and data, and a brand with a message that appeals to young, urban customers. Even Warby Parker's name, taken from two characters in a journal by the Beat Generation author Jack Kerouac, oozed hipness.

* * *

One of the friends-and-family investors who put money into Warby Parker in 2010 was Kirsten Green of Forerunner Ventures. The four founders were advised to meet her because she was familiar with the industry giant Luxottica from her days as a Wall Street analyst. "Like any investor, my job is to be skeptical," she recalls. "I wasn't quite sure how the Home Try-On thing would work. But I thought it was interesting that they were thinking about that as a means to ease the friction of buying, and I bought their thesis around the category."

Two years later, in early 2012, Green was raising a larger pool of money to seed Forerunner's first venture capital fund, which would enable her to build an ongoing business that would make more and bigger bets to test her investment thesis about the changing online retail landscape. On January 25, Green attended a dinner at Park Tavern's private dining room in San Francisco's North Beach neighborhood. The dinner was hosted by Alpha Club, an exclusive, invitation-only networking club for tech industry investors and founders, the former looking for ideas and the latter looking for money. A couple of days before the dinner, an investor with whom Green shared ideas asked her in passing, "Have you heard of Dollar Shave Club?"

"No, what is it?" Green answered. Told it was a men's razor start-up, Green thought to herself, "Geez, Gillette is a big, formidable company. They have a huge market share, huge presence, huge mind share, incredible loyalty, and a big budget to defend it. I can make only a few investments a year. Do I need to make that one?"

By coincidence, she found herself sitting at the same table as Michael Dubin and Peter Pham, who had come to the Alpha dinner from Los Angeles, looking for investors. Pham introduced Dubin, who explained his vision.

Years later, Green still hasn't forgotten that moment: "I definitely had the sensation—I remember the tape in my head going, *I have to invest with this guy*," she says, with a trace of amazement in her voice at how quickly she changed her mind about Dollar Shave Club's prospects. "I hadn't seen the video; I hadn't seen anything else. I wasn't exactly turned on by the headline of 'I'm going to sell razors.' But I don't remember a conversation super focused on razors. I felt that he 'got' the male consumer. The conversation was a much bigger one. The conversation was about the guy who was waking up to paying attention to his own health and wellness; who was waking up to owning his own decisions about what was in his medicine cabinet; who was peeking into his girlfriend's cabinet to see what she had. And I also was a believer already in my own right in pursuing things that were direct-to-consumer. When I heard him talk about that, I was like, *He gets it.*"

There was one problem: Green didn't actually have any money to invest in Dollar Shave Club because she was still working on raising her fund. But Dollar Shave Club needed money *now* to launch. If Green wanted in, she would have to move fast to find someone who would lend her the money.

At the top of her list of people to call was Sandy Colen. A San Francisco hedge fund executive, Colen for years had been Green's biggest financial backer. They had known each other since the mid-1990s, when Colen offered Green a job. Though she turned him down, they had stayed in touch. Like Green, Colen was intrigued by how e-commerce might change retailing, and the two were like-minded in thinking that advances in technology and changes in consumer behavior would cause disruption.

"She was perplexed that no one showed the same passion for these opportunities," says Colen, who put money into some of Green's early one-off investments before becoming a major source of capital for her, putting in $5 million as the sole investor in a Forerunner "angel" fund in 2010. "I was investor one," he proudly points out.

Colen's belief in Green's thesis had been reinforced, he recalls, when he traveled to an investment conference in 2011 and attended a talk by the founders of Warby Parker. "Kirsten had already made an initial investment in Warby Parker, and I was pretty much one hundred percent convinced this would work when I saw them at that conference," Colen recalls. "It was one of best presentations I'd seen by a disruptor."

So, when Green called asking for money for Dollar Shave Club, Colen didn't hesitate. He made what's called a "warehouse loan" of $250,000, with the agreement that Green would pay it back when she raised money from other investors to bankroll her new Forerunner fund. Colen had come to trust Green's instincts, and he knew that razors were a high-profit business, so he figured an upstart might have a chance at succeeding—even though he himself stopped using Dollar Shave Club razors after trying them. "I signed up for the product, and called Kirsten after cutting myself a number of times. I told her I love the company but not the blades," he quips.

In 2012, not long after making her first investment in Dubin's company, Green managed to raise $40 million from institutional investors (such as university endowments) and used some of it to pay back Colen's loan—to his subsequent regret. "Had she not been able to raise the money, I would have made a lot more!" he says.

Green got a seat on Dollar Shave Club's board as part of her agreement to invest in the start-up. "I had a conviction in a way maybe other people didn't because I was spending all of my time thinking about this group of companies. And that's what I wanted to hang my hat on, and this was a great example of one," she says.

As Dollar Shave Club's sales soared, Green invested more money in the company as it raised additional VC funds in subsequent rounds. And when Unilever bought the company in 2016, just four years later, proving her intuition right, Forerunner earned many multiples of what Green had invested.

Green's growing prominence has enabled her to raise ever-increasing amounts to invest in start-ups: $75 million for her second Forerunner fund in 2014; $122 million for the firm's third fund in 2016; and $360 million for another fund in 2018.

Though Forerunner's initial investment funds aren't large by venture capital standards, Kirsten Green has built the biggest portfolio of direct-to-consumer start-ups, with investments in nearly ninety e-commerce companies as of mid-2019. Forerunner has put money into children's clothing (Rockets of Awesome, founded by Rachel Blumenthal, wife of Warby Parker cofounder Neil), "smart" luggage with a built-in charger (Away, cofounded by two Warby Parker alums), cosmetics (Glossier), hair loss for men (Hims, founded by a Wharton grad), women's "slippers with style" (Birdies), outdoor gear (Cotopaxi, founded by another Wharton grad), women's apparel (Reformation), "handmade" Italian shoes (M.Gemi), "human-grade" pet food (The Farmer's Dog), sportswear (Outdoor Voices), household goods and apparel (Draper James, cofounded by actress Reese Witherspoon), women's vitamins (Ritual), customized shampoo (Prose), and customized acne treatment (Curology). Sprinkled among her investments are start-ups that, like purveyors of pickaxes and pans during the gold rush, cater to direct-to-consumer companies by helping them sell their products, including Lumi (packaging), Retention Science (marketing software), and Packagd (mobile shopping apps).

As much as Green looks for technology and online marketing smarts, she also seeks out entrepreneurs whose disruption strategy includes connecting directly with consumers. Brands that convey a sense of authenticity, rather than simply selling a product, can create a devoted community and take business away from bigger mass-market brands that by their very nature have a hard time identifying with consumers—for example, Dollar Shave Club, whose customers loved Michael Dubin's irreverent, stick-it-to-the-man (i.e., Gillette) attitude.

Green saw in Glossier's founder, Emily Weiss, the same thing she saw in Dubin. Weiss, then in her mid-twenties, in 2010 had started what became a wildly popular blog named *Into the Gloss* as a side endeavor while working at *Vogue*. A few years later she began approaching a number of venture firms seeking funding for a start-up, but had little luck—until she talked to Forerunner. Unlike the razor business, in which one dominant company charged high prices, the cosmetics field is crowded with many more players at all price ranges. Still, Green remembers sensing that Weiss had an "understanding what the customer wants three days before they understand themselves." She helped Weiss focus her business plan on a line of affordable basic cosmetics (including moisturizers and eyeliners), and Forerunner led the first "seed" investment round for Glossier.

Green's intuitive grasp of Weiss's vision was in sharp contrast to the response Weiss and her team received from other VC firms, says Henry Davis, who was president of Glossier for four years before leaving to launch his own direct-to-consumer start-up. "Some of the shit we would get was, like, spectacular," Davis recalls. "Assistants were brought into the meeting because they're women and understand beauty. Some VC guys who say, 'I'm going to give it to my wife and see what she thinks.' And I would leave meetings; I'd just get up and leave."

Thanks to Weiss's digital savvy, Glossier quickly built a huge following on Instagram, the social media app of choice for Millennials, who often use the site to post photos of their favorite products. Like Dollar Shave Club, Glossier has turned into a big winner for Forerunner. Green has invested in Glossier's subsequent fund-raising rounds, and the company's annual sales have topped $100 million. In the spring of 2019, it was valued at $1.2 billion—another Forerunner unicorn.

Green, like all VC investors, confesses to having passed on some ideas that now look like they could become big winners. One is Casper, the online mattress start-up. "One of the criteria I have is to look for businesses with repeat business opportunities," she explains. "When we looked at Casper mattresses, I asked myself, 'Is it a good mattress? Yes. Is the mattress-in-a-box buying experience better than going to a store? Yes.' But people buy mattresses, what, once every ten years? What didn't occur to me is that many houses have four to six beds. And I didn't think about other products that Casper has ended up selling, like pillows and sheets—all of which have high profit margins, like mattresses, so that gives a lot of room to operate." Her takeaway? "There is a delicate balance between following a set of criteria to determine what you invest in and being too married to that set of criteria."

David Pakman, the partner at Venrock who invested early in Dollar Shave Club, also turned down the opportunity to invest in Casper. "The big question I had was whether other copycats would come in, and I was right; lots of competitors have jumped into the market, because foam mattresses are fairly easy to make," he notes. But he concedes that it looks like he was wrong with regard to the larger picture. "It is a very big market, with good profit margins. You can't win them all."

Despite getting it right with Dollar Shave Club, Pakman has been far more selective than Green in placing bets on direct-to-consumer brands. In addition to looking for products or business models that can't be easily or quickly duplicated, he looks for categories where the dominant players sell largely through retailers and depend on broadcast advertising, and thus don't have a direct connection to customers; products with robust profit margins where the market leader likely will be reluctant to cannibalize its own business to thwart the start-up; and, ideally, products in what he calls "zero-sum" markets, where a customer buying your product doesn't buy your competitor's product.

Venrock's investment in Nest Labs, its first consumer product start-up, helped it develop this philosophy. Home thermostats may sound boring, but they are a multibillion-dollar-a-year business, one long dominated by Honeywell. At the time of Venrock's involvement, innovation in this area was glacial. Honeywell had pioneered programmable thermostats, which enabled homeowners to have their heating or air-conditioning automatically go up or down at preset times. Nest thermostats, introduced in 2011, were a technological leap forward. Connected to the internet, they used software to sense or "learn" users' habits, raising or lowering the temperature depending on their routines. Even when users were away from home, they could monitor and change the settings through their smartphone.

"No one in the business thought the idea would succeed," Pakman recalls. "A bunch of fancy sensors connected to the thermostat on your wall, using machine learning to control the temperature? And it costs two hundred fifty dollars, several times more than a Honeywell thermostat? Who needs that? No way." Honeywell, like Gillette, reacted exactly as Pakman expected: it did nothing initially. "The best opportunities are where the innovation is slow to be appreciated by incumbents," he notes. Venrock and other investors also anticipated that when Honeywell finally recognized the challenge, it would take several years for it to develop and begin selling a copycat "smart" thermostat. "Honeywell is a fine tech company but not a software company. What made Nest so great was that it integrated hardware and software. Honeywell didn't have the software engineering talent to do it faster."

By that time, Nest was so successful that Google bought it for $3.2 billion in 2014.

But not all Pakman's consumer product bets have paid off. In June 2016, excited by the success of Dollar Shave Club and Nest before it, Venrock led a group of several VC firms that invested $50 million in

Pearl Automation, a start-up founded by several former Apple executives. The idea was to add high-tech accessories to older-model cars. Its first product was a wireless rearview camera designed to be inconspicuously attached to the rear license plate so drivers, using their smartphones as displays, could see behind the car while backing up (technology common in new cars but not old ones).

Pakman thought Pearl could be for autos what Nest was for thermostats, but the company shut down a year later because there wasn't enough demand for its $500 cameras. "It was a premium, elegant product, like Nest," he says. "It met all my investment criteria. You can dream all you want about how well a product is going to do, but none of that matters if you don't sell enough. [Pearl] took too long and spent too much money getting their product to market."

Since then, Pakman has been approached by many entrepreneurs seeking money for new direct-to-consumer brands, and has declined them all. The sheer number of entrants means it's harder for a new brand to stand out. He concedes that some of the start-ups he has snubbed could well disrupt established brands and grow into very successful companies. But the huge sums of VC money pouring into start-ups means the odds are higher against delivering the payback Pakman expects, given the risk.

Indeed, venture capital investors who wouldn't even bother taking a meeting with an entrepreneur wanting to create a new physical brand before 2012 have begun pouring billions of dollars into start-up brands, all intent on disrupting and reinventing their category—sometimes the *same* category.

Not one but three direct-to-consumer organic tampon start-ups have been launched; about a half dozen online bra makers; several vitamin companies; dozens of mattress makers; three men's hair loss start-ups; a handful of makers of "smart" luggage featuring built-in electronic device chargers; at least a half dozen electric toothbrush start-ups; countless apparel companies specializing in everything from underwear to socks to belts; and shoe companies—merino wool shoes, handmade Italian shoes, plastic woven shoes. Also: couches, artwork frames, bicycles, laundry detergent, household cleaning products, teeth braces.

"It's not that most of these companies will fail," Pakman says. "I think it's been shown that it is not that difficult to create a brand online and reach $20 million in sales or even more. But the question is how many will become big enough, like Dollar Shave Club, to be acquired for a billion dollars?"

3

Making It in the World Bazaar

Ben Cogan and Jesse Horwitz, two young, bookish Ivy League graduates, don't have a clue about the finer points of making soft contact lenses. It is a highly automated, highly technical process that is accomplished in . . . well, the blink of an eye, and it requires precision equipment that operates in a super-clean plant to guard against anything that might risk contaminating a wearer's eyes.

"We know very little about lens manufacturing," Cogan confesses. "It could be a widget." Despite their utter lack of knowledge, in July 2015 the two friends, then in their mid-twenties, mapped out a plan to start a contact lens company as they ate dinner one night at a Chinese restaurant on Manhattan's Upper West Side. Cogan, who had studied philosophy at Princeton, was working at the razor start-up Harry's and had been accepted into the MBA program at Wharton. Horwitz, who had majored in economics and mathematics at Columbia, was an investment analyst for the university's endowment. Neither had ever set foot in a factory of any kind.

Undeterred, their first task was to find a manufacturer that would sell lenses online at a low price to wannabe entrepreneurs with no track record in the business. "Signing on with a good supplier is the top priority," says Horwitz. "If you get that wrong, it doesn't matter if you get everything else right." Like college students working on a term paper—which they had been doing only a few years earlier—they began researching possible suppliers.

Just over a year later, they were in business. Their online start-up, named Hubble, began offering a month's supply of daily disposable lenses for $33, roughly half the price charged by the industry giants Bausch & Lomb, Johnson & Johnson, and CooperVision. In 2018, Hubble's second full year in business, it had about four hundred thousand customers, and sales had grown to an annual rate of about $70 million. Horwitz estimated its U.S. market share of single-vision disposable lenses, for the most straightforward and simplest prescriptions, was about 8 percent. And it has expanded to Canada and twenty-eight European countries.

Hubble managed to do this with just two dozen employees, none of them in manufacturing or research and development, and without building a factory that would have cost millions of dollars to get up and running. Instead, after winnowing down a list of several dozen potential manufacturers, Cogan and Horwitz ended up buying lenses from a little-known Taiwanese company named St.Shine Optical, which has long had Food and Drug Administration approval to sell its contacts in the United States.

If you've never heard of St.Shine, well, Cogan and Horwitz themselves didn't know much about it before traveling to Taipei in the spring of 2016. And the St.Shine executives had definitely never heard of them; in fact, they were a bit puzzled when they met the two entrepreneurs. "We were surprised at how young they were," says Jason Ong, the company's international business director. "They were a start-up, and we had never dealt with a start-up. But the U.S. was an empty market for us, so we thought, Why not try it? We had nothing to lose." Why not, indeed. Thanks to Hubble, St.Shine now gets 10 percent of its sales from the United States, up from less than 1 percent, and it has expanded its production capacity to meet the growing demand of Hubble customers.

Welcome to the world's supply chain bazaar, where manufacturing expertise is just another commodity for sale. Globalization and technology have made it possible for entrepreneurs to launch new brands in just about any category and to bring them to market with astonishing speed. Never before has it been so easy to produce a physical product or to create a new consumer brand with so little investment. This has dramatically lowered one of the main barriers to entry that long posed an obstacle to entrepreneurs and safeguarded the incumbents that had built their own factories and employed legions of deeply knowledgeable specialists on their R&D teams.

Companies have outsourced production for decades, but in recent times, the global supply chain has become more diverse and sophisticated than ever. An abundance of potential manufacturing partners, many with excess capacity, can be found in Asia, the shop floor to the world. If anything, the challenge isn't so much finding a supplier as it is sifting through dozens of possible suppliers to find the right one.

This global market in goods of all sorts has been crucial to opening the doors for direct-to-consumer start-ups. Many start-up founders, like Cogan and Horwitz, have little to no background in the product they are planning to sell. Rather than a shortcoming, however, this often has proven to be an advantage. Entrepreneurs who come from outside an industry aren't afraid to rewrite the rules because they don't know enough to be constrained by how things were done in the past. While that may not raise issues with razors, Hubble's approach has stirred controversy, with some optometrists accusing the company of having skirted regulations to increase sales, an assertion that Horwitz and Cogan reject as an effort to thwart a new competitor.

But the debate underscores a new reality in the marketplace: not only are there more suppliers than ever willing to make every imaginable consumer product, but they are often more sophisticated than ever. In the early 2000s, many Asian outsourcing companies knew how to produce things efficiently and could make most any consumer product to a company's specifications. But few could help make the product *better*. Also, they expected large-volume orders, because that's the only way their factories could operate economically.

As trade boomed and more competitors emerged to produce goods for just about every industry, ambitious suppliers looked for a way to stand out. Today, if you want help designing your product, Asian factories can do that. Because they have been manufacturing so many products for years, at times on contract for big brand names, the best offshore outsourcing companies have built up knowledge about materials and parts, learning over time what distinguishes a higher-quality widget from one of lower quality. They have also developed engineering expertise and can suggest ideas to improve the design of the products they make. That way they can charge more or get more business, or both.

And as factories have become more automated, many suppliers have instituted lean manufacturing techniques that enable them to switch production lines in and out much more quickly and with less downtime. This means they can operate profitably on lower volumes— which means they are more willing to accommodate smaller orders while keeping their plants operating at a high capacity. Many Asian manufacturers that might have insisted on a minimum order of twenty thousand units will now accept an initial order of only a few thousand.

"It's much easier than ever to rapidly build a new disruptive company, at least in the early stages, with limited capital," notes Christopher Rogers, an analyst for Panjiva, which tracks import data and helps identify suppliers for an astonishing number of products, and puts it all online. Founded in 2005, Panjiva is part of an intricate network of companies devoted to every link in the global supply chain of goods. Information on suppliers that once was available only to big companies because it was buried in raw customs import data that was hard to access and decipher has now been democratized. "Smaller companies didn't used to have market intelligence," says Rogers. "Now they do."

* * *

In times past, the biggest bazaars had hundreds of physical stalls offering their wares. Today's global bazaar has hundreds of thousands of digital stalls that entrepreneurs can visit online. The scale is so vast that a cottage industry of advisers has grown to help users navigate the ever-expanding world of digital wholesale marketplaces. The biggest of all is Alibaba, the giant Chinese e-commerce company founded in 1999.

Let's say you want to sell mountain bikes. Plug in the words *mountain* and *bike* on alibaba.com, and the site lists hundreds of manufacturers selling mountain bikes for anywhere from $27.99 (for a bicycle with a cheap steel-alloy frame) to $988 (a high-quality carbon fiber frame). Some manufacturers will sell you just one, but most require that you order at least fifty bikes—still a tiny number compared with the minimum order of many hundreds or thousands most would have wanted a decade or two ago.

What about rechargeable electric toothbrushes? Alibaba spits out hundreds of suppliers of these as well, with the toothbrushes priced anywhere from $6.30 to $40.00 apiece, depending on the features, with minimum orders generally starting at around two hundred. Many offer free samples, should you want to compare the quality. Alibaba's site also lists the companies that have received the most inquiries in the last six months, the number of transactions they have done through Alibaba, and the amount of revenue generated.

Alibaba will even help you narrow down your list. If you fill out a "Request for Quotation" form with your specifications (color, size, material, etc.), Alibaba will match the request with the suppliers that best fit your needs—for free. If you are in a rush, you can pay ten dollars to get an expedited response, with a price quote in as little as one day.

When Alibaba first became a public company in 2014, with a multibillion-dollar stock offering, Bloomberg News journalist Sam Grobart decided to find out how easy it was to source a product using the site. He placed a request for bids for 280 pairs of denim pants in different sizes and colors (orange, purple, yellow, and green). Within a day, he had replies from manufacturers in China, India, Pakistan, and the Czech Republic. He whittled the list down to "gold star" companies, a status that suppliers can pay for but that also requires that they go through a background check by Alibaba to ensure they aren't scam artists. After judging responses based on price, delivery time, how well written the responses were, and whether they included a photo of the pants, Grobart picked a Pakistani supplier. "It's a little bit like online dating," he explained. The Pakistani supplier charged $9 a pair, for a total cost of $2,520. Shipping the order by air to New York added another $1,983. A buyer can pay using an escrow service called Alipay, which releases the money to the manufacturer only once the buyer is satisfied with what he has ordered. Twenty-five days after Grobart started the process, the pants arrived, with a Bloomberg label stitched on the back, per his specifications.

But if finding a supplier to make a product is easier than ever, finding the *right* supplier still requires legwork, as Ben Cogan and Jesse Horwitz learned when they were starting Hubble.

* * *

Cogan and Horwitz had become friends a few years earlier, while working as summer interns at the hedge fund Bridgewater Associates, and had apartments across the street from each other in Manhattan. Not long before their dinner in the summer of 2015, Cogan was buying a new supply of soft contact lenses for himself and learned that the price had gone up. This got him thinking. With their high price, contact lenses, an industry dominated by a handful of big players, were similar to razors, a business that Harry's (along with Dollar Shave Club) was trying to disrupt. The idea of disrupting the contact lens business intrigued Cogan. There were online retailers specializing in contact lenses, but they resold existing brands. While they offered discounts compared to what a customer would pay through an optometrist, the markup was still significant.

Cogan floated the idea by Horwitz, who agreed that it was worth pursuing, though both decided to stay in their jobs while working on a business plan. They quickly focused on daily disposable lenses because that was the fastest-growing part of the multibillion-dollar U.S. market for contacts, and they soon discovered that daily disposables could cost 25 to 50 percent more in the United States than they did abroad. So, there was room for a start-up online brand to undercut the existing players—assuming it could find a manufacturer willing to supply lenses at wholesale prices.

"Finding a good supplier was one of the most important things, because we felt it would give us a competitive advantage that would be difficult to match," Cogan says. But unlike many consumer products (shoes or underwear or toothbrushes), there wasn't a vast universe of contact lens makers to choose from. And because contact lenses were medical devices, approval from the Food and Drug Administration was required to sell them in the United States.

So, Cogan began combing through the FDA's online database for approved manufacturers. "While everyone else I knew was going to the beach, I spent a lot of the summer on my computer in FDA databases, poring over every single manufacturer. It was a slog," he recalls.

The search yielded several dozen FDA-approved companies in the private-label contact lens business that might be potential partners. Not sure which would be interested in making contacts for them, in the fall of 2015, Cogan and Horwitz dashed off emails to all of them. Hoping to impress the recipients, they mentioned that Horwitz had attended Harvard Law School (omitting the fact that he had dropped out after realizing he didn't want to be a lawyer).

The response? Deafening silence. "They had no idea who we were. It was a cold-call email, and they didn't bother getting back to us. I wouldn't have responded to myself, either," Horwitz admits.

The two concluded that they needed to bring in people who knew the contact lens business and who had reputations that could help open doors. One person they identified was a consultant named Bret Andre, who specialized in guiding foreign companies through the process of getting FDA approval to sell their lenses in the United States. Cogan had seen Andre's name pop up in a number of the regulatory filings he had scoured. In addition, a venture capital investor put them in touch with Brian Levy, a former chief medical officer for Bausch & Lomb. Since retiring about a decade earlier, Levy had been consulting and helping run small medical companies, and he knew everyone who was anyone in the lens world and had a deep knowledge about lens manufacturing.

As in the case of many of the initial investors Dollar Shave Club's Michael Dubin approached, the reaction of Andre and Levy at first was, Huh? "My dad works for CooperVision," Andre says, referring to one of the big contact lens makers, "and I never would have thought to take them on."

After hearing the pitch, however, each quickly signed on as an adviser. "It didn't take too much persuading," recalls Levy, who liked the idea so much that he decided to make an investment in addition to becoming an adviser. "If Dollar Shave Club and Harry's can do it with blades, why not contact lenses? It's a different product, but the same business model."

Levy had always been perplexed that one-day disposable contacts were used by only one-fourth to one-third of contact lens wearers in the United States, versus about 60 percent in Europe and 90 percent in Japan. It didn't make sense. He knew from his years at Bausch & Lomb that daily lenses are more comfortable for most users than monthly ones, and are generally considered safer: they are less likely to get contaminated and cause eye infections compared with monthly soft lenses, which must be taken out by hand, stored in a cleaning solution overnight, and put back in the next day.

Cogan and Horwitz got a better response when they dropped Levy's or Andre's name in their emails to suppliers asking about purchasing daily soft lenses for sale in the United States by their new company—at the time called Clarity Contacts. And once they had a list of potential suppliers, they used several criteria to whittle it down. One was the lenses' quality and comfort—to test this, they asked for samples and then wore them, recruiting friends to help. Next was the wholesale price—it would need to be low enough that they would still see a profit after pricing the lenses at about half the cost of established brands. Finally, they wanted to make sure the manufacturers had sufficient production capacity. "If our business worked, the need to scale up would be important," Cogan explains.

One issue that Cogan and Horwitz raised with Levy early on: their research had determined that in order to get the lowest price, they would need to buy from a manufacturer that made lenses with hydrogel rather than silicone hydrogel, a newer and slightly more expensive material. The two have similar properties—both are pliable and porous, so they absorb water and conform to the shape of the eye—but the newer material allows more oxygen through. How much that matters to people who wear contacts is a subject of debate. The industry is highly regulated by the FDA, which gives its approval only after a manufacturer demonstrates the safety of the lenses it makes and shows it has quality controls that prevent contamination during production.

For some wearers, lenses made with the newer material are more comfortable, though a 2018 study found it's a matter of personal preference and there is no measurable difference. Some optometrists steer their patients away from the hydrogel lenses, contending that the newer silicone hydrogel material is healthier for the eyes.

But Levy told Horwitz and Cogan that the older hydrogel material was still commonly used and is perfectly safe. "Obviously, big companies will say there are benefits to the new technology. But does it make old hydrogel obsolete? Absolutely not," he says. "All we need to know is that it is FDA approved, that the lenses are comfortable, and that they can get the manufacturing done at a low price." As was the case with Dollar Shave Club's blades, the hydrogel lenses may not have been the most advanced. But based on Levy's years in the industry, he believed that they were certainly good enough.

Even as they started working with Levy and Andre to find a supplier, Horwitz and Cogan decided to test their concept with potential customers by conducting what's known as a demand experiment. Traditionally, big consumer product companies go through a laborious series of steps before launching a new product. The process starts with market research, followed by in-depth meetings with focus groups of target consumers. If there is enough interest, the actual product often is introduced in just a few cities, to determine demand. Then, and only then, comes a national rollout.

Following this path can cost hundreds of thousands or even millions of dollars. But in the new world of digital-first brands, an online demand experiment can be run for next to nothing. You create a simple website, explain the idea for your product—in this case, contact lenses sold by monthly subscription—and ask visitors to provide their email addresses.

In February 2016, to make sure people saw their site, Horwitz and

Cogan posted it on the Facebook pages of several dozen friends. In a matter of days, not only had many of those friends signed up, but lots of them had reposted the link, so that people they knew would see it, and many of those people signed up and reposted it for *their* Facebook friends. By the time Horwitz and Cogan took down the website, a couple thousand people had provided their email addresses, giving the two entrepreneurs confidence that they were on to something—if they could find the right supplier.

After narrowing down their supplier list to four preferred companies, all in Taiwan, the two traveled to Taipei with Brian Levy in May 2016; Bret Andre joined them there. While Cogan and Horwitz would focus on negotiating price and other terms, Levy and Andre would concentrate on making sure the plants had state-of-the-art production methods and were in good regulatory standing with the FDA.

The latter two's industry knowledge proved crucial. Indeed, without it, the trip could have been a disaster. While visiting their preferred supplier out of the four on their shortlist, Cogan and Horwitz were working out final pricing details with the company's CEO when Andre interrupted them and pulled them aside. "Hey, guys, we have a problem," he said.

Digging into the company's regulatory filings, Andre and Levy had spotted something that neither Cogan nor Horwitz would have noticed. The manufacturer had received a letter from the FDA raising questions about the testing procedures the company used to ensure the quality of its lenses. "It's a potential land mine," Andre explained. "The FDA could put their shipments on hold if this doesn't get resolved, and you wouldn't be able to deliver lenses to your customers."

Cogan and Horwitz quickly ended the discussions—"We dodged a bullet," said Cogan—though they went ahead with a planned dinner with the company's executives that evening, which lasted for three awkward hours with everyone knowing there would be no deal.

None of the other three manufacturers they visited turned out to be right, either. Their production capacity was relatively small—something the group hadn't realized until seeing their factories—which would quickly pose a problem if Hubble sales grew as fast as they hoped. They hadn't initially set up a visit with a fifth Taiwanese company, St.Shine, because a U.S. middleman they met earlier had indicated that the company would charge too high a wholesale price for Cogan and Horwitz to be able to offer their lenses at 50 percent of the retail price of their bigger U.S. rivals. But they risked leaving Taiwan without a deal, so they decided to ask St.Shine for a last-minute meeting.

Fortunately, the supplier was interested. Though it had a 20 percent market share in Japan, it did very little business in the United States, selling in small volumes to optometrists who wanted to offer a private-label alternative to Bausch & Lomb and other big players. "Our pitch to them: You've been selling in the U.S. for fifteen years, yet you have a tiny market share and still haven't cracked the mass market," Horwitz recalls telling St.Shine's executives. "Give us a chance."

One critical negotiation point: The two insisted on exclusivity for online direct-to-consumer sales in the United States, a status that Cogan and Horwitz would lose if they didn't reach a certain sales level after a year on the market. If they succeeded, they didn't want St.Shine to be able to sell its lenses to copycat companies.

For Jason Ong of St.Shine, Horwitz and Cogan presented a persuasive case. "They were using our regular product that we already made, and they paid in advance, so we had nothing to lose," Ong says. But St.Shine did decline one proposal that Cogan and Horwitz suggested: that the Taiwanese company make an investment in the start-up. "We didn't want the risk," Ong says.

After some back-and-forth over price, the parties agreed to a deal. It cost St.Shine about 24 cents to manufacture a pair of lenses; it then sold the contacts to Cogan and Horwitz for about 38 cents a pair, or $11.40 for a thirty-day supply. With marketing and other costs, that left room for the two entrepreneurs to make a profit retailing lenses for $33, plus a $3 shipping charge to the customer. Other brands typically cost $45 to $70 for a month's supply, depending on the maker and whether the purchase was made through an online discounter. But whatever they charged, the biggest contact lens makers enjoyed much more robust profit margins. Indeed, Horwitz and Cogan estimated that Bausch & Lomb, with the efficiencies of scale that come with a higher production capacity, could make a pair of soft lenses for 12 cents a pair, one-third the cost Horwitz and Cogan would pay for St.Shine lenses.

Things moved quickly once the founders returned from Taiwan. With a supply of contact lenses assured, Horwitz and Cogan finalized a commitment for a $3.5 million investment from venture capital firms and quit their jobs to focus full time on their start-up. Cogan dropped his plans to pursue an MBA degree, forfeiting the deposit he had made to attend Wharton.

To appeal to Millennials, the most likely demographic to buy lower-cost contacts, the two consciously positioned their lenses as a lifestyle brand rather than a medical product. Upon determining that another favorite name, Iris, might pose trademark problems, they changed the company name from Clarity to the catchier Hubble (after the space telescope). "We couldn't believe 'Hubble' was available," says Malcolm Buick, a brand identity consultant hired to help with the launch. "It had been on our initial list, but we said to ourselves, 'Nah, that's not going to happen.'" After some testing, they chose baby blue as the main color for their packaging. "That's central to the brand's identity. Does it look cool? Can I take it out of my medicine cabinet and put it on my coffee table?" Buick explains.

Before Hubble could begin selling lenses, it had to set up a process for confirming that a customer had a prescription from an optometrist or ophthalmologist, as contact lenses are considered regulated medical devices. So, Cogan and Horwitz created a web page where customers could enter their prescription and their doctor's name. After the prescription was verified, Hubble could then ship lenses from among the range of standard, single-vision strengths St.Shine produced.

On their launch date in November 2016, Hubble got a boost with Millennial buyers when news stories dubbed it "the Warby Parker of contact lenses." One of the initial investors, Drew Tarlow of Wildcat Capital Management, recalls that his biggest concern was whether people would put a new brand of contact lens that they'd never heard of into their eyes. "The first week they launched, Ben and Jesse put alarms on their phones that would go off when a new order came in. I remember the first day or two, you'd hear a little bell go off, and everybody would get excited," Tarlow recalls. "After a week or two, they turned it off because they had so many orders. So, I figured demand wasn't going to be an issue."

Like Dollar Shave Club, Hubble combined price—"the more affordable daily contact lens"—and convenience. In addition to appealing to customers already buying pricey daily lenses from a major brand, their goal was to grow by getting consumers to switch from monthly lenses to Hubble daily lenses. "A lot of people wear monthly lenses because they are cheaper than daily," Cogan explains. "If you're paying three hundred dollars a year for monthly, you probably don't want to pay six hundred a year or more for daily lenses"—which is what the major brands typically cost. "But you might be willing to pay three fifty to four hundred for Hubble daily disposable lenses. If we convert more people to dailies, we could grow the market significantly."

As Hubble neared its first anniversary, the two founders—looking like a couple of clean-cut college kids in jeans and untucked shirts—shot a fifteen-second ad to run during Game 2 of the 2017 World Series. They booked the ad to air only if the game went into extra innings, and so paid half the price of a guaranteed slot. The game lasted eleven innings, which gave Hubble a big audience—many viewers had stayed glued to their sets given that it was a close and exciting game. "We started Hubble because contact lenses are too expensive," Cogan said in the commercial. The number of visits to Hubble's website immediately shot up, justifying the cost of the ad.

One potential risk for Hubble was that the major brands would decide to cut their own prices; they could do that and still be very profitable. But as a Wall Street analyst for HSBC bank concluded in a report to investors, "Given the lucrative margin for contact lens[es], we think it is not in the best interest of the big four players to cut prices now unless Hubble grows" much bigger.

Critics—including optometrists, who make money selling name-brand contact lenses to their patients—continue to take shots at Hubble both for selling lenses that use the old hydrogel material and for what they view as Hubble pushing the limits of regulations by not verifying prescriptions as rigorously as it should. About a year after Hubble began selling lenses, the business news website *Quartz* found that it filled some prescriptions for lenses from fictitious optometrists; after the article ran, Hubble says, it added an extra review layer to audit orders more closely and guard against this happening. And the *New York Times* subsequently reported that regulators were concerned that companies offering contact lenses online sometimes ran afoul of rules meant to prohibit substitution of a prescription with another brand made of a different material from what an optometrist prescribed. The Federal Trade Commission, which oversees contact lens sales, in 2019 proposed tightening the rules with stricter language. It didn't name Hubble but mentioned companies that "advertise directly to consumers, often through Facebook . . . and often sell their lenses through subscription services."

How much the criticism and the growing regulatory scrutiny might hamper Hubble over time remains to be seen. Early on, it doesn't seem to have deterred many customers, or investors. By mid-2018, Hubble had raised nearly $74 million from venture capital firms, which enabled the company to ramp up growth by pouring more money into marketing and expanding internationally. Its most recent financial backers include Colgate-Palmolive, the big consumer products company whose investment arm (perhaps not coincidentally) had profited by investing in Dollar Shave Club before it was bought by Unilever. Hubble also started a related business called ContactsCart in early 2019 that resells brands made by rivals such as Bausch & Lomb and Johnson & Johnson—much like websites such as 1800contacts.com—as a way to expand its business.

In 2018, to keep up with growing demand outside the United States and diversify its supply source, Hubble signed a contract to buy lenses from a second manufacturer, Ginko International, based in China. Unlike with St.Shine, Horwitz and Cogan didn't have to explain who they were when they approached Ginko. That made doing a deal "a lot easier," Horwitz says with understatement.

4

Survival of the Fittest

Just like the supply chain itself, the sourcing options used by direct-to-consumer brand start-ups vary widely. The model used by Hubble for contact lenses and Dollar Shave Club for blades is the simplest form. You buy what the supplier already produces, put your brand name on it, add your marketing special sauce, and target the weakness of the established players—price, convenience, image, whatever.

For Warby Parker, the formula was slightly different but still relatively simple. Rather than buying the frames that an eyeglass manufacturer was already making and putting the company's name on them, Warby Parker designed its own frames to give its products a signature look. To keep costs down, it initially offered only plastic frames in about two dozen styles, using cellulose acetate, a durable, lightweight, and flexible material. This gave Warby Parker a distinctive-looking product without having to make a capital investment in a manufacturing plant and production equipment or spend money on research and development.

Warby Parker has since expanded the number and type of frames it offers—there are more than one hundred each of men's and women's styles, made of titanium as well as acetate—but all are still designed in-house. And it now operates an optical lab, where it cuts some of its own lenses, though it still contracts out frame manufacturing.

In the end, Warby Parker, Dollar Shave Club, Hubble, and other direct-to-consumer start-ups are innovating not with a fundamentally different or better product but with better something else: a better price, better value, a better experience, better customer service.

While that is the path followed by many new direct-to-consumer start-ups, some have pursued another strategy: trying to build a premium product. It can be a riskier business plan, because the degree of difficulty is higher.

When Heidi Zak and David Spector, a husband-and-wife team in their thirties, started their company, ThirdLove, to sell brassieres online, they were taking on an iconic brand, Victoria's Secret, just as Michael Dubin had done with Gillette. With a U.S. market share hovering around 33 percent, more than 1,100 stores, and an annual televised fashion show that drew millions of viewers, Victoria's Secret towered over other lingerie makers.

But rather than simply sell a standard bra like those already churned out by many dozens of apparel manufacturers around the world, Zak and Spector decided to design their own bra and use high-quality materials for the thirty-some parts that went into it. Their strategy was to disrupt the category by building a better-fitting bra that wouldn't be sold at a discount but at a *higher* price than Victoria's Secret's and other popular bras.

Zak and Spector met in business school at MIT, where they started dating in the second semester of their first year. While there, Spector cofounded Scuba-Track, a company whose software enabled users to record and share data on their dives, including the depth, duration, and location. The company failed for "myriad reasons," he recalled, and he went on to work for Google on commerce initiatives, including Google Checkout and Shopping, before joining one of Silicon Valley's prominent venture capital firms, Sequoia Capital. Meanwhile, Zak worked in strategic planning at the clothing retailer Aéropostale and then went to Google to oversee marketing for business-to-business advertising sites.

While at Sequoia, Spector met with the four Wharton students who had recently started Warby Parker and were raising money. Sequoia declined to invest because the company was so young, but the meeting left an impression on Spector. "I thought their approach to building a direct-to-consumer brand and focusing on a stale and stagnant category, and taking a digital approach to retail, was unique," he says. "That meeting was an important part of building my interest in brands."

In 2011, tiring of their corporate jobs, Zak and Spector began talking about starting an e-commerce business, but they weren't sure which category they wanted to target. Then Zak found herself rummaging with frustration in her lingerie drawer looking for a bra she liked. That made her think. Most of her dozen or so bras were uncomfortable and didn't fit quite right. Plus, there were few things she enjoyed less than buying a bra. "No woman likes to bra shop. It's last on the to-do list of twenty things. I'd personally rather empty the dishwasher, right, than go bra shopping. Putting it online makes it much easier and convenient for a woman," she would later say in a television interview. "She can do it late at night, on the weekends, whenever, and not have to go to a store."

Though neither spouse knew much about manufacturing, or bras, they figured that they could combine design sensibility with technology to build a better bra. They quit their jobs in mid-2012 and together put $100,000 into their start-up, which they named MeCommerce Inc. because they were thinking of eventually offering other brands besides bras and they liked the idea that the name suggested personalized commerce. They soon chose the name ThirdLove for the bra business, to convey the three attributes—style, feel, and fit—that they wanted women to "love" about their bras (in contrast to most brands, which offered fashion or comfort, but rarely both, and even more rarely all three).

Their first hire was Ra'el Cohen, a lingerie designer who had worked for several fashion retailers and had even started her own boutique luxury bra company a few years earlier, though it hadn't worked out. Their second hire was a NASA engineer who had expertise in computer vision technology, using cameras to collect and analyze digital images, to create a better-fitting bra.

Even though Spector had come from the venture capital world, raising money wasn't easy. After all, this was in the early days of direct-to-consumer brands. But there was another reason: Zak recalls that they pitched their idea to more than fifty VC companies, almost always conference rooms full of men who didn't understand why women might need a better bra. Still, by early 2013, they got commitments for $5.6 million in financing.

Even as they were making the rounds to raise money, their small team had begun looking to source materials to make a premium-priced bra and working to develop an iPhone app. The idea was to use technology so women could get an even better fit at home than they could in a store. Following the app's voice prompts, women would use the phone's camera to take a photo of their upper torso while wearing a bra or fitted top and standing in front of a mirror. The photo's digital data—though not the photo itself, to avoid privacy concerns—would then be sent to the company, where an algorithm would translate the two-dimensional image's data into three-dimensional measurements to recommend the right size.

In early 2013, when a version of the bra app (whose computer-vision imaging technology has since received two patents) was ready for testing, ThirdLove placed ads on Craigslist (where most ad postings are free) and invited women to come to the company's small office in San Francisco wearing their best bra. About one hundred showed up and used the app, and then tried on the prototype bra that Zak and Cohen had created based on standard sizes used in the industry.

The session confirmed what they had hoped. Though the app could be tricky to use—the mirror had to be mounted straight, and the phone's camera held in a specific position—it provided accurate measurements when it worked right. But the app also generated some valuable information they hadn't expected. As the number of women testing and trying the app increased, and the company gathered more data, they found that for about 30 percent of women, the app had a hard time recommending the right size. "It would say, 'We don't know what to do with these people, because they're not actually a 34B size or a 34C,'" Spector explains. "We kept seeing this pattern."

This gave them an idea. To make bras that fit different-size breasts and shapes better, they would make in-between sizes—half sizes, like for shoes. Cohen went to work creating the new sizes. A 34B½ would fall between a 34B and a 34C, for example; a 34C½, between a 34C and a 34D. The differences between half-and full-cup sizes might seem small, but can be enough to make a difference in fit and comfort. "With bras, every quarter inch counts," Cohen explains.

ThirdLove wasn't the first bra maker to think that in-between sizes would be a good idea. In 2004, Playtex had offered "Nearly" sizes— "Nearly A," "Nearly B," etc.—before discontinuing them after several years because demand was weak. What ThirdLove claims is different is that its half-size measurements are derived from reams of actual data based on real women using the app. And because no other bra maker was offering half sizes, that would give ThirdLove a marketing pitch to distinguish it in a very crowded market.

"Ra'el, who has been in this industry for two decades, was, like, 'I've never had data like this. Nobody has,'" says Spector. After adding half sizes, ThirdLove would eventually offer nearly eighty sizes, about double what Victoria's Secret offers. Though some apparel companies, such as Lane Bryant, which specializes in large sizes, have about the same number of bra sizes as ThirdLove or even more, many don't because it's costly. More sizes in every style and color require more inventory. More inventory requires more retail space, both for in-store displays and for backroom storage, so women can try them on and buy them while shopping. But for an online retailer such as ThirdLove, which doesn't have to worry about shelf display space or retail storage, the number of sizes isn't a constraint.

After deciding to offer half-size bras, Zak and Spector were having a hard time perfecting their app, so in mid-2013 they bought another company that was developing digital technology used for fitting apparel. While fine-tuning this, as well as the bra design and sizing, they searched for a manufacturer. In 2012, they had culled a list of potential Chinese partners from Alibaba, Google, and LinkedIn, but that didn't work out as they had hoped. "We didn't have a brand yet, we had no website, we had no customers," says Zak. "We had an idea. That doesn't get you very far in China."

A complicating factor was that they wanted a supplier to produce the bra to ThirdLove's specifications, using the materials it had selected, rather than standard materials, shapes, and sizes. And to keep inventory costs low—to avoid having a lot of finished bras sitting around until they were sold—they wanted a manufacturer to make its bras on demand, as customers placed their orders.

For a newly designed bra, they found that Chinese manufacturers expected a minimum order of 3,600 for each color, style, and size. The number isn't particularly high for apparel, but it was more than Zak and Spector wanted to commit to before having sold a single bra. "Yes, you could buy smaller minimums if you bought the standard product they made." But, Zak explains, "we didn't want to use their cup shapes, we didn't want to use their materials. The whole point of our business was to build a better product."

So, they switched their search to Mexico. By being geographically nearer, they thought, it also offered the advantage of enabling them to more closely manage the fast-turnaround production schedule they envisioned. After numerous trips, they found a company in Mexicali, about an hour's drive from Yuma, Arizona, that already made bras, albeit lower-priced, lower-quality, store-brand ones. But Zak and Spector figured that if they managed the sourcing of the components that went into making a bra—the cups, the interior elastic, the underwire and wire channel, the straps, the front closure, the eyes and hooks, the padded label—they could ensure the final quality and better fit needed to justify charging a premium for their bras, which they planned to sell for between $45 and $68.

Yet things quickly went awry soon after ThirdLove began producing and selling its bras in August 2013. "We had bras coming off the line where the wire didn't match the cup. Threads were sticking out. The cups were a little off, rather than sitting the same on each side. The sewing lines need to be perfectly straight but weren't," Zak recalls. Many bras were being returned by unhappy customers.

Part of the problem was that the workers' sewing ability wasn't good enough for a high-quality bra. Zak and Spector realized they had erred by putting in place a production process that was overly complicated. On most assembly lines, workers perform the same task over and over, and become better and faster. That's not the way their made-on-demand system worked. "Each time a woman was sewing, it was a different cup and a different band and a different color," Zak says. "We came to them with a very Silicon Valley approach to building a bra. It made sense on paper, but in actuality it didn't."

For all the problems, however, when the bras were made correctly, ThirdLove buyers liked them. Of the initial half dozen bra styles, one model was especially popular, giving optimism for the company's prospects if they could just get the quality consistently high. "Our basic bra had a single-digit return-and-exchange rate," Cohen recalls. "I'd never seen it that low before in my career. Typically, the rate is more like 20 percent."

Still, the production snafus soon cost ThirdLove hundreds of thousands of dollars on wasted materials, a large sum given the amount they had raised initially from investors. "We got to a dead end in Mexico, with not a lot of money left," Spector says.

He and Zak then decided they had no choice but to find another manufacturer. They went back to China, to a company that had more sewing expertise than the Mexican factory. They had to agree to higher minimum orders than they preferred and pay penalties if their order volume fell short. They also scrapped the complicated on-demand production that had been part of their business model. But the Chinese company's R&D team worked with ThirdLove to create a lightweight, soft memory foam that better molded the cups to the shape of women's breasts. The bras still would be constructed of the materials and parts made to ThirdLove's specs by other, specialized factories. But the Chinese contract manufacturer sewing the pieces together would manage the supply and delivery of components needed to meet production requirements, which ThirdLove had been doing when it was manufacturing in Mexico.

It took months to make the switch, but in mid-2014, production

was finally moved from Mexico to Asia. Even though the initial manufacturing glitches almost killed ThirdLove, Spector says, "We learned
a lot about what not to do, and the experience of us learning how to
make a bra, component by component, enabled us to pivot to Asia. We
knew what could go wrong, and how to work with a manufacturer to
make a really good bra. And we also learned that we should focus more
on our bestselling bra, which was renamed the 24/7 Bra."

Zak and Spector realized they were fortunate in one respect: Third-
Love's early quality problems hadn't damaged its reputation with
women permanently because sales had been so low that first year. Now,
with its manufacturing issues resolved, they figured it should be easy
to jump-start sales.

That would become their next challenge.

* * *

In March 2015, Zak and Spector convened a meeting of a dozen senior
managers in the company's office in the gentrifying Dogpatch neighborhood, a couple of miles south of downtown San Francisco. Their
message: the start-up was in danger of running out of money and
needed to find a way to increase sales.

ThirdLove had already survived its near-death experience from its
manufacturing problems, but now a new crisis loomed: even though
most women who purchased ThirdLove bras liked them, not nearly
enough were buying them. "If we don't figure out how to sell more bras
and get women to try them, then we will not be here in six months to a
year," Zak advised her colleagues. "We will truly not exist."

Achieving success at ThirdLove was proving more difficult than
expected. "How hard could this be?" Zak recalls thinking. "We'll figure
it out. We're smart, we'll work hard. Then, all of a sudden, you're staring
at each other over the kitchen table. I had that moment, like, 'Oh God,
what did we do?'"

Adding to the challenge, Zak and Spector weren't the only ones
with the idea to start an online bra company. They faced a half dozen
other VC-backed competitors, who were making it hard to rise above
the noise.

ThirdLove was struggling even though its measurement app, designed to deliver a better-fitting bra, had received an avalanche of attention. Zak and Spector had been interviewed by *Fast Company*, *Forbes*, and *Inc.*, and the app was featured on fashion sites such as *InStyle* and *HelloBeautiful*. ("Would you try a boob selfie fitting app?") It was the type of overwhelmingly positive free publicity that start-ups dream about but rarely get. Alas, it didn't boost business nearly as much as the founders expected, and annual sales were still running well below $1 million.

Nothing seemed to appreciably move the sales needle. "No orders are coming through. We refresh our website, and it's crickets. Nobody is hearing us," Zak told the group gathered in the conference room. One problem they had to overcome, they all knew, was that other companies had touted better-fitting bras in the past and had never really delivered on the promise. "This is a product that women have always been skeptical about, and with ThirdLove being online only, people were especially skeptical of us," Spector says. "There's been this barrier of trust, and for decades and decades women felt they have been let down. We need to do something to lower that barrier."

Then, someone—nobody remembers who it was—tossed out an idea: "What if we let women try it for free for thirty days? Wear it to work and make sure they like it before paying?" The group batted around the risks. "There could be a lot of inventory out there for no money back initially, right? No sales until day thirty," Spector said. And what if the return rate was high? A bra that someone had not just tried on but had worn for a few weeks wasn't like a pair of Warby Parker eyeglass frames that had been returned. Those could be cleaned and then sent out for a try-on by another customer. A used bra couldn't be resold to someone else.

But everyone agreed that ThirdLove had to try something bold. A free trial would send a message to potential customers that the company was confident that its bras would fit women better than their old ones.

And so, in May 2015, ThirdLove inaugurated its "free trial program" advertising campaign (later renamed Try Before Buying). It was largely on Facebook, not on television or in newspapers or women's magazines, where bra makers such as Victoria's Secret traditionally do most of their advertising. Like most direct-to-consumer brand start-ups, ThirdLove couldn't afford a multimillion-dollar advertising campaign.

The ads were simple and straightforward, the better to catch a woman's attention as she scrolled through her Facebook News Feed. They featured a photo of a ThirdLove bra and a straight-to-the-point message: "30-day risk-free trial. If it's not the most comfortable bra you've ever worn, return it for free" (with the word *free* in boldface, to make sure the point wasn't missed). Or: "The World's Most Comfortable Bra. 30-day free trial. Signature half cups. Try it for free" (with the last line highlighted in a purple box). Occasionally, the ads would include testimonials from existing customers. For the free trial, customers had to pay a $1 shipping fee initially charged to their credit card, and they would be billed $64 for the bra only if it weren't returned within a month.

The advertising took advantage of Facebook's "look-alike" targeting feature, which directed the ads to people most likely to be customers: women between the ages of twenty-five and sixty-five who fit the demographic of being able to afford a higher-priced bra or who had been searching online for bras or other intimate apparel. The targeting helped to keep their spending down, which was critical, given ThirdLove's need to conserve cash.

ThirdLove started cautiously, in case a significant proportion of women who ordered the bras returned them, which would have been a disaster for the company. Indeed, some employees were nervous about the program. "I remember walking in the door, and we were talking about scaling the program," recalls Veronique Powell, vice president of operations and strategy, who had left a job at Gap and joined Third-Love not long after it launched Try Before Buying. "That blew my mind. I thought, 'There's no way this can work.'"

There were some anxious moments early on. About 10 percent of the orders went awry. In some cases, credit cards used by buyers expired or were lost between the order's being placed and the end of the thirty days, or purchases were made with debit or prepaid cards that didn't have a sufficient balance to cover the price of the bra, meaning that ThirdLove had to write off the sale or contact those buyers to try to collect the money for bras that hadn't been returned. Powell shakes her head in amazement when recalling how some buyers gamed the system. One woman even went so far as to buy six bras over a six-month period, returning each at the end of thirty days, before ThirdLove caught on and blocked her from the free-trial program.

Still, sales started ticking up immediately. Even better, Zak says, "The keep rate"—the percentage of people who liked the bra and paid for it at the end of the free-trial period—"was high, around seventy to seventy-five percent." By January 2016, confident that the Try Before Buying campaign was working and that the payment kinks had been worked out, ThirdLove increased its Facebook ad budget to about $100,000, and sales rose to 3,000 bras per month. By the next January, monthly bra sales had risen to 38,000 as the company increased its Facebook spending to $2 million.

With orders pouring in, ThirdLove had more revenue to plow back into marketing the Home Try-On program, helped by instantaneous feedback from Facebook. The data revealed the best time of the day, and best day of the week, to get the most sales for the least money spent. ThirdLove's staff knew what percentage of the people who saw the ad clicked on it and went to ThirdLove's website and, of course, how many actually ordered a bra.

This meant they could track precisely how much it cost in advertising for each click and each sale. Before the free-trial program, Third-Love was spending several hundred dollars in advertising for each bra it sold. With the new ad campaign, the customer acquisition cost plummeted to about $40 to $50. "We put a lot of money behind it and ran with it," says Zak. In 2016 and 2017, the free-trial campaign, advertised almost exclusively on social media, generated about 80 percent of the company's sales, which increased from around $1 million in 2015 to nearly $20 million the next year, then jumped to about $75 million in 2017 and more than $130 million in 2018.

With social media advertising, ThirdLove managed to break

through the clutter by spending a small fraction of what it would have needed for a television or print ad campaign. It also got a boost from a new online "Fit Finder" quiz, which replaced the smartphone sizing app in 2016. Because the app was tricky to use and was available only for iPhone owners, lead designer Ra'el Cohen worked with ThirdLove's data team to develop a detailed questionnaire that was as accurate as the app in determining a customer's size. It walked website visitors through a series of questions about their current bra—the maker, the size, the fit of the cup (*cups gape a little . . . cups overflow a lot*), band, and straps. And it asked them to select, from a series of drawings of different-shaped breasts, which pair most resembled theirs. Among the nine options: Asymmetric (*one breast is larger than the other*), Bell (*slimmer at the top, fuller at the bottom*), East West (*nipples point outward, in opposite directions*).

By 2018, eleven million women had taken the Fit Finder quiz, and ThirdLove had largely ended the Try Before Buying program. "We don't need it because now people know our brand and our product, and they have friends who have worn it," Zak says. "But figuring that out changed the course of our business. Without that program, truthfully, we would not be here today." Thanks to the strategy's success, ThirdLove would go from a start-up facing the abyss to a fast-growing company with a valuation of more than $750 million, about ten times the amount of VC money it had raised as of 2019.

5

From Mad Men to Math Men

For ThirdLove, as for so many direct-to-consumer start-ups, social media advertising was a game changer. "Facebook's quick ability for targeting a look-alike audience, and reaching people who are similar to people who have recently purchased from you, made it a huge part of our growth," Heidi Zak explains. "It's limitless how much you can test. You can find out what kind of imagery and graphics and words work, and mix them up to find the best combination. If the ad we put up is a video, we know how many [users] click on it. How long they watch the video. How many watch to the end of the video. How many click through to our website."

As recently as the 1990s, advertising was dominated by the big agencies on New York's Madison Avenue. In the cacophony of the marketplace, if you wanted to be a national brand, you hired an advertising agency to create what you hoped would be memorable TV commercials, and then spent huge sums to air them. Even then, you couldn't be sure if the money was well spent, certainly not in the short term, giving rise to the adage that 50 percent of advertising works and 50 percent doesn't, you just don't know which. But there was really no alternative, which put start-ups with new brands at a huge disadvantage.

In the 2000s, Silicon Valley became ascendant in the world of advertising. The change started with Google, whose search engine algorithm allowed anyone, even start-ups, to spend as much or as little as they wanted to find potential customers by bidding for popular search words and posting sponsored links.

The rise of social media opened an even bigger spigot of options, as brands could tap directly into networks of like-minded consumers. Some of that promotion grew organically, as happy customers posted photos of themselves using the products—Dollar Shave Club razors, Warby Parker eyeglasses, Hubble contact lenses, Glossier cosmetics— endorsing them for free. Other companies recruited and paid "influencers" who enjoyed large social media followings.

But first a company had to generate interest and sales, and for ThirdLove and hundreds of other new, direct-to-consumer brands, Facebook (and Instagram, which Facebook bought in 2012) emerged as the great equalizer. For as little as few hundred dollars a day, a start-up could buy ad space on social media platforms. The ads could be produced for a pittance, because they didn't have to be fancy. In fact, simplicity conveyed authenticity.

Facebook wasn't always an advertising behemoth. Before it began using sophisticated algorithms to rake in tens of billions of dollars in revenue annually, its initial forays into marketing were fairly basic. In the early days, it created an icon that let its users "like" things, such as Facebook pages set up by companies; then those companies could direct ads to people based on their "likes." Most advertisers in Facebook's early days were big corporations that treated the platform as just another advertising channel, much like TV, to increase brand awareness. It wasn't yet recognized as an ideal venue for "performance marketing," that is, funneling in new customers and driving sales growth. Facebook then began introducing a series of features to make it easier for advertisers to identify people who weren't already customers but who demographically fit the profile of potential customers.

To build its advertising business, Facebook started cultivating alliances with digital marketing firms, many of them start-ups themselves. "Facebook was trying to figure out how we differentiate ourselves, because Google was so dominant with search in the digital advertising space," recalls Patricia Lai, who joined Facebook in December 2009, as it was looking for ways to determine how best to combat Google.

Facebook began scouring lists of those advertisers who were increasing their spending on the site, to learn what they were doing and to find ways to encourage them (and other potential advertisers) to spend even more. Among the top one hundred, amid familiar names such as Pepsi and Samsung and Kellogg's, someone spotted a San Francisco company called Ampush, a digital marketing firm that no one at Facebook had ever heard of.

Who are these guys? Lai wondered.

Ampush was founded in the fall of 2009 by three friends who were roommates in the undergraduate program at Wharton. After graduation, they went to work for big consulting companies or Wall Street firms and were soon earning several hundred thousand dollars a year. But after a few years, they were bored and decided to start a business. Two of them, Jesse Pujji and Aniket (Nick) Shah, moved to California— initially to Pujji's childhood home in San Diego, where they lived with his parents to save money—while the third, Chris Amos, continued working and shared his income to fund the trio while they started their business, Ampush. (The company's name comes from the first two letters of each of their last names: AMos, PUjji, SHah.)

"My dad wasn't exactly supportive of me leaving Goldman Sachs," Pujji recalls. "He said, 'I paid for you to go to an Ivy League college!'" That pretty much sums it up, his father agrees: "I didn't think it was a smart move. He was clueless what he was going to do at first, working out of a little office, living at home with us."

Indeed, the three young men didn't have a specific business plan. But they were digitally savvy and understood the growing importance of data, and decided that something related to online advertising might be worth exploring. "Digital media and online marketing were the spinal cord of the internet," Pujji explains. "We call it sandbox entrepreneurship. Play in the sandbox, and something good will come up."

The three moved Ampush to San Francisco after less than a year because . . . well, it's the center of the digital world, and San Diego isn't. They also decided to focus their efforts on the educational market. For-profit colleges are a multibillion-dollar-a-year business, with an insatiable appetite for students. To find them, these institutions pay advertising agencies for "leads" they generate; the schools figure they will be able to enroll a certain percentage of people who express interest. In February 2010, Amos, Pujji, and Shah went to a conference in Las Vegas, where they persuaded a half dozen for-profit schools such as Kaplan University and the University of Phoenix to give them contracts that would pay Ampush for attracting potential students.

But they quickly learned how little they knew about internet advertising.

They set up a website called DegreeAmerica.com and began bidding for Google search words. When someone clicked on the ad Ampush had placed, he was taken to the site and asked for his email address, which was passed on to an educational institution that would contact him and try to sign him up. Like other advertisers specializing in this "lead-generation" business, Ampush was paid around $50 for each email address it collected and forwarded.

At the start, it was a disaster. Ampush was spending $800 to $1,000 on Google advertising for each lead it managed to generate, losing hundreds of dollars on each potential student it found. "We ran up $100,000 in credit card debt. It was costing us far more to get each lead than we expected, and more than a school would pay us," Pujji recalls.

Through trial and error, they managed to turn a modest profit several months later, after they figured out how to better tailor their ads so that a much higher percentage of people who clicked and came to their site would provide their email addresses. Still, it was a crowded market, with a number of other online ad agencies going after the same pool of potential students.

While brainstorming about how to stand out and find more potential students at a lower cost, the founders began to think about an alternative to Google. "We asked an intern, 'Go figure out this Facebook thing,'" recalls Nick Shah. "'How would we use this thing?' And she created this whole playbook." Ampush then had to develop the software over time to make the concept work at scale on Facebook's platform, and to keep improving it.

Both Google and Facebook require advertisers to place bids for keywords. The winning bid is based on a formula that includes the amount of the bid and the likelihood that someone will click on the ad. The critical difference when it comes to advertising, Shah says, is that Facebook is an audience platform, while Google is an "intent" platform. Google is great at identifying people who enter a search term—that is, those who actively express an intent or an interest in something. Facebook is better at identifying a target audience, people who *might* be interested in something but haven't yet expressed that interest online.

"With Google, you can go find a thousand people who might be searching for a master's in teaching today," he explains. "But on Facebook you can find tens of thousands of people who identify themselves in their profiles as substitute teachers who might be thinking about getting an advanced degree but haven't searched yet. That was the insight. You can target the right people, catch their eye, and sign them up."

It was their "aha" moment. Facebook in 2010 was like Google a decade earlier, its power as an advertising platform not fully understood or appreciated. "We wanted to be the 'it' company for social media marketing," Pujji says.

To test its ideas, Ampush began to target its advertising toward Facebook users who indicated in their profiles that they were substitute teachers. The straightforward pitch: "Sick of being a substitute teacher? Go back to school." It worked beyond their expectations. "There was an amazing click-through rate," Pujji says, referring to people who saw the ad, clicked on it, and provided their email addresses.

With fewer advertisers on Facebook at the time, there was less competition. So, if you knew what you were doing, you could bid less to advertise on Facebook than on Google and could generate more leads. It was a bit like Wall Street, where the Ampush founders had learned that you could mint money with smart arbitrage, that is, taking advantage of different prices for similar assets—the assets in this case being keywords for digital advertising. "We'd been banging our heads against the wall advertising on Google. This was way less expensive. The price for a click was 60 to 80 percent cheaper."

To scale their spending on Facebook, Ampush wrote software that plugged into the site's advertising platform; the software automated the way Ampush placed ads and bids on Facebook and made it easier to target groups of potential customers and to bid at the lowest possible cost. With Ampush's software, Pujji explains, "You could quickly customize and personalize the ad on Facebook. It could automatically target different cities, likes, and interests; ages and other variables; and push thousands of ads. It would then change the price bid of the ads dynamically based on how they performed." It was a decision that would help make Ampush one of the pioneers in social media advertising.

In March 2011, Ampush was improving its internal technology to optimize Facebook results when Pujji got a call from Patricia Lai at Facebook, who about six months earlier had been assigned to reach out to the founders of Ampush and work with them after the company's name had popped up as a top advertiser on Facebook. She invited him and his colleagues to meet with her bosses at Facebook, even though the type of advertising Ampush was doing "was not the model that Facebook wanted to be known for," Lai says, given the somewhat unsavory, high-pressure sales reputation that some for-profit colleges had. "We were trying to understand their business model."

Pujji and a handful of colleagues piled into two cars and drove to Facebook headquarters in Silicon Valley. He recalls, laughing, "I don't think they were expecting Penn graduates and Goldman Sachs alumni to show up. They expected to find online hustlers."

In the meeting, the Facebook executives quizzed the group about the software tools Ampush had developed for their Facebook advertising. "They knew the Facebook algorithm really well," Lai recalls. "They had done little things to optimize bidding, like not competing with themselves for the same bids, and trying A/B tests"—variations on an ad, to determine which performed better—"so had figured out how to get the best return on investment from ad spending." Those insights, it turns out, were in Facebook's interest as well as Ampush's, because making it easier to advertise more effectively on Facebook would give companies a reason to switch more advertising there. Facebook was taking a page from Microsoft's book when it rose to dominance decades earlier by encouraging software developers to write their word processing, spreadsheet, and other programs for its operating system, thus making Microsoft's product more useful and eventually an essential component of a PC.

Not long after the meeting, Facebook invited Ampush to become one of its "Preferred Marketing Developers," a program in which marketers are granted special access to Facebook's platform so they can write increasingly sophisticated software that would make it easier for advertisers to target specific audiences. The recognition prompted Ampush, one of the smaller companies in this program, to expand its horizons and pivot away from for-profit-college lead generation and look for new advertising clients. In 2013, it was granted entry to the even more exclusive "Strategic Preferred Marketing Developer" group, whose members were granted access to Facebook's advertising platform changes.

One evening early that year, as Ampush executives were discussing a list of potential advertising clients, they watched a new video that Michael Dubin had released for Dollar Shave Club's second product, wet wipes called One Wipe Charlies. The group loved it, and reached an immediate consensus: "These guys are really funny. We should be working with them," recalls David Hawkins, who had been hired by Ampush that February as a salesman to drum up new business.

Dollar Shave Club was still a small company at the time. Its sales in 2012 had been $4 million, so it didn't yet have a big advertising budget. However, Ampush learned that Dubin was in the process of raising a $12 million round of VC funding that fall. Ampush's founders got an introduction to Dubin from Peter Pham of Science, one of their advisers—Pham had a small ownership stake in Ampush—and pitched a proposal for Dollar Shave Club to spend heavily on Facebook to speed growth.

With the additional financing in hand, Dollar Shave Club brought in Ampush to test its ideas. The ads targeted users in several distinct groups based on what Facebook had gleaned from their activity: one group they dubbed "whales," the highest-value customers, who bought shave cream and wipes as well as razors; another they called "executives," those who subscribed to Dollar Shave Club's most expensive, six-blade razor; and "fans," who had "liked" Dollar Shave Club on the company's Facebook page but hadn't yet subscribed.

Ampush raised or lowered the amount of money it bid to advertise on Facebook based on the expected LTV (or "lifetime value") of people in each targeted group, determined by calculating how long customers likely would remain a subscriber and what mix of products they would purchase. "Back then, for each customer who would buy $150 from you over a lifetime, it would only cost you $25 to $40 [in Facebook ad spending] to get," Pujji recalls. The payback was so good that Dollar Shave Club's daily Facebook spending quickly rose from about $2,000 to $10,000 to more than $50,000.

In what has since become standard practice for social media marketing, Dollar Shave Club experimented with as many as fifty different ad messages to see which ones would get the highest response. In contrast with traditional TV or print advertising, this is easy on Facebook because the ads are shorter and tend to be less polished.

Ads featuring photos taken by customers of newly delivered razors were among the most effective. "Because of how inexpensive our razors were, there was a lot of skepticism around 'Are these razors really that great?'" recalls John Brian Kim, who headed customer acquisition at the razor start-up. "You pay for what you get, right? By showcasing real boxes from real members talking about how great, how high-quality, our razors were, that led to people giving us a shot." Another ad that brought in lots of subscribers was a straight-up price comparison with Gillette. For a third ad, targeted at women, "we coined the 'pink razor tax' to highlight the fact that Gillette's women's razors were more expensive than its men's razors," Kim says.

By mid-2014, Dollar Shave Club was signing up 55,000 new subscribers a month from Facebook alone, more than double the rate at the beginning of the campaign. Its sales for the year rose to $65 million, triple the year before. Kim says Ampush gets a lot of the credit. "We got a better sense of the Facebook ecosystem working with them," he notes.

The campaign's success helped Ampush as much as it did Dollar Shave Club. In 2015, Ampush ranked number 61 on the Inc. 5000, the magazine's list of the fastest-growing private companies based on their percentage rate of growth. It no longer had trouble getting in the door to make pitches. "As a by-product of our work with Dollar Shave Club, a lot of good things happened," Hawkins says. "A lot of buzz was created because of our success there. It got talked about a lot in the start-up community." Ampush's client list would grow to include not only new direct-to-consumer brands such as Hubble and Madison Reed hair coloring but also larger companies such as Uber and StubHub. In 2015, a much bigger digital marketing company named Red Ventures paid $15 million for a 20 percent stake in Ampush.

Ampush's success sent a clear signal to direct-to-consumer start-ups. While not everybody could develop a viral video, as Michael Dubin had for Dollar Shave Club, anybody could copy Dollar Shave Club's Facebook strategy of using social media to target its most likely customers and constantly testing and iterating its ads using data that revealed what was working and what wasn't.

Over time, Facebook's ad targeting would become significantly more sophisticated. As the number of active users grew from tens of millions to well over a billion, Facebook collected more and more data on each user. It built "black box" algorithms that could identify "look-alike" audiences by aggregating billions of bits of data to predict who was most likely to respond to an ad message—even if a person at first glance did not seem similar to others in the selected group.

Facebook posted a how-to guide on its website and offered to do much of the work for the advertiser: "When you create a Lookalike Audience, you choose a source audience . . . and we identify the common qualities of people in it (example: demographic information or interests). Then we find people who are similar to (or 'look like') them." Facebook also helped select different target audiences and advised advertisers on the optimum size of the audience for each message for best results, typically anywhere from a few thousand to hundreds of thousands.

No wonder that just about anyone who spends time on Facebook and Instagram is bombarded with a steady flow of ads pitching new brands. There, among your cousin's new baby photos, your friend's pictures of hiking in the Himalayas, and fake news posts from Russian operatives, are ads for Away luggage, Hubble contact lenses, Quip electric toothbrushes, Glossier cosmetics, Allbirds or Rothy's shoes, Prose shampoo, Madison Reed hair coloring, Dollar Shave Club razors, MVMT watches, Brooklinen bedding, Purple mattresses, Brandless (yes, that is the name of a direct-to-consumer brand) groceries . . . and ThirdLove bras.

* * *

At first glance, the fourteen different ThirdLove video ads placed on Facebook and Instagram over a two-week period in the fall of 2018 looked pretty much the same. They all featured women wearing ill-fitting bras, to highlight ThirdLove's marketing message that this wouldn't be a problem if only you bought one of its bras.

But the text accompanying the videos differed slightly:

> Say goodbye to that gape, dig, or itch. ThirdLove bras have memory foam cups, no-slip straps, and tagless bands. Take the Fit Finder quiz to find your perfect fit in 60 seconds and receive a recommended size and style!

> It's time for a bra that actually fits. Say goodbye to bras that dig, gape, or fall down and try a bra with premium details instead.

> Say goodbye to bras that dig, gape, or slip. ThirdLove bras have a 60 day fit guarantee. Wear it. Wash it. If you don't love it, for any reason, we'll take it back.

The videos also have minor variations. Some show a model wearing a bra that is "gaping" because the cups are slightly too large for the woman's breasts. Some show a woman putting back in place a strap that has slipped off her shoulder, and others show a model struggling to adjust the band riding up on her back. These run fifteen seconds. A few videos run twenty seconds and show a combination of two of these problems. And others run thirty seconds and show all three problems on the same video.

Do these minor differences matter? The data says they do.

In the world of television, measuring accurately how a commercial has performed can be difficult, especially in the short term. But in the world of Facebook, this task couldn't be easier or more precise. Third-Love knows instantaneously what's working and what's not, through the volume of data captured for each iteration of every ad it shows: the percentage of people who clicked on each version, how long on average they watched it, how many watched to the end, how many responded by taking ThirdLove's online Fit Finder quiz, and, most important, how many purchased a bra after seeing the ad.

Every two weeks, a team gathers to dissect the numbers for the latest batch of Facebook ads. During the fourteen-day period tested for these particular videos, the data showed that ThirdLove spent $52 in advertising on Facebook for each sale, and the ads had a 4.2 percent conversion rate, meaning that 4.2 percent of those people who clicked on the ad ended up buying a bra. But there was a wide range of performance among the ads, with the fifteen-second "gaping cups" ad accounting for 25 percent of those sales, highest among the fourteen ads, with others accounting for as few as 7 percent of the resulting sales. ThirdLove uses these results to determine which ads to show more often and which to drop from the lineup.

In a constant search for the best results for the least amount of spending on Facebook, ThirdLove will produce and post variations of hundreds of different videos a month. This requires what resembles a factory assembly line—from the shooting of the material to a team that slices and dices the images into multiple videos to the people who post the videos and then analyze the data. And it requires a huge volume of images.

On a warm mid-September afternoon in San Francisco, in a studio a few miles from the corporate office, ThirdLove creative director Gabrielle DiClemente is overseeing a rapid-fire photo shoot of two models, each wearing fifty different bras and undergarments. The models are fuller-figured, in keeping with ThirdLove's positioning strategy. Victoria's Secret sells sexy. ThirdLove sells natural, and wants women to look at its models and say, "I can see myself in her."

For Facebook ads, cheap and fast trump polished. In the pre-Facebook world, a photo shoot like this would have aimed to produce perhaps eight exquisitely framed shots a day; now the goal is twenty-five to thirty more natural shots—each selected and digitally edited while the shoot is still in progress, to speed up production. "We can take all these different clips, piece them together in different orders, and then upload them onto Facebook to see what the audience is interested in," DiClemente explains. "If they didn't like it, you['d] have all this content sitting on the cutting room floor." From shooting the models in the studio to posting the ads, it will take a month or less, versus two to three months in the past.

But relying on Facebook to catapult online sales has become harder than in the early days of direct-to-consumer start-ups. To avoid overwhelming its users with ads, and thus causing them to tune out, Facebook limits ads in newsfeeds on its mobile phone app to about one in every five items posted. By 2018, it had more than six million advertisers, versus one million in 2013. With more companies advertising, that means more competition. ThirdLove and everyone else now has to bid higher to place ads.

To stand out, and keep people clicking, ThirdLove and other online brands have increasingly switched to videos from photos in their social media ads. "Facebook basically told us, hey, you have to move to video, that's where we're seeing a lot of results. There's not a lot of production quality but, oh my God, it worked," says Nisho Cherison, ThirdLove's head of growth marketing. The amount of money ThirdLove had to spend to get a customer on Facebook, which had been steadily rising, declined 25 percent as a result—although it still was slightly higher than when it began spending heavily on its Try Before Buying program in 2015.

Before joining ThirdLove in 2016, Cherison ran digital marketing at One Kings Lane, an online home décor start-up. "Back in 2011," he recalls, "there were not many advertisers on Facebook. My cost per click used to be twenty to thirty cents. Today it can range anywhere from a dollar fifty to three dollars and even four dollars." And clicks aren't sales—it is just someone opening an ad on Facebook to view it.

With annual sales racing past $100 million for the first time in 2018, ThirdLove's success posed a problem. The bigger the pool of customers you try to reach on Facebook, the more you have to include groups whose profile is less like that of your existing customers—meaning that you risk spending more money to target people less likely to order your product. Even though Facebook remains effective, you start getting diminishing returns for every incremental dollar spent. Moreover, despite Facebook's huge audience, it doesn't reach everyone.

As recently as 2017, about 80 percent of ThirdLove's marketing dollars went to Facebook and Instagram, typical for many direct-to-consumer brands. By late 2018, that figure had dropped to roughly 50 percent. Like established brands, ThirdLove and other start-ups have found they need to diversify their advertising spending, with podcasts, old-fashioned direct mail, billboards, and even newspaper, magazine, and television advertising. So, in the fall of 2018, ThirdLove tried something it hadn't done, and couldn't afford to do, before. It hired a big advertising agency that helped it develop a new marketing campaign that included a polished TV commercial costing about $950,000 to produce, many times what the company was spending monthly just a few years earlier. ThirdLove's advertising budget for all of 2018 would exceed $50 million. And the ads increasingly drew a contrast with Victoria's Secret, following Dollar Shave Club's playbook of trying to attack what it saw as its bigger rival's weaknesses.

In the case of Dollar Shave Club, it was Gillette's high prices and the inconvenience of buying blades locked behind a store counter. That wouldn't work for ThirdLove's bras, which cost more than most of Victoria's Secret's bras. So, instead, ThirdLove has targeted what some in the #MeToo era see as Victoria's Secret's outdated, even offensive, emphasis on sexy models with the hourglass figures few women have.

To highlight the difference, ThirdLove's ad campaign features women of all ages, shapes, and sizes, with the tagline "To Each, Her Own."

Victoria's Secret's image, along with the entry of various new online players led by ThirdLove, has put it on the defensive. Though it remains the biggest bra maker, its U.S. market share fell to 24 percent in 2018, from about 33 percent two years earlier. ThirdLove is growing fast but is much smaller, with around 2 percent of the U.S. market in 2018. But sensing its rival's weakness, ThirdLove has gleefully engaged in public tête-à-têtes with Victoria's Secret. In an interview with *Vogue* in November 2018, a senior executive at L Brands, which owns Victoria's Secret, derided the idea of featuring plus-size or transgender women in its annual televised fashion extravaganza, saying, "The show is a fantasy." And then, in a parting shot, he added, "We're nobody's third love. We're their first love."

If the idea was to put down ThirdLove, it had the opposite effect, prompting fierce criticism of Victoria's Secret and putting ThirdLove in the spotlight with free publicity. Heidi Zak was inundated with interview requests, and she appeared on the *Today* show shortly afterward. Though she and her husband are equals in the company, cofounders and co-CEOs, it isn't uncommon for people to think that she founded and runs ThirdLove herself. That's because there is one area where they don't share co-billing: the savvy couple recognize that it is smart strategy for her, a woman, to be the public face of the company.

In a full-page ad in the Sunday *New York Times*, written as "An Open Letter to Victoria's Secret"—signed by Zak alone as "Founder, ThirdLove"—she wrote, "You market to men, and sell a male fantasy to women . . . We believe the future is building a brand for every woman, regardless of her shape, size, age, ethnicity, gender identity, or sexual orientation." This got more media coverage for ThirdLove, as did Victoria Secret's hiring its first transgender model in 2019 in belated recognition that it was out of step with the times. Even this news was an occasion for reporters to remind readers that, in the earlier spat, ThirdLove had scored points against its bigger rival.

Even Facebook advertising couldn't deliver that.

6

The Algorithm Is Always Right

The customer, a woman in her mid-to late forties, knows what she wants when she logs onto eSalon.com to order its customized hair coloring for the first time: dye to match her natural blonde color, and cover up her grays, with the lightest blonde shade it offers. As she clicks through a series of about a dozen questions, the algorithm inside eSalon's computers starts churning away. By the time the customer finishes answering the questionnaire, the algorithm, without anyone from the company having met this customer or even spoken to her, will understand her hair color better than she does.

How long is your hair? it asks. *How much gray do you have? How straight or curly is your hair? How thick is your hair? What is your ethnicity? What color are your eyes? What is your natural hair color? Which is the closest shade to your natural color? Would you like to maintain your current color?*

To help her, the questionnaire shows thirty-one photos of different shades of blonde, with very small gradations from lighter to darker colors. At the end, she selects the lightest blonde color eSalon offers, just as she intended. But that's not exactly what she will receive.

eSalon has collected data from more than five million people. Based on this woman's answers, it knows the best color formulation to achieve the blonde look she wants, regardless of what she thinks. eSalon's computers have learned from crunching the data that many first-time customers who fit her profile and ordered the lightest blonde dye have been disappointed; they felt their hair came out looking too blonde—too "hot," in hair color jargon. The data showed that a higher number of customers asked for a slightly darker color for their next order, so their hair wouldn't come out looking quite so light.

Knowing all this, eSalon automatically sends the customer—without telling her—a formulation that has 98 percent of its lightest blonde shade with 2 percent blue added to soften the color, or cool it, rather than 100 percent blonde. "After seeing this data, we adjusted our algorithm so that new customers who are a natural pure blonde and want to keep that look automatically get that little bit of blue added," explains Thomas MacNeil, eSalon's chief technology officer. "They're happier with the result, even though they're asking for the blondest of blonde that we have."

For eSalon, and almost all direct-to-consumer brands, data is the coin of the realm. The data they collect directly from each customer provides a significant advantage over bigger, long-established brands. Clairol doesn't have this data because the customers it deals with directly are retailers. The people who use the product are largely anonymous to Clairol and most big companies; they walk into a drugstore, pick a box of hair color off the shelf, pay for it, and walk out.

eSalon's shelf is its website, and it collects information about each customer who walks through its digital door and answers its question-naire. The longer a woman remains a customer, the more eSalon knows about her—and not just her. eSalon aggregates all of that individual data and uses machine-learning algorithms and predictive analysis to inform virtually everything it does: from adjusting its product formu-lations to introducing new products (e.g., color for highlighting hair) to testing seemingly insignificant word changes on its web pages. "In the end, we're a tech company selling a beauty product," says Tamim Mourad, one of eSalon's cofounders.

Data mining is critical to the biggest challenges facing all direct-to-consumer brands: holding down the cost of attracting customers and keeping them after a purchase or two. Using the data it has gathered, eSalon has improved its retention rate from below 50 to about 70 percent on its customers' initial orders. One of the key metrics, especially for subscription companies such as eSalon, Dollar Shave Club, and Hubble, is a customer's lifetime value, or how much she will spend over time. The cost of acquiring customers can be offset only if a lot of them become repeat customers who buy month after month or, even better, year after year. "It's all about retention, because nobody makes money on the first order," explains Francisco Gimenez, another cofounder.

Businesses have used predictive analytics for the past couple of decades, but the growing power of computers, along with the ability of online brands to gather huge amounts of data from customers and potential customers, has made machine learning central to their success. "It's such a big deal, the fact that these companies' sales are largely digital. The fact that they have a consistent digital trail for all their customers is a huge windfall," says Eric Siegel, who runs his own predictive analytics firm.

Direct-mail companies were pioneers in using data analytics to target consumers, Siegel notes. "If you've got a list of five hundred thousand customers, and you're going to spend a few dollars per individual to actually send them something physical in the mail, and then some very, very small sliver actually responds, the name of the game is discerning the patterns that define customers that are much more likely to actually respond. If I can find the 20 percent who are a few more times likely than average to actually buy what I mail them, and I only mail to that top echelon, even though I don't get any business from the other 80 percent I've left off the list, the bottom-line profit of the marketing campaign skyrockets by many times over."

Predictive analysis of consumer behavior has become far more sophisticated in recent years. As commerce has increasingly moved online, companies have collected much more data from customers. And the computing power to run algorithms and make correlations has increased exponentially, too. Virtually every company, big and small, uses predictive analysis, from banks determining who qualifies for a credit card to online dating services divining which couples would be good matches.

Netflix put predictive analytics in the spotlight in 2006 by announcing a competition, with a $1 million grand prize, for creating the best algorithm that would improve its in-house user movie recommendations. Three years later, a team won by writing an algorithm that was 10 percent better at predicting which movies Netflix viewers would like, which resulted in higher customer retention rates.

Among e-commerce start-ups, one of the earliest power users of data analytics was Stitch Fix, an online styling service that provides personalized shopping, selecting clothes that meet a customer's fashion sensibility and budget. The company was started in 2011 for women who didn't have time to shop or who wanted help picking out clothes. (It has since expanded to include men and children.) Customers are mailed a selection of five items and can keep what they want and return what they don't want, at no charge—except for a $20 styling fee, which can be applied to a purchase. Stitch Fix's success depends on customers keeping some of the items, making it imperative that the company anticipate, without having met the customers, what items they are most likely to keep.

To figure this out, Stitch Fix starts with a questionnaire, to ascertain a customer's preferences, which are then analyzed by a human stylist. Like eSalon, Stitch Fix uses predictive analysis based not only on the customer's initial answers but on what she keeps and doesn't keep—and what other customers who fit her profile keep and don't keep. In this way, it applies algorithms similar to those developed by Amazon to recommend books that you would like based not only on what you have bought but also on books purchased by customers who bought the same books as you.

These algorithms use different types of computer number crunching. A "decision tree" algorithm, as its name implies, correlates a cascading series of dozens or hundreds or thousands of data points (like branches on a tree) to winnow out items you probably won't like and add things you probably will. "Random forest" algorithms are ensembles of dozens or even hundreds of different simpler algorithms that work together and correct for possible errors.

Stitch Fix, which employs a chief algorithms officer and more than a hundred data scientists, probably is the only consumer product company ever to post on its website an "Algorithms Tour." An elaborate and lengthy online graphic, it explains how Stitch Fix uses data (some not having an obvious correlation or connection) to act as a clothing match-maker. "Each attribute that describes a piece of merchandise can be represented as data and reconciled to each client's unique preferences," Eric Colson, Stitch Fix's chief algorithms officer, explains on the company's *MultiThreaded* blog. "For example, the way a certain blouse fits tightly on the shoulders and flaunts the upper-arms may provide value to some clients while being an undesirable quality to others . . . Machines are great at finding and applying these relationships."

As Stitch Fix has developed more sophisticated algorithms, it has incorporated the use of computer vision to help select clothing. "We have our machines look at photos of clothing that customers like (e.g., from Pinterest), and look for visually similar items," the website explains. And while the company initially sold apparel and accessories made by others, its data scientists in 2017 started designing "Stitch Fix exclusive brand" items by combining different style characteristics from popular clothing. In-house designers create these "Hybrid Designs" by taking ideas generated by artificial intelligence about the kinds of clothing its customers might like.

Predictive analysis is now employed by a wide variety of digitally native brands. Warby Parker uses information from its questionnaire to help you select the five eyeglass frames it will send to you for their Home Try-On program. ThirdLove's algorithm helps pick the bra likely to fit you best. The Farmer's Dog, which sells fresh, personalized pet food online, uses a questionnaire to figure out the right mix and portions for your pooch. Winc, an online wine retailer, uses the answers to its questionnaire to determine which wines to send you and, like Stitch Fix, has started making its own brand of wines from varietals using an algorithm that processes data from the wines its customers like most. Care/of makes a customized selection of vitamins tailored for you based on your answers to its survey, and Prose uses its questionnaire to customize shampoo for its online customers.

Tamim Mourad and several of his colleagues at eSalon have learned from experience the importance of technology to a start-up. In 1998, before the direct-to-consumer brand revolution began (indeed, before many of the entrepreneurs behind many of these start-ups had graduated from college or even high school), they started an internet company while they were in their twenties. The company, PriceGrabber, was one of the original online price-comparison sites.

Mourad and his colleagues founded PriceGrabber after they noticed that an electronics company was selling zip drives, an early data-storage device, as a loss leader, to attract customers. The devices typically retailed for $80, but this company was selling them for $20. "So, we bought as many as we could, and we used twenty to thirty different shipping addresses so they would keep selling to us. Then we resold them," Mourad recalls. "This made us think, what else is this retailer selling below cost? We wrote software that crawled its site, saying 'show me everything with the biggest price difference.'"

They quickly expanded PriceGrabber to compare prices from all over the Web, sorting the products by zip code and retailer, and made it a go-to location for people looking for the best prices online. PriceGrabber collected a per-click fee from retailers whose prices it listed. In 2005, Experian bought the company for $485 million, yielding a huge gain on the founders' total investment of $1.5 million.

After taking a couple of years off, the PriceGrabber founders began brainstorming about starting another business. One idea they considered, but dropped, was language translation online; they concluded it would be difficult to do well, and there wasn't a clear way to generate revenue.

Then, in the fall of 2008, Mourad and his wife were having dinner with a couple who owned a beauty salon in Beverly Hills. The other woman, who was a hair colorist, tossed out a business idea. "She said that women who color their hair at home don't do it well because there is a dearth of information," Mourad says. What about starting a website that explained how to dye your own hair? He didn't see a way to make money from that, but he asked her, "Is it possible to formulate color for someone sight unseen, and mail them something they apply at home? If that works well, then you're delivering a product that is better than the standard hair coloring in a box at a drugstore, that would approximate what someone could get at a hair salon. If you could do that, you could charge a price that was a premium. There's a business model."

He went back to his former PriceGrabber colleagues, all men who knew nothing about hair coloring. Still, the more they thought about the idea, the more they liked it. It was a business ready for disruption, they decided, for several reasons. Though at-home hair coloring may be a niche business, it was a big niche ($2 billion in annual U.S. sales) dominated by a handful of established companies. And their friends-and-family research found that women often aren't satisfied with the options. Off-the-shelf packaged brands were fine, but most offered only up to around fifty premixed shades. "Many people who color their own hair at home in general are not happy because the results are mixed," Francisco Gimenez notes. "But it is affordable, which is why they do it. At the high end, salons charge on average around $60 for base color, though it can go as low as $45 in some cities and is more like $100 or $150 in bigger metro areas."

Next, they asked themselves another critical question: Would L'Oréal, Clairol, or Revlon counter with a customized "box" coloring of their own sold through retailers? After doing some research, they made a calculated bet that the answer would be no. Why? All the big players not only sell packaged brands through retailers, but also offer "professional" product lines with premium ingredients to salons.

If L'Oréal were to offer a customized, at-home brand, that might well antagonize salon owners and stylists, who account for a healthy portion of the company's sales. "It's a conflict for them," Gimenez says. "These big companies have centralized R&D for all their products, but the professional side has access to the better formulations and ingredients than the consumer side does."

The PriceGrabber guys concluded that there could be an opening for a new brand priced somewhere in between. In today's global marketplace, it would be easy to find suppliers to sell them professional-grade ingredients that go into hair coloring formulations: dyes, modifiers (to stabilize color tones), vitamins (to moisturize the hair), antioxidants, hydrogen peroxide (to remove the old color and activate the new dye), among others. The biggest challenge would be to figure out how to combine all these ingredients to mimic what a stylist does in customizing color for each woman who comes into a salon. "Can you formulate hair coloring for someone sight unseen?" Mourad says. "We had to figure out how to test that idea."

They first did a proof-of-concept test to see if women might be interested in buying customized color online. They created a rudimentary website and then hand-mixed colors for about fifty women who had signed up, submitted a photo, and said what color they wanted. Then the women were asked if they liked the color better than the results they got with a do-it-yourself kit at a drugstore. "We recruited people who were willing to put this product on their hair, with no idea who we really are. The results were positive enough for us to say we have something. Now what?" he recalls.

The next step: tapping their knowledge of tech and data science to figure out how to replicate color customization for sale to fifty thousand women, not just fifty. "We wanted to do something that was really innovative, not bullshit innovative," Mourad says. "Really different and value added."

Omar Mourad, Tamim's younger brother and another of Price-Grabber's cofounders, read everything he could about dyeing hair. "I didn't have any tangible color experience applying it on any person's hair. But I became a theoretical expert in hair color," he says.

Over the next several months, he and Gimenez took the lead in translating the rules of hair coloring into software that would determine the right customized mix to get the desired color. That can depend on numerous variables: a woman's natural color, her current dyed color, the desired color, how recently she dyed her hair, how much gray hair needs to be covered up, the texture and length of her hair. One rule of hair coloring is that it is easier to go from lighter to darker hair rather than darker to lighter hair; another is that changing your hair color by more than two shades is tricky, and is best done gradually.

"You basically look at all of the combinations, and then build out a matrix for how to formulate for all of those scenarios," Omar explains. Tamim adds, "While you can engage with color professionals to help you, in the end taking what they say and translating that into software is not a simple task."

Using the knowledge that Omar Mourad had gained, the team developed a questionnaire that included queries that a stylist would ask a first-time customer. The questions themselves aren't rocket science. The rocket science happens when hundreds of thousands or millions of people answer the questionnaires, enabling you to gather more and more data to analyze and correlate.

After translating the hair coloring rules into software and writing the questionnaire, the next step was to automate the formulation of the customized colors. Mixing the ingredients by hand could take a couple of hours, so they bought paint-dispensing equipment that could be programmed to combine different liquids in precise amounts.

It worked great, or so it seemed at first. "A week later, all the hair dye went bad," Tamim Mourad recalls. "We didn't know, and what the people who sold hair dye to us didn't tell us, and what the paint-dispensing equipment people didn't know, is that hair dye oxidizes. It doesn't like exposure to air. Paint has no trouble oxidizing. The guys who make our hair dye didn't think of saying anything, because the idea of putting it in a canister and mixing a little bit of this and a little bit of that as orders came in didn't exist."

So, eSalon had to spend several months creating an entirely new production line so that the dyes wouldn't be exposed to air. It built machinery that would dispense precise amounts of liquid, measured by weight with a high-grade medical scale (which is more accurate than measuring by volume), into each two-ounce bottle of coloring traveling down a conveyor belt. Each bottle would then be labeled with the customer's name: "Mia's Color" might consist of a mixture of 60 percent

Lightest Blonde, 5.9 percent Ash, 19.1 percent Gold, and 15 percent Pearl.

In September 2010, under the name eSalon, the product was launched. The price initially was $22 for a one-time purchase, since raised to $25. But to build repeat business, the company charged $10 for the first order and $20 for subsequent orders for anyone who subscribed to buy its hair coloring at regular intervals, with women choosing between four and eight weeks, depending on how often they colored their hair.

eSalon initially targeted women who colored their hair at home. "But we have found that 20 percent to 30 percent of our customers are people who have been going to a salon and, likely for cost reasons, said, 'Wait a minute, you're telling me I can get a product that approximates what I get in a salon for a fraction of the price?'" Tamim Mourad says. "That message was appealing to them."

Many customers liked the product early on. But eSalon wanted, and needed, more of them to love it. "When we first started, we were analogous to a colorist coming out of cosmetology school coloring hair for the first time," Tamim Mourad recalls. Which is to say, eSalon's customized formulations were good, and better than an off-the-shelf kit, but not as good as an experienced hair stylist who had been coloring hair for many years.

As with an apprentice stylist, eSalon's formulations improved over time, as the company got more customers and was able to gather more information. "To update formulas and update your logic, you need history: history of data [for the] people coming to you with parameters, you formulating a particular way for them, and then [their] giving you feedback that changes the way you formulate for that person, and possibly the next time for someone with the same set of parameters," Tamim Mourad explains. "We're now formulating color much better than we were at launch."

In addition to analyzing data points such as repeat orders (the best single measure of how much a customer likes her formulation), eSalon also tracks the percentage of women who ask that their formulation be tweaked, and how. A little darker? A little lighter?

From the start, eSalon also has employed colorists on staff to answer calls, guide women through their first orders, and field their questions, suggestions, and complaints; a colorist might even recommend adjustments to the mix. All this qualitative data is collected and stored, too, along with the quantitative data. Customers are now asked to submit a photo if they would like (something that eSalon didn't offer initially), which adds another data point for the human stylist to feed into the algorithm that determines the right color mix.

As of 2018, eSalon had dispensed 165,000 different formulations. That's out of a total, it calculates, of 2.2 *octooctogintillion* pigment variations (that would be 22 followed by 266 zeros).

Omar Mourad and his team constantly analyze the data, searching for anomalies that suggest ways to improve color formulations and make customers happier. At one point, they noticed that women who used the default formulation for the company's Dark Blonde-Natural Golden color didn't reorder at the same rate as for similar colors in that palette. So, they reduced the percentage of golden tone in the formulation and increased the dark blonde base, to get better coverage of gray hairs. The changes led to a 20 percent improvement in third-order retention rates.

Improving the third-order retention rate is especially important, because eSalon's data shows that customers who place three orders typically remain customers for a much longer period—and the longer a customer stays, the more valuable she is, because the cost of acquiring new customers is higher than the cost of keeping an existing one. "If we can get them through three orders, we know that they're going to keep going to seven, eight, nine," explains Thomas MacNeil, the chief technology officer. "If we get them past that, they're, like, going to stay for thirty, forty orders."

To reduce customer churn, eSalon has been working on predictive analysis algorithms that look for clues on how to retain more customers at these recognized break points. What do the customers who stay with eSalon past that second level of orders have in common? Have they requested adjustments to their customized color formulation between their third and eighth orders? If so, eSalon might consider tweaking the orders of other women with similar profiles, to see if their retention rate increases. That's what it did for women who have long hair and a similar profile based on variables such as their natural color, their dyed color, how long they have dyed their hair, and their coloring frequency. "We will know to give you two different formulas, one for your roots and one for your ends, so it will give you that salon look rather than just a color fill, where you put the same color over everything," Mac-Neil says.

This attention to detail has won eSalon many loyal customers, including those who used to go to salons and those who bought cheaper off-the-shelf kits. Jenny Sewell, a beauty blogger, wrote that she used to pay $75 to get her hair colored by a stylist at a salon, but decided to try eSalon because the price was lower and it offered customized color. "It just makes more sense to use eSalon," Sewell says. "The quality is high, the cost is reasonable and the product is easy to use." Another customer, Ann Lingley, also is a convert. "When I was working full time, I could afford $200–$250 color at the salon. Now, being retired, that isn't in the budget. . . . Since I found eSalon on the web, I was very impressed by the quality," she wrote on an independent review site.

eSalon uses the data it collects for more than hair coloring formulations. Like most direct-to-consumer brands, it analyzes just about every aspect of the customer experience. While its main product is hair coloring, the company also sells related products such as shampoo. And to entice first-time customers just before checkout, it offers a discount on their initial purchase of shampoo (normally $12 to $15) to those who sign up for a regular subscription. To determine the optimal price that would yield the most revenue, eSalon tested three different prices, $7, $8, and $9. "The best result, the combination of the number of people buying times the price, was eight dollars," Omar Mourad says.

Data also showed that YouTube, which eSalon initially thought would be a cheap advertising channel to attract first-time customers, wasn't especially effective. Analyzing the numbers, Omar Mourad and his team realized that much of the YouTube traffic consisted of women in their twenties who just wanted to experiment with hair coloring. Few made subsequent purchases. Better to spend more money elsewhere, to target older women who buy hair coloring to cover their gray, and who are more likely to make multiple purchases. "Not all users are equal," he notes.

In 2019, L'Oreal did what eSalon's founders predicted it wouldn't do and decided to offer customized hair coloring online. L'Oreal introduced a new brand, Color&Co, that copied key features of eSalon, including an online quiz or a consultation with a colorist to help determine the "a unique custom-blend [color] made only for you." The price of $19.90 for repeat customers who signed up for a subscription was virtually the same as eSalon's. Facing increased competition from a much bigger rival, eSalon—with sales still a modest $30 million a year, giving it a tiny market share—agreed to sell a 51 percent stake to the German multinational Henkel. Henkel, which already sold a number of hair coloring brands, such as Schwarzkopf's Brillance and Natural & Easy, cited the growing trend toward personalization of beauty products and eSalon's "valuable customer insights" as reasons for its investment.

7

Eyes on the Customers

A few days after Warby Parker began selling prescription eyeglasses online in February 2010, it ran out of the inventory of frames the company was mailing to prospective customers under its free Home Try-On program. Soon it started getting queries from people who didn't want to wait until the company had restocked its supply.

"I heard you're in Philadelphia. Can I come to your office and try on glasses?" the emails typically asked.

But there was no Warby Parker office at the time. The four founders were still MBA students at Wharton. They hadn't been sure whether enough people would actually buy glasses online to make Warby Parker a viable business, so some of them had backup job plans in case the venture didn't get off the ground.

In response to the queries, Neil Blumenthal, one of the founders, recalls, "We were like, 'Oh, we're working out of my apartment. You're more than welcome to come.' And we invited five people to come, thinking if we ruined our reputation, it would only be five customers."

At the apartment, Warby Parker eyeglass frames were laid out in neat rows on the dining room table pushed up against a wall where a mirror was mounted, so the visitors could see what the frames looked like when they tried them on. "When people came in, they'd also see us working, literally on the couch, replying to customer emails. It was a peek behind the curtain," Blumenthal says.

One of the customers that day was a doctor in residence at the Hospital of the University of Pennsylvania. "He was in scrubs," Blumenthal remembers, "so that's how we knew." Most of the visitors who showed up placed an order, which was a good sign. But what happened afterward got the founders' attention.

"Literally, the following week we started to get all these orders from people with email addresses at the hospital. We thought, Wow, there's something going on here. First, we know that some people want to touch and feel the glasses," Blumenthal says, confirming that the Home Try-On program could help overcome any hesitancy in customers to buy eyeglasses online. "Second, if you deliver an unexpected experience, like going to someone's house, or more important, seeing behind the scenes at a start-up, that leads to a conversation and connection, that brands can build relationships with customers just like human beings can build relationships. And that's through vulnerability. So, if we're showing our warts, that's okay, whereas conventional wisdom is that brands have to be super polished."

This premise was quickly tested by an unanticipated problem. The company initially had ordered just ten thousand pairs of frames, to avoid being stuck with lots of inventory in case there wasn't much demand. But the most popular frames quickly sold out, and by mid-March the company had run out of fifteen of the twenty-seven styles Warby Parker had designed. Customers coming to the website didn't know this. Not expecting sales to take off so fast, the founders hadn't bothered to include a way to indicate when a particular frame was sold out. So, people kept ordering glasses and paying with their credit cards.

"We quickly circled up as a team and said, 'What are we going to do here?'" recalls Blumenthal. The lenses were produced on demand in the United States, but it was going to be a while before the company had more frames, because its Chinese supplier had to manufacture and ship them.

They debated whether to keep accepting orders. For a start-up, it's painful to turn down sales. While they were conferring, Dave Gilboa, one of the other cofounders, kept checking his phone, which he had set to notify him every time an order was placed. "Guys, while we've been discussing this, we've gotten five new orders," he said to his colleagues. They quickly called their website developer and told him to add "Sold Out" messages. They then wrote emails to the customers who had placed orders, apologizing that they wouldn't be getting the glasses any time soon and crediting their account. "That engendered some good-will, and where people would have been extremely frustrated, they had patience and tolerance," Blumenthal says.

Most of these customers came back and reordered after the inventory was replenished. "There was a big lesson learned, that when you explain something to people, they can understand," Blumenthal notes. "When you make mistakes, the most important thing is to own up to them and try to solve them as quickly as possible."

Warby Parker's founders realized early on that creating a new brand in the digital age was as much about creating a good customer experience as about creating a good product—maybe even more.

Warby Parker wasn't, in fact, the first company to sell eyeglasses online, and it wasn't the cheapest, either. Well before it came along, Eyeglasses.com, Goggles4u, FramesDirect, and Zenni Optical were all selling eyeglasses for a lower price than you could get at an optical store.

Tibor Laczay, the cofounder of Zenni, can hardly contain his exasperation when asked about Warby Parker. Bring up its name, and he launches into an extended monologue. "When they first started, they were constantly claiming they invented the online eyeglass business. They repeated it so often that they got all the PR repeating it. Now they are out there as some great, innovative company, but I'm not sure what they have innovated," he says. "They're not even that much less expensive than a brick-and-mortar store, maybe forty or fifty percent. We're ninety percent cheaper." And, he adds, "They're all Wharton School graduates. I've certainly met enough Wharton graduates I wouldn't want to hire."

Laczay is right about who came first. In 2003, seven years before Warby Parker had sold a single pair of glasses, he helped start Zenni, then called 19dollareyeglasses.com. While it offers a range of prices based on the type of frame, its eyeglasses with a straightforward single-vision correction can cost as little as $42, or half the price of Warby Parker's cheapest glasses. Since then, Zenni has sold more than twenty million pairs of glasses, compared to more than five million for Warby Parker.

Yet it's Warby Parker that is by far the best known of the online eyeglass start-ups; Warby Parker that has raised about $290 million from VC investors and, with estimated annual sales between $400 million and $500 million, is valued at around $1.75 billion; Warby Parker that is one of the darling brands of Millennials; and Warby Parker whose name has entered the lexicon as a verb, as in "I'm going to Warby Parker this product category," or, as a 2015 headline on the *Huffington Post* declared, "4 Industries Currently Getting Warby Parkered." Go online and you can find references to the Warby Parker of hospital scrubs, the Warby Parker of cowboy boots, the Warby Parker of paint, the Warby Parker of self-care.

Neil Blumenthal readily concedes that the physical differences between Warby Parker's glasses and other brands are insignificant. Yes, he says, Warby Parker prides itself on its stylish, classic frame designs. And it boasts of using a premium cellulose acetate from a family-run Italian company to make its plastic frames and a high-quality, ultra-lightweight titanium for its metal frames. But so do many eyeglass companies.

To stand out from the online rivals that preceded it, Warby Parker focused on something more than selling eyeglasses: building a stronger connection with its customers. "The world is getting far more competitive. Most products that are sold do what they at least say they want to do. So, product quality is converging rather than diverging. It's the same thing with dishwashing detergent," Blumenthal says. "If we think that product quality is converging, then suddenly these other attributes that were lower priorities in the consumer's mind now have a higher priority. As a direct-to-consumer brand, we can create a far better experience.

And it's not just about having a customer-friendly policy like free shipping and free returns."

Warby Parker's ethos—since mimicked by many digitally native start-ups—is one of the early online examples of what their Wharton professor David Bell calls "bonding, not branding."

To explain the distinction, Bell points to one of the most iconic brand symbols. "Philip Morris created the image of the Marlboro Man and sort of told people that's who they should aspire to be," he explains. "A bond is something much more personal, where you feel an affinity with the seller, as if the seller were talking to you directly. You might even subscribe to the brand's social [media] channel. In Marlboro days, there was no real way for consumers to express their affinity for brands in the way they now can. There was no Instagram, where you could take a picture of your cigarette or send out tweets. That's why we've moved from a pure branding to a bonding. Customers will interact with a brand in a social channel, they'll share it with their friends."

Another successful direct-to-consumer brand, Glossier cosmetics, built a connection with the women who became its customers before it even had a product to sell. The views posted by Emily Weiss on her *Into the Gloss* blog about what she liked and didn't like in the world of beauty products proved so popular that she decided to seek VC funding and started Glossier in 2014.

Weiss then deepened the bond by soliciting advice from her customers. Glossier selected the soft pink color used on its packaging after Weiss used Instagram to post different shades of pink and followers weighed in on the one they liked best. Even as it has grown, Glossier still listens to product ideas from fans such as Devin McGhee, an African American graduate student in Atlanta. McGhee started a popular Instagram account, GlossierBrown, and at one point publicly chided Glossier for not having shades of some of its products that worked well for black women with darker complexions.

"I remember when Emily saw that," recalls Marla Goodman, a former Glossier vice president. "We knew we had a limited shade range, but hearing and seeing that—that post made its way around the company." McGhee's post prompted Glossier to look more closely at expanding its number of shades. "I had once worked at Ralph Lauren," Goodman adds, "and you could not have done anything like that there. There's absolutely no way."

In 2018, the company invited McGhee to visit its R&D labs in New York. "They reached out and said we really want to partner with you on expanding shades," she says. "When I went to headquarters, I got to play in the product development room. They showed me a lot of things. What do you like about this? What do you not like about this? I got to give them really personal feedback." Then, she met with Weiss and Henry Davis, Glossier's president at the time. Subsequently, Glossier increased the number of shades for its concealer and skin tint from five to twelve, including some darker shades. "Glossier genuinely listens," McGhee says.

Davis says that tapping directly into Glossier customers like McGhee is central to the company's strategy. "Glossier was born out of the *Into the Gloss* community. Its mandate was community. That's what direct-to-consumer is really about. It's not about distribution. It's about connection. Access to and relationship with the customer is the most important, number one factor," he notes. "How do you listen to customers and work with them? The way you make someone feel you're listening is you talk back to them." In contrast, he says, "P[rocter] and G[amble] doesn't know who their customers are. They have to pay ad agencies a bunch of money to tell them what their average customer looks like. And they do pretty sophisticated market research and ethnographic research and all that kind of stuff. But it's not their actual customers."

Sometimes, creating a good customer experience might seem counterintuitive from a business point of view. When you subscribe to Dollar Shave Club, you get razors sent to you every month. A few days before the shipment goes out, you get an email reminding you that the package will soon be on its way. Click on the email and you can add to your order (e.g., shaving cream or hair gel). And if you have a stack of unused blades sitting in your bathroom cabinet, you can cancel or reschedule that month's shipment.

Why does Dollar Shave Club make it so simple to postpone a shipment, potentially reducing its revenue—in contrast to, say, suspending your cable TV service for a month, which is virtually impossible? Because by doing so, it is more likely to keep you as a customer and make you more likely to recommend its razors to a friend.

Warby Parker, Glossier, Dollar Shave Club, and many new direct-to-consumer brands recognize that as important as a good product is, creating a good customer experience fosters loyalty, and loyal customers spread the word on social media and bring in more customers. "In the digital economy, your audience has an audience," says David Bell.

In a world where products are commoditized, Neil Blumenthal says, a company needs to create moats to fend off the competition: "How do you create moats? You continue to provide more value. How do you provide more value? You create a more holistic experience. That's a barrier to entry."

* * *

The night before Thanksgiving 2018, Mark Ely noticed a small scratch on the lenses of a pair of Warby Parker glasses he had recently purchased. The glasses came with a one-year scratch-free guarantee, so he sent a text message that evening to the customer service team. Given the timing, he says, "I figured I wouldn't hear anything until the next week, and probably have to email again, it being the holiday and all."

He quickly learned otherwise. "A half hour later, I got two emails," he recalls. "The first one said your new glasses are on the way. Then the second one was 'Here's your return label to send us back the glasses that you have. Just make sure you send back the old ones so that we can check and see why they failed like that.' That blew me away, especially at nine o'clock at night the day before Thanksgiving. But the most surprising part was I got the email that everything was in progress before they even said, 'Hey, that's a problem, we'll get you taken care of.'"

For anyone who has worked for Warby Parker, none of this is surprising—nor is it for many of its customers, judging by Twitter messages about the company's customer service:

@WarbyParker customer service is so good I'm
almost happy my eyesight is failing.

Absolutely wrecked my favorite Burke frames
the other week, and @WarbyParker swung and
replaced them for me. 10/10, some of the best
customer service I've received.

Ya'll I called @WarbyParker today and someone
picked up the phone. No phone trees.... Just a
person saying hello. I was shocked.

Tweets like these are common, which is the whole point of Warby Parker's customer service. For many years, until Warby Parker starting expanding its network of retail stores, it had more employees in customer service—or "customer experience" (CX), as Warby Parker and most direct-to-consumer brands call it—than in any other department. In 2019, about 350 of the company's 2,000 employees worked on the CX team, making it the second-largest department after the retail store staff. Many American companies have outsourced their call centers overseas, often to India or the Philippines. For the customer, this can mean talking to someone with a hard-to-decipher accent who speaks English as a second language, but it saves the company money.

By contrast, Warby Parker viewed its call center workers as critical to creating a bond with customers, because they were the first personal point of contact. "You call Warby Parker, and we want somebody to answer within six seconds. So many e-commerce sites were trying to hide their 1-800 number, and they viewed customer service as a cost center that should be minimized," explains Blumenthal. "We've always viewed it as profit center, as an investment in our brand. Our customers are our biggest driver of traffic and sales because of referrals. We make somebody happy, and it benefits the company."

The model Warby Parker embraced was similar to the "ninja" customer service offered by the e-commerce men's clothing pioneer Bonobos. Its marketing promised better-fitting pants, but in the end, they were still pants. "You could buy similar-looking and similar-priced things, but people came back time and time again because they knew if they had a problem, it was going to be fixed. It's something people cared more about than the clothes themselves," recalls Aaron Bata, who worked at Bonobos's call center and went on to run customer service for the direct-to-consumer mattress start-up Tuft & Needle. "Every single one of us in that room was vastly overqualified to be a customer service rep. On one side of me was a woman who had just graduated from Princeton. On the other side was someone who had just graduated from Barnard."

Until 2014, Warby Parker's call center team worked at its corporate headquarters in New York, which at one point was in the historic Puck Building in Lower Manhattan, which probably made it the most expensive call center office space in the world. Even after opening a second customer experience team (now numbering three hundred people) in Nashville, Tennessee, Warby Parker keeps about fifty call center workers at its new downtown New York City headquarters on Spring Street, underscoring the symbolic importance of customer service to the company's success.

Colleen Tucker, a recent graduate of Cornell University with a degree in psychology, was one of Warby Parker's first hires in early 2010, not long after it began selling glasses, when the founders were working out of Blumenthal's apartment. She was brought in as an "operations associate," but she spent much of her time answering customers' phone and email queries, processing returns, and taking orders to UPS for delivery. Tucker confesses that she took the job because, after the 2008 financial crisis, she couldn't find work and was living with her parents. "The economy wasn't great. It wasn't like I was getting all these job offers," she recalls.

Among her early memories of working at Warby Parker—in addition to Blumenthal conducting staff meetings while barefoot—was fielding a complaint from a customer. She doesn't remember what the customer was unhappy about, but she very clearly recalls what one of the founders said to her: "Just give them free glasses." "He just threw it out there," Tucker recalls. "That was a signal to us that they really care, they're not so focused on short-term costs, they're in it for the long run. They gave us the autonomy to tell the truth and apologize and go off script."

Another call center employee, Patrick Mahoney, had worked on Wall Street for a couple of years after graduating from the University of Pennsylvania with a degree in philosophy, politics, and economics. Although his salary and bonus exceeded $100,000 a year, he didn't like the job, so he quit—to work answering phones at Warby Parker for $15 an hour, or about $30,000 a year. "My parents thought I was absolutely crazy," he confesses. It was 2012, when the company was still small. But Mahoney had bought a pair of Warby Parker glasses and liked them, and he wanted to do something entrepreneurial.

It was what most people would consider a lowly call center job. But Mahoney takes exception to that. "'Call center' is not at all how I would describe it," he says. "We had a very customer-first mentality. That's why I hate the 'call center' connotation. We had an expression: 'to surprise and delight.'" He recalls a customer who lived in New York calling frantically on a Friday because the glasses she had ordered hadn't been delivered on time, and she had been counting on wearing them to a wedding that weekend. He tracked the glasses to a distribution center across town and, realizing they wouldn't be delivered until after the weekend, left the office, picked up the glasses, and took a taxi to deliver them in person to the customer's apartment. "To her, it was outside the realm of possibility that she was still going to get her glasses for the wedding. But that was the mentality. Whatever it takes. It was the antithesis of customer experience at the time," he recalls.

His colleagues on the call center desk included other graduates of prestigious universities, many of whom were promoted after a few months to a year. Mahoney himself was moved onto the finance and strategy team before leaving to pursue an MBA at Harvard Business School. But many of his colleagues have stayed, and as recently as 2019, about a dozen high-level managers at Warby Parker, such as Colleen Tucker, had begun in customer service.

Some have taken what they learned at Warby Parker and started other direct-to-consumer brands or departed for senior jobs at such companies. Around the time Patrick Mahoney was hired, another call center worker named Steph Korey, who had graduated from Brown University, was promoted to run the company's supply chain team. In 2015, she and a fellow Warby Parker alum, Jen Rubio, would start Away, a direct-to-consumer luggage company that four years later had a valuation of more than $1 billion.

At Warby Parker, creating a good customer experience is about more than answering calls quickly and responding to complaints. Sometimes it involves whimsy. Early on, the company began offering prescription monocles, starting at $50. It doesn't sell many—only a few hundred a year—but having monocles makes trendy, young urbanites feel that Warby Parker identifies with them. Then there was the new website that popped up on April 1, 2012, warbybarker.com, featuring glasses for dogs—because, as the founders explained, glasses for dogs, like glasses for people, are too expensive. Some people thought it was serious, until they noted the date: April Fool's Day. It was classic Warby Parker. The idea had come from two employees who noticed that Warby Barker was the most common misspelling in Google searches. "It gives a peek behind the curtain of who we are," Blumenthal explains.

The idea is to constantly find ways to connect customers with the company, and to make interactions with the company as easy, seamless, pleasant, and fun as possible. "We often use the quote that 'Happiness equals reality minus expectations.' So how can we be constantly creating a reality that's above customers' expectations to keep them happy?" Blumenthal says.

As touchy-feely as this sounds, most everything Warby Parker does—as with most digitally native brands—is driven by data. What percentage of each frame style is sent back for an adjustment because they don't fit quite right? Which prescriptions don't go well with certain frames because the correction is so strong that the lenses look too thick? What percentage of customers have old prescriptions that need to be updated before they can purchase new glasses? At what point in the online checkout process do potential customers get frustrated and stop?

Each of these data points presents an opportunity to improve customer experience.

This is critical in taking on a bigger, established competitor like Luxottica, Blumenthal explains: "Everything we do we need to get better. How do you get better? You make informed decisions. How do you make informed decisions? You get data and analyze it."

From the start, two drivers of Warby Parker's sales were its Home Try-On program and the Virtual Try-On feature on the Web. But it became clear that both had issues that frustrated customers and both needed to be improved.

When Warby Parker first started selling glasses in 2010, it offered just twenty-seven different styles of frames, with a total of about forty if you count different colors for some frames. With a limited selection, picking five frames to be sent to you at home to try on was relatively easy. But as Warby Parker added more frames—by 2016, there were about 240 styles, counting different colors but not including prescription sunglasses—it took longer and longer to browse through the offerings online, which discouraged some customers. To improve the experience, Warby Parker decided to test ways to narrow the options and make it easier and faster to choose five frames.

Initially, it created curated Home Try-On boxes, preselected assortments of five frames that it would send to customers who didn't want to take the time to scroll through the many styles and make their own selections. The curated boxes were based on just a couple of variables supplied by customers, including their gender and face width. "That didn't really work," recalls Erin Collins, the senior director of e-commerce and consumer insights. "We tested it and saw that the results didn't lead to an increase in more people getting Home Try-Ons. We didn't get enough information for us to give good recommendations. People like to have some control of what they're choosing. We allowed people to swap out stuff, but it wasn't resonating."

So, Collins and her team decided to try a more elaborate quiz—akin to the quizzes that eSalon uses to help determine the hair coloring mix for new customers and that ThirdLove uses to determine the right bra size. "Why don't we actually ask you more questions, then give ten to fifteen recommendations? You're still picking the five [frames], but we'll narrow the set that you choose from," she says.

To determine which questions would result in the most people taking the quiz and having frames sent to their homes, Collins's team conducted several dozen online A/B tests over a few months. They tried various combinations of questions, and also different numbers of frames to choose from, and then studied the data.

They ended up with just seven questions, with five being used to help determine the recommendations:

> *What are you looking for?* Men's styles or Women's styles.
> *What's your face width?* Narrow, Medium, Wide, or I'm not sure.
>   Let's skip it.
> *Which shapes do you like?* Round, Rectangular, Square, Cat-
>   eye, or No preference.
> *Which colors do you like?* Bright, Neutral, Black, Tortoise,
>   Crystal, Two-tone, or No preference.
> *Which material do you like?* Acetate, Metal, Mixed material, or
>   No preference.

The other two questions serve different purposes. *When was your last eye exam?* is meant to alert you if you need a new eye test before placing an order for prescription glasses. And *Want sunglasses recommendations too?* gives the company an opportunity to sell you two pairs of glasses at the same time.

The trickiest question was face width. "Who knows their face size?" Collins explains. In one of the tests to determine the best questions to pose, the Warby quiz featured an illustration of people wearing hats and the query *How do hats fit you?* The answer options were along the lines of "usually too tight" and "usually too big." This was quickly dropped, as many people either said they didn't know or answered, "I don't really wear hats." The final quiz instead has three drawings of different-size faces, along with brief wording below each to help you choose:

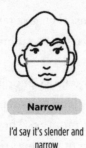

Narrow

I'd say it's slender and
narrow

Medium

Not sure? This is a good
place to land.

Wide

It's definitely on the
wider side

After Warby Parker introduced the quiz in January 2017, the number of people asking for a Home Try-On rose. The quiz results had
the added benefit of helping the company improve its frame selection.
More customers than expected said they had a narrow face, so the
company's designers added about a half-dozen narrow styles.

The Virtual Try-On proved more challenging to fix. The idea behind
it is straightforward: Upload a photo of your face when you visit Warby
Parker's website, then select the frames you want to "virtually" try on and
they are superimposed over your photo. Most of Warby Parker's online
eyeglass rivals use similar software, because people want to visualize how
frames will look on their faces before committing to buying them.

The problem: the technology available when Warby Parker started
selling glasses in 2010 had limitations. It was hard to make sure the
frames would be scaled properly when superimposed on the face in the
photo, in part because of variations in the size of the photos uploaded.
As a result, the visualization often was distorted. This was one of the
reasons Warby Parker added the Home Try-On option when it opened
for business, rather than relying solely on the Virtual Try-On.

The company continued to offer the Virtual Try-On until 2015,
and then decided to suspend the feature and take it off the website
altogether, having learned that a smaller percentage of people who used
the Virtual Try-On ending up buying glasses than those who didn't. "It
was not only not helping; it was hurting," Collins says. "So, we had a
whole strategic discussion and decided we would rather have nothing
than have this. It's actually pretty rare to see something actually hurt
conversion. So, for us, it was like, *This is bad*."

Still, surveys showed that some customers missed the feature. So, in the months after Apple introduced its iPhone X in late 2017, with a more sophisticated camera, Warby Parker began looking into a new and improved Virtual Try-On. The new iPhone featured what Apple calls a TrueDepth camera, which can collect thirty thousand data points on a face, allowing it to map the proportions more accurately when it captures a face's image. The image can be rotated and still convey proper proportions. "The quality of 3-D modeling and 3-D rendering and design is light-years ahead of where it was before," Collins says.

A team of Warby Parker engineers began working on an augmented reality product called Blueprint, to create a lifelike visualization when frames were superimposed over a live facial image viewed on the iPhone X. After about six months of work, the team found it could get the fit to look realistic and proportional. But getting the technology to show the colors of the different frames was a challenge. When the team showed an early version to a group of users, a typical response was "I don't get it; I want to see the colors." Lacking the in-house expertise for that, Collins decided to hire an outside 3-D artist partner specializing in technology that could accurately depict colors. "We worked with them back and forth, back and forth. We went through many iterations, and tests on employees and users with lots of different face types," she says.

After about a year of R&D, and about a dozen versions, Warby Parker introduced the new Virtual Try-On feature in February 2019. It captures a live image of your face from your iPhone and allows you to swipe quickly and seamlessly through dozens of different frames to see how they look. You can even move your face around, and see how the frames look from different angles, including from the side. Though the new Virtual Try-On works only with an iPhone X, it was an instant hit—in part because it includes a social media–sharing feature, so you can ask your friends what they think of the frames you like.

"One thing we found early on was that buying glasses is very social," notes Blumenthal. "People in the U.S. buy glasses once every two years, so it's not a frequent purchase that you're good at. You want validation from your friends or your partner, and we found that people were taking pictures of themselves during the Home Try-On and post-ing it on Facebook and asking friends for feedback. That helps the virality of the brand as well."

Warby Parker also has found a technological solution to one of its more vexing problems: when someone falls in love with and orders a particular frame, but her prescription requires lenses that don't work well with that frame. The lenses might be too thick, or the vision isn't as sharp as it should be because the size of the lens doesn't allow the center to be aligned properly.

Typically, what works and what doesn't is left to the optician's subjective judgment. But when the optician guesses wrong, the customer returns the glasses and has to find new frames and place another order, which is frustrating for the customer and costly for Warby Parker.

So, the question is no longer left to chance. By collecting and ana-lyzing data showing how often each frame is returned by unhappy cus-tomers who have a certain type of prescription, says Corey Frederick, manager of store operations, "We have what the math is, and it uses your prescription strength and knows when you select a frame [that is] not well suited. We can tell you if this frame is too wide or too small, that the size and styling may look good, but it isn't fit for your prescrip-tion." When that happens, an alert pops up in red letters at the top of the order form.

Sometimes, delivering a good customer experience means not doing something—or not doing it until Warby Parker thinks it can do it well. Progressive-lens prescriptions, the modern-day version of bifocals, account for about half of all eyeglasses sold in the United States. But Warby Parker didn't start offering them online until 2014, after it had been in business for four years. The reason was that progressive lenses are harder to fit properly; they require precise measurements of where the center of the eye is in relation to the lens, because you see faraway objects through one part of the lens and close objects through another part, and the center is different with each frame.

Calibrating this correctly when you are selling glasses online can be especially tricky. "Every frame sits differently on everyone's face, so usually the measurements had to be taken in person," explains Kaki Read, senior communications manager. Warby held off on offering progressives until it could develop technology that would enable its online opticians to walk customers through placing their orders with a high degree of confidence that they would get it right and the glasses would not be returned at high rates.

When it comes to customer experience, almost no detail is too small to measure. To determine how long it took a salesperson to enter every bit of information when a customer was buying glasses at one of its stores, Warby Parker used timers to calculate which steps could be speeded up. "Trying on glasses can be fun, because that's a social experience. Checking out is not fun. Once you've made your decision, it's time to get the fuck out of there," Blumenthal notes. "But we need to know your address, your email address, your billing information, what have you. I call these low-value interactions, whereas finding the right frame for you is a high-value interaction."

In examining the data, Warby Parker zeroed in on something that took several seconds longer than necessary: entering the person's email address. "It's a real obvious one," says Blumenthal. "Why don't we create a button, so that instead of doing @-g-m-a-i-l, we just created one button for @gmail.com. It's super, super simple and easy, right? Is that going to turn us into a $100 billion company? No. But if we do a billion of those things, it will."

8

Delivering the Goods

At 5:01 on a Monday afternoon in July, an online shopper in Brooklyn clicks on his computer's Buy button and places an order for two pairs of Bonobos trousers: blue Weekend Warrior Straight Fit Pants and gray Stretch Washed Chinos.

They arrive on his doorstep the next day.

How does that happen?

The journey starts in a sprawling warehouse tucked away in a bucolic exurb forty miles northwest of Boston. It looks like most warehouses, with hundreds of brightly illuminated aisles lined with row after row of shelves. But gliding silently around this warehouse's maze are several dozen robots, each standing five feet tall and weighing one hundred pounds, with a rounded base and elongated neck but no arms—akin perhaps to a tall, stylish R2-D2. These robots were engineered to do just one thing, but to do it very efficiently: get e-commerce orders out the door, fast.

Within seconds of the Bonobos order arriving electronically at the warehouse, its computer system assigns it to one of these Locus robots. Scattered throughout the warehouse are seven hundred thousand different items, but the robot doesn't hesitate. An algorithm dispatches it on the best route to bins containing the right size and color of trousers.

When the robot arrives, a worker picks each pair of trousers and places it into a rectangular tote the robot is carrying. At many warehouses, workers can walk five to ten miles a day, selecting orders along the way; an efficient worker might pick up to fifty items an hour. But at this warehouse, the robots do the walking—rather, the rolling—while people are strategically stationed around the warehouse. Working in tandem with a human picker, a robot can gather as many as two hundred items an hour.

In a tad over an hour, at 6:05 p.m., the robot has collected the trousers, along with many other items it was assigned to gather along the way, to optimize its journey. A minute later, the robot delivers the pants to a packing station, where a worker folds them neatly into a box that is quickly loaded onto a UPS trailer truck waiting at the warehouse dock. From there, the trousers are sent to a regional UPS sorting center nearby, transferred to another UPS trailer en route to New York, and then, for the "final mile," the last stage of the journey, placed on a brown UPS van with other deliveries destined for Brooklyn's 11208 zip code.

At 6:23 p.m. on Tuesday, the package lands on the customer's front door step. The shipping is free—to the shopper. The cost to Bonobos: $12.

This will occur millions of times a day at warehouses across the country. Getting that many goods to that many homes in that little time would have been impossible a decade ago. To make it happen, the modern supply chain has evolved into a highly automated and tightly choreographed ecosystem, where every hour, every minute, counts. It is something that online shoppers never see or even think about, unless their order is late or gets lost. But it's something that direct-to-consumer brands obsess about, from the speed to the accuracy to the cost.

The robots at work in the Massachusetts warehouse are the second generation of robots deployed by Quiet Logistics, founded in 2009 by two industry veterans intent on creating the automated warehouse of the future. Initially, they had used robots from another company, only to be informed that they would no longer be serviced. Their future in jeopardy, Quiet Logistics' founders—with no robotics experience—scrambled to build their own, better robots under a new company called Locus Robotics. They are now selling these robots to other warehouses around the world that are also racing to automate.

How Locus robots came to be built is part of a broader tale of the revolution and fierce competition sweeping the logistics world. Once a staid business personified by barrel-chested warehouse workers laboriously loading and unloading crates, it has become an industry increasingly driven by computer science PhDs writing algorithms and developing cutting-edge technology for every step in the delivery process. Supply chain management has become one of the fastest-growing majors at universities across the United States, with tens of thousands of students enrolling every year.

In 2019, roughly eighteen billion e-commerce packages were shipped in the United States alone, generating more than $180 billion in logistics revenue—many multiples greater than a decade earlier, figures that are expected to keep growing. At the same time, the expectation for how long it should take for an online order to be delivered has fallen. In the early days of e-commerce, if an order arrived within five to seven days, the customer was happy. Now, if it takes that long, the customer wonders what went wrong—and maybe even stops doing business with that online retailer. The enticement of getting a slice of the billions of dollars in delivery revenue has resulted in a frenzied race to make every step along the way faster or cheaper or better for the consumer.

Some start-ups have focused on the shipment of cargo from an overseas manufacturer to a U.S. port; others, on moving goods from the dock to the warehouse; some on building robots and highly automated warehouses to provide the most efficient handling after an order is placed; others, on developing smartphone apps that help truck drivers to fill empty space on their rigs, or apps that allow online shoppers to track an order every step of the way. Many are tackling the last-mile problem, a growing issue as the number of packages delivered to doorsteps is growing exponentially. There are even start-ups focusing exclusively on "reverse logistics," the business of making it easy for online customers to return goods they don't want, which happens with 5 to 30 percent of all online purchases.

There's Schlep, ShipCalm, ShipHawk, Shippo, Shipsi, Shipt, Ship-waves, Shipwire, Shotput, Shyp, Stord, Stowga, Swapbox, and uShip; Darkstore, Deliv, Dolly, and DoorDash; Cargobase, Cargohound, Cargomatic, Convoy, and Curbside; Returnly, Rickshaw, Roadie, and Routific; Flexe, Flexport, and Freightos; Parcel Pending, just plain Parcel, and Postmates; Lugg and Lockitron; TruckTrack, KeepTruckin, and YouTruckMe; Instacart and MakeSpace; and Narvar and Optoro.

And Locus Robotics.

* * *

Techies at heart, Bruce Welty and Michael Johnson have been in the logistics business since the 1980s. Welty studied math and computer science at Colorado College and then used his skills to write software that managed warehouse operations. In 1987 he started a company, AllPoints Systems, and partnered with some investors and with Johnson, a computer programmer he met while looking for talent at Boston College.

Back then, warehouses were just emerging from the Dark Ages, when they tracked inventory with pen and paper and workers moved goods around with hand-operated pallet jacks and forklift trucks.

Warehouse-management-systems software, offered by AllPoints and various competitors, dramatically improved efficiency. For the first time, warehouses could computerize everything from tracking inventory to mapping the location of what was stored in every rack. The new technology enabled workers to find the right pallet in the shortest amount of time and helped make sure that trucks were full and took the most efficient route when making deliveries. Walmart rose in prominence as America's biggest retailer in part because it spent billions of dollars improving its logistics network.

But even with the new software, the essential nature of the logistics business, delivering pallets and cases of goods to retail stores, hadn't changed. It was, in the parlance of the warehouse world, a many-to-one business, with large volumes of products going to a single store.

Welty and Johnson built a roster of prominent clients for their software, including Toys "R" Us, Eveready batteries, and May Department Stores. And in the mid-1990s, they began targeting online retailers as well.

In 1996, Welty became particularly intrigued by a fledgling company selling books online named Amazon, and was determined to get it as an AllPoints customer. He repeatedly called the company but couldn't get anyone to respond. "I even flew to Seattle and I tried to get into one of their warehouses," he recalls. "But I couldn't find any, so I found a UPS driver and I said, 'Hey, is there an Amazon warehouse around here?' and he said, 'Oh, yeah, it's over there.' So, I walked over to it and I literally jumped on the loading dock and started wandering through the warehouse trying to find people."

AllPoints never got Amazon's business, but it did secure a contract to help set up a state-of-the-art warehouse for another prominent Seattle start-up, the online retailer Drugstore.com.

The project meant rethinking how warehouses traditionally worked. Rather than sending large pallets or cases of goods to a relative handful of store locations, e-commerce requires sending huge volumes of small packages to many different locations. Doing this efficiently is far more complicated. Many orders can be for more than one item—toothpaste, mouthwash, shampoo, and face wash, for example. This requires locating individual items quickly and then making sure every package is filled with the right products and sent to the right address.

The automated warehouse that AllPoints helped set up for Drugstore.com in 2000 used a series of conveyors coursing through the warehouse to carry orders to packing stations after workers had picked the items from shelves. Advanced for its time, it still required a lot of manual labor and was prone to bottlenecks if, for instance, a conveyor broke or slowed down.

Having built a successful business, and looking for new challenges, Welty and his partners sold AllPoints in 2001 for $30 million. After dabbling in investing and consulting for a few years, Welty and Johnson began hearing about a start-up named Kiva Systems, which was in the early stage of developing warehouse robots. Kiva had been founded by former executives of Webvan, an online grocer that had gone bust, in part because its warehouses weren't sufficiently automated.

Welty's immediate reaction was "I don't believe you. Robots in a warehouse? Not a chance." But as he and Johnson heard more, they became curious. Kiva robots had been installed in the mid-2000s by a few big retail chains, such as Staples, for their company-owned warehouses. Welty persuaded a former customer to sneak him into a warehouse employing Kiva robots. "I was completely blown away. 'This is the coolest thing I've ever seen,'" he recalls.

Welty and Johnson knew that creating a new kind of warehouse focusing on e-commerce would be difficult. "Everyone says, 'This is nice, that I can get my stuff at my doorstep.' But, oh my god, this changes everything," Welty explains. "In fact, back then, it wasn't a little more expensive on a unit cost basis to ship something to a customer's home rather than to a store. It could cost *much* more. Everything was set up wrong—the software, the storage, the packing. We needed a real answer for that."

Kiva, he realized, was the technology breakthrough that was needed to reinvent warehouses. "They would solve a lot of the problems," Welty says. So, he and Johnson created a new company, Quiet Logistics, which would operate warehouses for e-commerce companies, and in early 2009 it became the first independent warehouse operator to deploy Kiva robots. Quiet Logistics soon built a reputation for delivering goods quickly and inexpensively. Depending on the size, weight, and distance, it could deliver orders to a shopper's home for as little as $6 to $8 (including the UPS or FedEx fee). This amounted to a savings of 50 percent or more from what online retailers had paid a few years earlier.

Start-ups such as Gilt Groupe, a Web-only fashion and home furnishings retailer, and Bonobos signed on as early customers. Music Parts Plus found that the error rate in shipments to its customers fell to virtually nothing after it switched its warehouse business to Quiet Logistics; before then, customers received a product they didn't order about 10 percent of the time.

Since its founding in 2012, Mack Weldon, an online retailer of men's briefs and undergarments, has used Quiet Logistics as its warehouse. Its overall shipping costs have declined over time to about 10 percent of revenue, from nearly 16 percent, thanks to increasingly sophisticated technology used by Quiet Logistics and Mack Weldon's own increased sales volume, says the company's founder, Brian Berger. The average delivery time has declined as well. "From the start, they helped us think about things like packaging, and how best to have our products land in their warehouse for maximum efficiency," he notes.

Though Quiet Logistics was relatively small by warehouse industry standards, Welty was frequently quoted as an industry pioneer by journalists from *Businessweek*, CNBC, the BBC, and *60 Minutes*, in addition to many trade publications. As it flourished, the company quickly outgrew its initial tiny warehouse of twenty thousand square feet in Wilmington, Massachusetts, and began adding space, eventually expanding into three new warehouses totaling more than eight hundred thousand square feet in the nearby town of Devens.

Quiet Logistics even became a showcase for Kiva, which often asked to give prospective customers a tour of Quiet Logistics's warehouse, to see the robots in action. It was flattering, a validation to Welty and Johnson that their vision for reengineering warehouses had been right. "We thought, This is cool. Kiva wants to show off our warehouse," Welty says.

Even as they grew, like all entrepreneurs they constantly eyed and worried about possible threats from bigger rivals—and none more than Amazon, which had expanded far beyond its days as an online bookseller. Amazon was rapidly building a warehouse empire to distribute all sorts of goods sold on its website, and to offer logistics services to e-commerce companies such as Quiet Logistics's clients.

"We'd be fucked if Amazon bought Kiva," Welty told his colleagues while discussing the competitive landscape at a board meeting in the fall of 2011. At which point, Johnson recalls, "Everyone laughed, and said, 'That would never happen. Har, har, wouldn't that be funny?'"

A few months later, in early 2012, Kiva brought employees from an unidentified company to Quiet Logistics for a tour. The visitors spent about an hour and a half in the warehouse. "They were very stoic," recalls Johnson, who accompanied the group. "I could tell the gears were turning, like they were trying to absorb it all. When people first see our warehouse, they're like, 'Wow, this is really simple.' It's not a normal warehouse. You're thinking, 'Where's everything else, where are all the forklifts?'"

After they left, something crossed Johnson's mind: *I think that was Amazon.*

He was right. Initially, he and Welty were proud that Amazon was paying attention, but that didn't last long. "We got the bad news a couple of months later that Amazon liked what they saw so much that they decided to buy Kiva," Welty says. "And then, a year later, we got worse news: that they were going to stop servicing our Kiva robots in a few years, so we would have to find new robots for our warehouse."

Welty and Johnson were unnerved. They had built their entire business model around an automated warehouse. Kiva robots were essential to their business. After starting with just ten Kiva robots initially, their warehouses now deployed two hundred. In search of an alternative, Welty flew around the world to visit companies developing robots. But even as he did, he and Johnson worried: What if Amazon ended up buying the company whose new robots Quiet Logistics decided use to replace the Kiva robots? Wouldn't they find themselves in the same bind again?

* * *

Behind Amazon's purchase of Kiva was Jeff Bezos's maniacal obsession with logistics. To get online shoppers to change lifelong habits and buy anything and everything from Amazon, the company had to make the experience just as easy as going to a store—or, better, even easier than going to a store, and cheaper, too. What is easier or cheaper than having something you order delivered free to your home in a day or two?

Amazon, of course, wasn't the first retailer to view delivery as a competitive advantage, or the first to build a business by delivering goods where and when a customer wanted them. More than a hundred years before Amazon sold its first book, both Sears, Roebuck and Montgomery Ward used logistics to become retailing giants in the late nineteenth century. Their shoppers browsed mail-order catalogues, and it could take as long as several weeks for a product to arrive, but that was good enough to help the two retailers win the loyalty of customers—especially those living in rural areas, where the selection of goods often was limited and local shopkeepers charged higher prices.

There is a reason that Amazon is driving much of the innovation in logistics: it shipped five billion packages in 2017, far more than any other company. Amazon has built a sprawling network of warehouses around the United States that puts distribution centers close to customers everywhere and thus speeds the delivery of goods. In the early 2000s, the company had only a handful of warehouses. But then it went on a building binge. By 2019, it operated 390 warehouse and logistics facilities of various types in the United States (more than 50 of them at least a million square feet in size), covering a total of 142.3 million square feet, with another 35.6 million square feet of warehouse space planned. Its warehouses, if placed side by side, would cover about one-fourth of Manhattan.

Amazon once was in the spotlight for working its warehouse employees to the point of exhaustion. While the company is still criticized, working conditions in its warehouses are in the news much less often. With more than two hundred thousand robots of various types deployed, and highly automated conveyor systems in place, much of the picking and carrying is done by machines, not people. Amazon is testing new warehouse automation equipment, such as machines that take goods off a conveyor belt and package them for shipment, and along with rivals such as UPS it wants to deploy small drones for air delivery.

Not satisfied with spending billions of dollars on distribution centers, Amazon also has poured resources into every link in the supply chain. To rely less on traditional shipping giants to deliver its goods, Amazon is amassing its own fleet of long-haul trucks. It has created "vertical" warehouses in urban centers that have heavy concentrations of online shoppers, so it can offer delivery in two hours or less for frequently ordered items under its Prime Now program.

To alleviate the problem of traffic congestion caused by the huge increase in package deliveries, Amazon is experimenting with Amazon Locker, a neighborhood "self-serve" facility where goods are delivered to secure lockers at places such as 7-Elevens and are picked up by the buyer, rather than being delivered to their front door.

Amazon is also trying different approaches to speeding up "last-mile" delivery. After starting Amazon Flex for drivers to earn money by delivering packages in their spare time, the company went a step further by helping the more ambitious drivers set up their own franchise local delivery business, called Amazon Delivery Service Partner, with the benefit of being able to tap its logistics technology and economy-of-scale discounts for the equipment needed to get started. It also is testing a "sidewalk" delivery robot about the size of an ice cooler to carry and deliver goods from the curbside to a customer's doorstep. Amazon's chief financial officer, Brian Olsavsky, said that Amazon would spend $800 million in the second quarter of 2019 alone "to evolve the two-day free shipping program into a one-day free shipping program." In the summer of 2019, in a sign that it views Amazon increasingly as a competitor and not just a customer, FedEx said it planned to stop providing its ground-delivery service as well as its Express Air Freight service in the United States to Amazon.

Retail rivals of Amazon are frantically fighting back as well—in some cases by poaching Amazon logistics executives. In 2016, Target stores lured away Arthur Valdez, who rose through the ranks in a sixteen-year career at Amazon to become a vice president overseeing supply chain and transportation. Amazon sued Valdez, alleging that he had violated a noncompete agreement by joining Target, and it dropped a tidbit to underscore how highly it values experienced logistics talent: that his Amazon compensation was more than $1 million a year.

Many of the logistics and supply chain start-ups being financed with billions of dollars in venture capital funding are aiming to replicate Amazon's innovations. "Amazon is the behemoth in logistics," says Tim Laseter, a supply chain expert who teaches at the University of Virginia's business school and has closely followed the company's evolution. "It has a network that is hard to match, and its whole mindset has been to layer on tech and do it better and better and better over time, so it will be the lowest-cost shipper."

* * *

Bruce Welty and Michael Johnson weren't alone in worrying about the threat posed by Amazon's purchase of Kiva. About a dozen other companies were racing to develop highly automated warehouses equipped with robotics to take advantage of the growth of e-commerce, and to fill the void after Amazon announced it would stop selling Kiva's robots to outsiders.

In the fall of 2013, Welty spent a month visiting robotics companies in Germany, England, and Japan, but he couldn't find any robots that would be ideal for warehouse work. "I remember coming back and saying, 'We should build a robot, not buy someone else's,'" he says.

Johnson's initial response was "You're crazy." But Welty argued that they had advantages over many robotics companies. Having used Kiva robots in their warehouse, they knew Kiva's limitations and the features that would make for a better next-generation warehouse robot. "Over time, we had developed a long laundry list with Kiva that we didn't like. So, why don't we fix those problems?" Welty says.

Kiva's workhorse robots don't look like what most people think of as a robot. They look like giant orange ladybugs, squat boxes on wheels, measuring about two feet by two-and-a-half feet and one foot high. After getting an order for a product, they follow markings in the warehouse and position themselves under the stack of shelves that includes the bin where that product is stored; then they carry the entire stack to a station manned by warehouse workers, who pick out the item before the Kiva robot returns the stack and goes on to pick up another stack to collect its next order.

As cumbersome as this sounds, it yields huge productivity gains. The robots do the traveling, not the warehouse workers. They know exactly where to get products, rather than wasting time searching if they don't remember where each item is stored. But Kiva robots are slow. In addition, it can take a lot of time and money to configure warehouses for Kiva.

Welty and Johnson wanted faster robots that could navigate autonomously along an infinite variety of paths, like a human can, without having to follow marked routes. They wanted them to be inexpensive. They wanted more flexibility than Kiva allowed, to increase or decrease the number of robots operating depending on the number of orders a warehouse was filling, which can vary widely from the summer to the winter holidays. And they wanted a warehouse to be able to get the robots up and running in a few weeks, simply by placing bar codes throughout the warehouse, rather than installing special shelving or other equipment.

While the task was daunting, Welty says, "Technology had improved a lot since Kiva had started. Sensors were better and way cheaper. The software had improved a lot. We could buy that stuff, and wouldn't have to invest and build it from scratch. That's why we were confident we could build a better, faster, cheaper robot."

They began by purchasing a $300 hobbyist robot kit—basically, a bunch of mechanical parts, a motor, and an electronic control board. They tinkered with it to see if they could program it to go forward and backward. That accomplished, they bought a TurtleBot, a more sophisticated robot kit, and experimented with features such as wireless communications.

Initially, the project was part of Quiet Logistics. Then, as the development costs grew, they set up Locus Robotics as a separate company, funded at first with $7 million from Welty, Johnson, and their backers, and later with $59 million from venture capital investors.

A warehouse robot might sound mundane, but Locus didn't have a problem recruiting robotics scientists for their project. Mike Sussman, who had worked at Kiva and another robotics firm, signed on in early 2014 as head of hardware engineering at Locus. "I always like to get a blank slate and create something," he says, explaining his decision. "There was a huge unmet need in a booming market where the right approach hadn't been figured out." Soon, a team of about a dozen scientists and engineers was assembled.

The biggest hurdle, they quickly realized, would be to write software that would send complex instructions to the robots' "brains" (the computer chips and circuitry) and to state-of-the-art cameras and laser sensors built into the robots so they could buzz around without bumping into things.

It took a year to program the robots so they could navigate smoothly in a crowded warehouse. "Think about walking down a street in Manhattan, all the calculations you have to do constantly and instantly to avoid running into another person," Welty recalls. "It was quite comical. Just when you thought you had written the [software] code right, the robots would drive at high speed and crash into each other."

During this period, Bradley Powers, who joined Locus as principal roboticist from another industrial robot company, occasionally worked three or four days straight without leaving the R&D lab at the company's headquarters in Wilmington, Massachusetts. "You kind of lose track of time," he says. "The robots would see something that they didn't recognize, and that would cause them to get a little lost and go to the wrong place." Fixing the problem involved the laborious task of writing algorithms, testing the robots, rewriting the algorithms, testing them more, and doing this over and over and over.

All told, the team built about a dozen prototypes before the robots were ready to be let loose in a warehouse. The battery-powered Locus 'bots, as the warehouse workers call them, don't have mechanical arms or legs. Instead, they have a low, rounded base, or "body," that sits atop four wheels. Attached to the base is an elegantly designed long "neck"—Locus calls it an *armature*—with a platform that can hold up to three plastic totes for collecting and carrying items from warehouse shelves. At the top of the neck is the "face," a color-coded computer screen that displays the next item the robot will collect.

In late 2015, after extensive testing, Locus deployed a few robots in Quiet Logistics' warehouse. They performed even better than expected. In a couple of hours, robots working with just one person managed to collect as many orders as it took two workers to do in eight hours.

A few months later, Johnson took several robots to a logistics trade show, hoping to drum up interest. Locus set up its booth so the robots could move around and simulate collecting warehouse orders. He remembers being nervous, and hoping that fifty people would stop by. In the end, nearly five hundred people visited the booth, including executives from Walmart, Amazon, and DHL. "The lights would be going off at the end of the day, and people would still be in the booth, saying, 'Can you show me how they work?'" Johnson recalls.

In May 2018, Locus Robotics got a visit from a team of examiners from the U.S. Patent Office. "We've been filing for so many patents in logistics"—they've filed several dozen, with more than ten having been granted—"and they rarely see so many patents from one place. They wanted a tour. Who would have thought that warehouse guys could build a robot?" Welty says.

Locus has helped Quiet Logistics expand its business in the year since it was cut off by Amazon and Kiva. By 2019, it had begun expanding to the West Coast and operated two million square feet of warehouse space, with plans to double that amount by 2021, and it had doubled its number of customers to more than sixty, adding brands such as the luggage start-up Away and the online mattress brand Tuft & Needle.

With only about 10 percent of warehouses nationwide having installed robots, Welty and Johnson are confident that their bet on Locus will pay off. "Amazon has created an arms race in this industry, and Locus is an arms dealer in that arms race," says Rick Faulk, the chief executive of Locus. "They're our best marketing arm, and it's not even close."

Locus faces lots of competition. One of its rivals, an autonomous mobile robot start-up named 6 River Systems, was acquired by Shopify for $450 million in late 2019. But Locus is recognized as one of the industry leaders. It leases its robots for $1,000 a month to make them affordable for warehouse operators who don't want to pay $30,000 to buy them outright.

Among its first customers was DHL, the giant parcel shipping company, which tested six Locus 'bots for about a year. "We're a metrics-driven company, and we found we were getting substantial increases in productivity with Locus, up to two times as much," says Adrian Kumar, a vice president for DHL's North American business. It quickly scaled up to more than one hundred robots.

Locus has turned down one potential client, Welty says: Amazon. "They called us, and we've said no." Why do anything that might help Amazon? he asks.

Quiet Logistics is girding for another battle with Amazon. In May 2019, the company was bought for about $100 million by two big real estate firms, including Related Companies, the developer of the multibillion-dollar Hudson Yards in Manhattan. The mission, says Welty, is to become the anti-Amazon by building "vertical" warehouses in big cities to facilitate same-day deliveries, just like its giant rival. And, naturally, he expects the new warehouses will be filled with robots—Locus robots.

* * *

The cavernous warehouse in Ontario, California, about thirty miles east of Los Angeles, contains 1.6 million square feet, covering the size of nearly thirty football fields. Inside are fifty miles of conveyor systems. Outside are one thousand parking spots for big-rig trailers. The warehouse was built in 1980 by Kmart, which acquired Sears, Roebuck in 2004. For more than thirty years, the warehouse was filled with inventory.

But by 2017, as the fortunes of Kmart and Sears declined, hundreds of aisles with fifteen-foot-high stacks of metal shelves stood eerily empty. The retailers didn't need nearly as many goods as they once did, because shoppers were staying home and buying online, usually from other retailers.

A year later, many of the shelves had been replenished—not with goods for Kmart and Sears stores but with the products of more than a dozen e-commerce companies. This inventory had been brought to the warehouse by what might be best described as the Airbnb of the warehousing world, the brainchild of Karl Siebrecht.

Siebrecht was at a cocktail party in Seattle when he bumped into a friend of a friend who had launched a barware business that sold stir sticks, shot glasses, coasters, and the like. Things were going okay, the man said, but he lamented having to pay for warehouse space he often didn't need. That's because most warehouses required customers to commit to a fixed amount of space for a term of at least a year, even though a business's sales can fluctuate for a variety of reasons—such as seasonality. That's especially true of start-ups, which can't predict how fast their sales will grow.

That got Siebrecht thinking. A serial entrepreneur, he was in the process of selling his second digital-advertising-software company and was starting to consider what he might do next. What about pairing businesses like this man's barware company with warehouses that had unused space, as many often do? If he did, both could benefit. The warehouse would earn money by filling some of its empty racks, and consumer product companies could get as much, or as little, space as they needed, for as long as they needed it and where they needed it, without the expense of having to sign a long-term lease. Plus, the concept could be easily explained to customers. Like Airbnb, which pairs up travelers with people seeking to rent rooms in their homes, Siebrecht's company would collect a fee for making it easy for people on both sides of the transaction to find each other.

For e-commerce entrepreneurs, there would be another advantage. If Siebrecht could build a big enough network of warehouses, a start-up could afford two, three, or even more warehouse locations, strategically placed around the country, thus speeding delivery and making them more competitive with Amazon, with its network of warehouses nationwide. "One of the fundamental challenges for a start-up is, 'How fast I can get my stuff to consumers and how much it is going to cost to do that?'" Siebrecht explains.

So, he started Flexe. Though it seemed a no-brainer to Siebrecht, recruiting enough warehouses to join the network was harder than expected. That was because until you have a critical mass, it isn't much of a network. "Warehouses are an old-school industry, not at all cutting edge," he explains. A typical reaction from a warehouse: "Why pay Flexe a 10 to 15 percent commission when we've always found our own customers?" His response: "We'll find customers for you, so there's no cost to you unless we bring in more revenue for you."

For the first year, Siebrecht worked from his basement, slowly signing up warehouses while his small team created a website to match customers with warehouse space and software that all the warehouses in the network would use to provide the same level of service and quality. After all, a bad experience with a few warehouses could taint everyone in the network. He managed to raise $21 million in two early VC funding rounds and focused initially on two cities, Seattle and Los Angeles, because both are major West Coast ports and transit hubs with lots of warehouses.

As with Locus Robotics, what helped most, Siebrecht says, was the growing power of Amazon. "In the past few years there has been an urgency to change, and that has put the wind at our backs," he observes. From only a few dozen warehouses in its network in 2015, Flexe had grown to more than one thousand in 575 U.S. cities and 40 Canadian cities by mid-2019—a number, Siebrecht points out, that far exceeds Amazon's total logistics facilities of nearly four hundred.

Flexe's website looks similar to Airbnb's. If you are a business looking for warehouse space in Los Angeles, you go to Flexe.com and up pops a map showing warehouses of various sizes and in different locations—including the 1.6 million-square-foot Innovel warehouse in Ontario, owned by the parent company of Kmart and Sears.

In late 2016, the struggling retail giant was selling off warehouses because falling sales meant it didn't need as many as before. "We had a lot of space empty," says Ryan Gorecki, a senior manager at Innovel headquarters, in Chicago's suburbs. He pauses. "Everywhere," he adds for emphasis. That's when he spotted a Flexe brochure on a colleague's desk.

Gorecki was intrigued and called Flexe. He quickly was sold on the concept, but his bosses were initially skeptical. "Remember, we're a legacy business," he says, echoing what Siebrecht said about the difficulty he had getting traction. Gorecki managed to persuade them, saying there was little to lose, especially given the difficult straits their business was in. After putting just a few of its warehouses in the Flexe network, the benefits quickly became apparent. Innovel soon expanded its participation to more than two dozen warehouses, filling empty space and bringing in "many millions of dollars" annually in added revenue.

Among the early Flexe customers at the Ontario warehouse were the online mattress retailers Casper and Lull; Mohawk, the maker of hOmeLabs brand minifridges and other small appliances; Vive, an online medical device store; and Kangaroo, an outdoor appliance e-tailer. The warehouse's smallest Flexe customer was Cargo, which sells boxes filled with breath mints, lip balm, beef jerky, candy bars, energy drinks, and aspirin (small-ticket items carried by convenience stores) to Uber and Lyft drivers, who can resell them to their riders and make a few extra bucks. Vive occupied about 50,000 square feet, but Cargo initially occupied fewer than 1,000, with the ability to expand to 2,500, an amount of space that would have been unheard of for a large warehouse to provide to a customer in the past. "When we look at some of these e-commerce clients, we ask what's the potential for growth," Gorecki points out. "A start-up may only require five hundred square feet today, but in a year that could be twenty thousand."

Flexe already has a competitor: UPS, the giant shipper. Looking to fill the empty nooks and crannies of space in its own network of warehouses, and in other companies' warehouses, UPS launched an internal start-up, Ware2Go, that is a virtual copy of Flexe. "Scale whenever you want. Wherever you want," Ware2Go's website promises.

To Flexe and its investors, UPS's suspiciously similar initiative confirmed that they had tapped into a potentially huge market. In mid-2019, Flexe raised $43 million from VC firms, increasing its total funding to $64 million, to help it expand and fend off its new rival.

Bring it on, Siebrecht says. "After we started this business, I found myself staring at trucks and planes and ships and trains," he says. "Logistics is larger than the financial system. It's right in front of you, all the time and wherever you go, but you never really notice it."

9

The Mattress Wars

Walk into just about any mattress store in America. Gaze around the showroom. Take a deep breath. You are about to embark on one of the most befuddling and irritating shopping experiences you will ever encounter—one that makes buying a car look easy and pleasant.

You may have tried to prepare by first doing some research online, but that is unlikely to help. That's because you are going to be presented with a deliberately confusing overabundance of choices.

At the Sit 'n Sleep in a strip mall in Culver City, California, 134 mattresses are on offer, with prices ranging from $500 to $11,000. There's the Sealy Premium Joy King for $993.99, the Serta Perfect Sleeper Sandalwood model for $1,382.99, the Serta Blue Fusion 1000 LF King for $2,659.99, the Aireloom Laguna PL King for $5,978.94, the Tempur-Contour Elite Breeze Split/Dual California King for $7,598, and the Tempur-Ergo Premier for $11,396. And on and on. Oh, and if you don't like the mattress—because you only had a few minutes to lie down on it in the store, when you really need to sleep on a mattress for at least a few nights to know if it's right for you—forget about getting your money back. Sit 'n Sleep allows you only to exchange the mattress for a different one, and doing so will cost you a 20 percent "restocking" fee.

You say you want to compare the prices with any of a half dozen mattress stores within a fifteen-minute drive, or with the prices you saw while doing research online? Well, good luck with that. The other retailers carry many of the same mattresses from the same manufacturers, but they likely will have different names. The confusion is by design, because retailers, whose salespeople work on commission, don't want you to be able to compare prices. And Serta Simmons and Tempur-Sealy, the two companies that have long controlled about 70 percent of the U.S. mattress market, which is roughly split evenly between them, have been happy to cooperate. It's a very comfortable relationship, one designed to maximize profits for the manufacturers and retailers, and earnings for the commissioned salespeople, who can do very well selling just a couple of mattresses a day.

It was at a mattress store in the San Francisco Bay Area that John-Thomas "JT" Marino and his wife bought a Tempur-Pedic foam mattress in 2010 for more than $3,000. For Marino, a recent math and computer science graduate of Penn State University, the mattress was one of the most expensive purchases he had ever made. He recalls trekking to several stores and trying to compare prices but finding it impossible. Then he had to take two days off work waiting for the mattress to arrive, because the delivery crew didn't show up on the scheduled day. "It was a nightmare, one of the worst experiences of my life," says Marino. And he and his wife didn't even like the mattress after sleeping on it, but they kept it because of the store's onerous return policy.

About eighteen months later, in the spring of 2012, Marino, then twenty-seven years old, and a good friend from Penn State, Daehee Park, who was twenty-four, were working at a start-up developing an app Marino describes as "a Pinterest for shopping," and they realized they were unhappy. "We were software guys who wanted to get out of software and solve a problem, and we wanted to start with a problem that we had experienced personally," Marino recalls. "We spent about two weeks listing everything that we got pissed about." One of the potential businesses on their short list was selling a customized package of vita-mins online (a direct-to-consumer idea that others have since launched). "But the one we kept going back to was mattresses. It was the most bor-ing of all our ideas, but the reason it stood out was the experience I had in 2010 shopping for a mattress."

So, the two pulled out a legal pad and wrote down a "hate list," filling the page with things everyone disliked about buying a mattress and how those things might be fixed. "It wasn't rocket science," Marino concedes, recalling that the list included pushy salespeople, high markups, expensive delivery and returns, and a confusing array of too many mattresses.

Marino and Park agreed to put in $3,000 each and began drawing up plans for the first salvo of an assault on the $16 billion-a-year mattress-industrial complex. As it turned out, this attack would be launched not just by one or two start-ups but by dozens. If the barriers to entry have fallen in many consumer product categories, in the mattress business, they've collapsed. The competition for sales would become a free-for-all—underscoring not just how difficult it can be for entrenched incum-bents to defend their turf, even when they try to mimic the newcomers' tactics, but also how hard it can be for fast-growing disruptors them-selves to turn a profit in a market crowded with me-too rivals.

Back in 2012, it was still unclear if enough people would go online for a major purchase. Razors? They cost a few dollars. So what if you don't like them? But a mattress that costs hundreds of dollars that you haven't had a chance to lie down on, even briefly? Hmm.

That's the question Marino and Park wanted to answer. So, even before they had a product to sell, they used their programming skills to conduct a test. They created a dummy web landing page for their fledgling company, which they had named Tuft & Needle. The page displayed a stock photo of a mattress and offered fast, free delivery and returns, and included a button to click and place an order, to see if any-one would provide their credit card information. "We'd been advised by some of our founder friends that if you get somebody who isn't family or friend, someone who doesn't know you, to try to give you money, that is your validation that you're on to something," Marino explains.

One evening in June 2012, the online test went live. Marino headed for a coffee at Coupa Café in downtown Palo Alto, where tech lumi-naries such as Google cofounder Sergey Brin and the late Steve Jobs had been known to visit. Park called Marino to say that he had placed a Google search ad in the hope of attracting visitors to the site. Fifteen minutes later, Marino got another call from Park. "Dude," Park told him, "we just made a sale."

Marino jumped out of his chair: "'Jackpot!' I said, very loud, and the chatter stops, and it goes dead quiet. They all turn and look at me, grinning and nodding their heads. They're in the Silicon Valley world, and they know what happened." (Because they didn't yet have a product to sell, Marino and Park didn't accept the credit card payment, Marino hastens to add.)

The online test clinched it. Marino and Park decided to locate the company in Phoenix, where costs were lower and it was easier to hire people. "In Silicon Valley, you're either an engineer or designer who works for one of the top twenty companies or you're a founder of your own business. Try to get one of those people to quit and join a mattress start-up that's not funded," Marino explains.

But they first had to figure out how to make a mattress. They started by cutting open the mattress Marino had bought in 2010. After doing some research, the two concluded that the materials that went into the mattress, mainly foam and fabric, cost a couple of hundred dollars.

It turned out that Marino and Park had chosen a product that was technically easy to produce, thanks to the rise of the foam mattress. For many decades, the market was dominated by mattresses made with innerspring coils that were heavy, bulky, and unwieldy. They were complicated to manufacture and costly to ship. Then, along came a new type of mattress material, based on "viscoelastic" memory foam developed by NASA's Ames Research Center in the 1960s to improve the comfort and safety of aircraft seats and backs. The material had the ability to conform to the body, absorbing pressure and then springing back to its original shape. Initially it was difficult and expensive to make, but the technology improved over time, and in 1991 a Swedish company introduced the "Tempur-Pedic Swedish Mattress."

Once a niche product, in part because it was sold at a premium price, foam mattresses grew to about 30 percent of mattress sales (as measured in dollars) over the next two decades. Foam prices fell, as foam became a bit of a commodity, made by lots of U.S. producers. But the retail price of good foam mattresses remained high. The main reason: with mergers of mattress companies—Tempur-Pedic bought Sealy in 2013, and Serta and Simmons became majority owned in 2012 by the private equity firm Advent International—price competition was limited. And competition among mattress retailers, once a highly fragmented business, was curtailed as well, as the industry giant Mattress Firm gobbled up rivals and grew to more than 3,500 stores.

To get a foam mattress made for Tuft & Needle, Marino drove up and down the East and West Coasts knocking on doors of suppliers and contract manufacturers. Many wouldn't speak to him. "They didn't want to work with a disruptor, with a company that wants to take down the industry that they're supplying," he says. Finally, he reached a manufacturer who told him, "We can't make you a mattress, we can only supply the foam. But I'll teach you what you need to know."

Armed with this knowledge, Marino and Park teamed up with a manufacturer in Connecticut, which didn't work out, and then switched to a small, family-owned furniture manufacturer in Buena Vista, California, that made products such as foam couch cushions and was looking to diversify. Foam mattresses had another advantage for an online start-up offering free shipping: Compressed, a foam mattress can fit into a relatively compact carton and can be shipped for as low as $50, versus double or triple that cost for an innerspring mattress, which must be shipped flat and requires two people to maneuver it for delivery. The Buena Vista factory didn't have a machine to compress the mattresses, so initially, the compression was done manually. A shop vacuum cleaner sucked air out of the foam, and a worker—sometimes Marino himself—would kneel on the mattress so it could be folded and crammed into a box.

(Tuft & Needle was not the first to sell mattresses online or even, it turns out, to come up with the bed-in-a-box idea, though the packaging was central to its strategy and image. BedInABox, in Johnson City, Tennessee, claims that distinction, starting in 2007. "We're a small, family-owned company. Our competitors have done a fabulous job of taking what we started and going to the next level," laments Melissa Clark, chief marketing officer and daughter of the company's founder.)

In October 2012, Tuft & Needle, self-financed, without having raised any venture capital money, began selling mattresses. The initial version of its mattress was very basic, just five inches thick and priced at $350 for a twin bed. Unlike Warby Parker and Dollar Shave Club, Tuft & Needle didn't get much attention initially, and sales didn't take off. "We had to do quite a few returns at first," Marino admits, "but we iterated constantly until our customer satisfaction was high enough for us to start getting referrals."

As it improved the quality of its mattresses, Tuft & Needle went from selling on its own website to offering its mattresses on Amazon, and high ratings from Amazon buyers helped it sell more mattresses without having to spend too much on advertising.

Marino and Park, however, weren't the only ones thinking the mattress industry was ripe for disruption. In September 2012, just before Tuft & Needle began selling mattresses, a blog called Priceonomics ran a short, eight hundred-word article headlined, "We Need a Warby Parker for Mattresses." The message was blunt: "The mattress industry is rotten. It's controlled by a handful of players that make Google-esque margins for no intrinsic reason. Through a combination of an oligopolistic market structure, heavy-handed sales techniques and opaque product naming conventions, mattress manufacturers profit far in excess of the value they provide consumers."

Around the same time, Ben Lerer, a venture capitalist at Lerer Hippeau in New York, one of the early investors in Warby Parker, went shopping for a mattress. "I went into a Sleepy's, and it was gross and weird and impersonal," he recalls. Lerer commissioned a consultant, Eliot Pierce, to study the mattress market and what it would take to start an online company. The report to Lerer in May 2013, titled "Sleeper Cell," identified challenges (most prominent: finding a manufacturer) but concluded, "There is an opportunity to create a compelling new brand in the mattress space." It also identified other revenue sources, such as selling pillows, sheets, and headboards. The report was remarkably prescient about the potential for a direct-to-consumer mattress start-up but was laughably conservative in its revenue projections (at least in retrospect), estimating sales growing slowly and reaching $15 million in 2017.

Lerer was convinced that mattresses could be like eyeglasses. "I got word out: 'Is anyone interested in building a mattress company? Let me know,'" he recalls. A group of entrepreneurs already working on a mattress start-up, tentatively named Duke's, answered Lerer's call. The group's leader, Philip Krim, had sold cheap, no-name mattresses online in the early 2000s, when he was a student at the University of Texas. "They had done basically the same research that we had, but it was more informed," Lerer says. "For example, they had great conviction about why the price should be around $1,000, rather than $500 or $2,000."

In February 2014, Lerer Hippeau became the lead investor in a $1.6 million seed investment round in the new start-up, which had changed its name to Casper. Its playbook was the same as Tuft & Needle's: it started with just one foam mattress model at half or less the price of similar major brands, a thirty-day free trial, free delivery, and free returns, with the mattress being donated to charity if you didn't like it. Shortly before Casper launched, JT Marino of Tuft & Needle recalls bumping into some of its founders in New Orleans at the convention of the International Sleep Products Association. "I went partying with them. I told them, 'We're going to turn this industry upside down,'" he says. After a pause, he adds, "We ended up becoming enemies."

In April 2014, Casper began selling mattresses to great fanfare, thanks to a savvy media campaign that resulted in stories in the *New York Times*, Bloomberg News, and many other outlets. By the end of the year, the number of articles about Casper totaled 158. In its first month, Casper's sales exceeded $1 million, or about what Tuft & Needle's sales had been for all of 2013. Casper marketed itself as more than just a way to avoid the miserable experience of going to a mattress store; it made buying a mattress seem fun. Customers began posting videos on YouTube of unpacking their Casper foam mattress from its box, watching it expand, and then jumping onto it. Other YouTube videos showed Casper mattress boxes being balanced on bicycles by deliverymen. Orders poured in so fast that at times they exceeded the number of mattresses Casper had in stock.

To foster goodwill, and to avoid bad reviews or complaints online, Krim recalls, "We would call people up with an apology and offer to buy them an air mattress" as a stopgap until their mattresses were ready. "We did this with hundreds and hundreds of customers. Amazon shut us down multiple times, because we were buying so many air mattresses that they thought we were buying them to resell them."

Meanwhile, Tuft & Needle, operating in relative obscurity in Phoenix, was growing steadily—sales rose to $9 million in 2014, its second full year, from $1 million the year before—as it replaced its original five-inch mattress with an improved ten-inch version. Not only was it thicker, but Marino found scientists who formulated a better foam for a more comfortable mattress. Though the company was far from the media spotlight in New York, it finally started to get attention: a Hacker News post online in December 2013 was followed by a story in *Fortune* magazine in January 2014 headlined—that's right—"Meet the Warby Parker of Mattresses." Marino and Park, who still hadn't raised any outside money, got calls from venture capitalists asking to invest, but the two turned them all down. "We actually had two separate VCs say, 'If you do not let us participate, we will find somebody else who will,'" Marino says. "One of them ended up investing in Casper."

The online mattress wars were just beginning. But just as with Gillette facing Dollar Shave Club and Harry's, the big players didn't yet understand the threat.

* * *

Michael Traub knew little about the mattress business when he was recruited to become the president of the Serta mattress company in September 2014. Having worked for years running the North American business of Bosch and Thermador home appliances, he was trying to get up to speed on the competitive landscape. So, he posed a question to his new colleagues: What should we make of these start-ups selling mattresses online?

"What is Casper? What is Tuft & Needle?" he asked his executive team. At the time, the annual sales of all the start-ups combined probably totaled less than $50 million annually, and certainly under $100 million, or well below 1 percent of the market. The response: "Don't worry about them. They're a bunch of crazy kids. Their mattresses are a piece of shit. People will realize that in a couple of years and be gone."

The executives at Serta and its sister company, Simmons, firmly believed their mattresses were superior. The company employs about fifty scientists and technicians, who constantly test and develop the materials that go into its mattresses. At its lab outside Atlanta, R&D head Chris Chunglo enjoys giving tours to visitors and showing off some of his favorite test equipment: There's a machine that uses a bowling ball cut in half to mimic people sitting down on a mattress 100,000 times, to simulate ten years of wear. Another machine, which resembles a massive, six-sided rolling pin, called a rollator, goes back and forth, pressing down on mattresses through 120,000 cycles to simulate the wear a bed gets from people sleeping on a mattress for years. Then there's a high-tech mannequin that can be adjusted to simulate different weights and body types sleeping. A pad embedded with 2,000 sensors generates a map of all the pressure points when a person lies on a mattress. A "foam compression recovery" testing apparatus—for which Chunglo received a patent—measures how quickly a mattress returns to its proper shape depending on the weight or pressure applied, for example, when a sleeper changes positions through the night. And another mannequin tests for heat and humidity given off by a body nestling on a mattress.

Don't suggest to Chunglo (who has a plaque hanging outside his office that reads, "Foam Whisperer") that all mattress foam is created equal. One of the most common complaints about foam mattresses, he explains, is that they can get hot when you're sleeping on them. To provide a more comfortable experience, the best foams are embedded with what are called phase-change materials that help maintain a uniform temperature. "When you get into bed, your body usually is warm. Then you start to cool down," he explains. "The material absorbs the heat when you are hot, and then releases the heat back to you when you get colder.

"Most new players go to the foam suppliers and look for foam with a particular feel and never really know what the actual physical properties are," Chunglo asserts. "They don't understand how the components will interact with each other and how they would affect a good night's sleep. We test all of our competitors all the time." What does he think about the start-ups? "Casper is a very vanilla bed," he says, matter-of-factly and dismissively.

Nonetheless, judging by growing sales, shoppers seemed to be perfectly happy with the mattresses made by Casper, Tuft & Needle, and others. So, after Michael Traub became head of Serta Simmons Bedding in 2015, overseeing both the company's popular brands, he commissioned a study of the online upstarts. It concluded what many people inside the company wouldn't acknowledge: "We found that most of the customers were not returning their beds. They like them. They didn't want to have to go to a mattress store and deal with a salesman," he recalls. "This can be a very self-satisfied industry, very old-school and set in its ways. Nobody thought the newcomers could find a way to enter the market, that the business had high barriers to entry. There was arrogance. Hearing this from consumers, we knew we had to fix something."

Serta Simmons couldn't risk ignoring the direct-to-consumer trend, Traub decided, even though that could mean cannibalizing sales of its higher-priced mattresses. To compete with the upstarts, it would first have to compete with itself.

Traub and his aides deliberated about whether to buy one of the start-ups, but they rejected the idea. "There is not a lot of value in these companies," he explains. "Very little intellectual property." Instead, they turned their focus to launching their own bed-in-a-box product, and to determining whether it should be a new brand or should carry the name of one the company's existing brands. "There was a lot of heated debate back and forth," he confesses. Some managers argued that they should have control of any new direct-to-consumer mattress, rather than see R&D and marketing dollars go to a new brand that could take sales away from their brands. In the end, Traub vetoed that idea. "We decided to start with a new brand. I didn't want the baggage of modernizing Serta. Plus, how do I explain to Mattress Firm"—the giant retail chain that sells a lot of Serta Simmons mattresses—"that I'm going to sell a new Simmons Beautyrest mattress online and bypass them?"

Traub also decided it wouldn't make sense to appoint a longtime Serta Simmons executive to run the start-up. Anyone already at the company would be too tied to the traditional way of doing business, he figured, and less likely to be able to think creatively and compete against his or her friends inside the company. So, Traub brought in a headhunter to find an outside executive with entrepreneurial moxie.

High on the short list was Bryan Murphy, who in his twenties had started an e-commerce company selling auto parts and built it into a business with $2 billion in annual sales. This caught the eye of eBay, which bought Murphy's start-up and put him in charge of eBay Motors. "We sold eight billion dollars of parts and cars annually on eBay. I tell people I was the number one used-car salesman in the country," Murphy quips.

When he got a call from the headhunter asking if he might be interested in starting an online mattress company for Serta Simmons, Murphy was skeptical. Make that highly skeptical. "My first reaction was . . ." He pauses. "Mattresses? I don't know."

But the call came at a time when Murphy, now in his forties, was looking for a new challenge. So, he decided to listen. "I realized mattresses are a sixteen-billion-dollar-a-year business, with huge profit margins to work with." Still, he expressed another concern. "The second thing I said was, 'I don't believe you when you say that you want to disrupt yourself.' I'm not aware of any—repeat, *any*—successful disruption by a company of itself. History has shown that internal start-ups like this get their ass kicked one hundred percent of the time by a new company totally committed to disrupting a business. The only way that I will do this job is if I can compete on the terms of the market, not on artificial terms. Or we will fail."

Finally, he insisted that the online company's office be in New York, far from Serta Simmons's headquarters in Atlanta. Otherwise, it risked succumbing too much to the parent company's traditional ways of thinking.

To Murphy's surprise, Traub agreed. "We had to do this," explains Traub.

After joining the company in September 2016, Murphy found that even with Traub's vocal support, he wasn't the most popular person on his visits to Serta Simmons's office in Atlanta. "There are two types of people at headquarters. People who really are happy to see me, and people who pretend they are really happy to see me," he notes. The more successful his online venture was, the more it would cut into sales of the company's higher-priced mattresses—and potentially result in lower overall profit margins, and job cuts. But the alternative, he argued, would be worse. "You can concede one hundred percent of the direct-to-consumer business to others and lose all of that revenue, or you can aim to capture fifty percent of the online business and lose some of your current revenue."

Murphy and Traub understood that competing against the company's existing brands by creating a new brand and business model wouldn't be easy. Murphy, who grew up in the Detroit area, knew this well from the recent example of General Motors. In 1990, the automaker created Saturn as "a different kind of car company," GM's answer to lower-priced, energy-efficient imports from Toyota and Honda that were stealing its sales. Saturn aimed to mimic its rivals. Instead of an expansive but overlapping array of models offered by GM's established nameplates (Chevrolet, Buick, Pontiac, Oldsmobile, GMC, Cadillac), Saturn offered just two models initially. Its dealerships prided themselves on a "no haggle" pricing policy. Saturn also tried to foster a cooperative management-worker spirit in an industry known for contentious labor relations. Despite some early success, however, Saturn could never match Japanese production efficiencies, and managers running other GM divisions in Detroit grumbled that it was siphoning off billions in investment dollars that could have been used to improve their brands. Over time, Saturn became an afterthought, and GM discontinued the brand in 2010.

"If this works," Murphy said of the Serta Simmons online venture, "we will be a Harvard Business School case study."

So, the new division, which was named Tomorrow Sleep, became a Casper and Tuft & Needle wannabe, even setting up an office in Midtown Manhattan that boasted all the requisite features of a respectable e-commerce start-up. Ping-Pong table? Check. Computers sprouting unsightly cords and sitting atop tables that are scattered about an open loftlike space? Check. Boxes of takeout food from nearby Szechuan restaurants sitting open, half eaten? Check. Workers in their twenties and thirties slouching around in casual dress? Check. Murphy would show up wearing a blue-and-green checkered lumberjack shirt and blue jeans. The whole ambiance had an uncanny resemblance to Casper's office, about thirty blocks to the south, near Union Square.

Tomorrow Sleep's business model mimicked that of the online, bed-in-a-box start-ups: Price your mattress for half or less what retail stores charge for similar-quality beds made by the established firms. Offer free delivery, a free trial at home (from 100 to 365 days) and free returns, including shipping. Tomorrow Sleep's website told its "story" in videos, including "behind the scenes footage" of the factory where its mattresses were made, flattened by a giant press, and rolled and stuffed into a box about the size of a minifridge.

By the time Murphy started, his mission had become even more urgent. In 2014, there had been only a handful of online mattress start-ups. Now the number had grown to dozens, because it was so easy to find a manufacturer and launch a mattress business online. Many were small, but Murphy estimated their combined annual sales in 2016 at $600 million to $700 million—and growing by at least 75 percent a year. "There are few industries where your suppliers become your biggest competitors, but the foam manufacturers are happy to sell to anybody," Traub laments.

In an effort to carve out a niche and differentiate itself, Tomorrow Sleep's first offering was a hybrid mattress with foam on the top and springs on the bottom, combined into one piece. While praising and copying the business model of the online start-ups (free deliveries, long home tryouts, and free returns) Murphy expressed confidence that a differentiated mattress could effectively counter them. "I will tell you, my beef against all of those companies is that the product is lacking. Their products are okay, not great," he said.

Tapping the expertise of Serta Simmons's R&D labs, the foam in the Tomorrow Sleep mattress was formulated with a gel-like cooling material, to offset the tendency of foam mattresses to retain body heat and make sleeping less comfortable. A Tomorrow Sleep king-size mattress was priced at $1,200, about the same as the start-ups' foam-only mattresses and one-half to one-third the price of the higher-end Simmons and Serta brands. To hold down manufacturing costs, the Tomorrow Sleep mattresses were thinner than the company's existing brands (ten inches versus twelve to fifteen inches).

But launching the new business took time. The Tomorrow Sleep mattress didn't go on sale until the summer of 2017. It received good online reviews for being firm and comfortable, and for providing good quality at a reasonable price, but the competition had become even more intense. By Murphy's count, in the year between his joining Serta Simmons and the introduction of the Tomorrow Sleep mattress, the number of online mattress companies (including start-ups and existing regional players that started selling bed-in-a-box mattresses) had grown to more than one hundred. He estimated that online sales had increased to about $1.3 billion, or 8 percent of the overall mattress market.

As a late entrant, Tomorrow Sleep had a hard time getting traction. "A few days after we started selling mattresses, I got a call from my private equity bosses" at Advent International, Traub recalls. "Where are we? What's happening? How many sales?" He explained that it was slow going, but they needed to be patient. Moreover, the online mattress business had become a raucous, bare-knuckle brawl. With so many look-alike start-ups vying for attention, mattress buyers often were swayed by "independent" review sites. If a shopper went to Google and plugged in the words "best mattress," review sites popped up at the top. A good review could steer a lot of sales to a new brand, while a bad review could cause damage.

JT Marino recalls Tuft & Needle getting a call early on from Derek Hales, who ran a review site called Sleepopolis, saying he wanted to review the company's mattress. "I'm like, wow, that's awesome," Marino says. After the generally positive review, Hales called him back and said, "Hey, so I wrote this article and, you know what would be really awesome is if there's some way I could get a little bit of a kickback, a little bit of commission" from people who read it and then followed a link to Tuft & Needle and bought a mattress. Marino figured it was like an advertising expense, and could increase sales, so he agreed to what's known as an "affiliate" relationship that would typically pay Sleepopolis 10 percent for each sale that came through its site.

Sleepopolis had similar deals with other start-ups, he learned, including Casper and another popular brand called Leesa. But the commission relationships (which a shopper might want to know about when reading a supposedly "independent" review) were buried in a corner of the review site. "Then we had an epiphany," Marino says. "Wait a second, these are mattress salesmen. They're the new mattress salesmen, reincarnated online. So, Google is the new mattress store." There were so many new bed-in-a-box mattress companies selling the same thing with the same free shipping and return policies that shopping for one had become as confusing as walking into a mattress store.

Still, how this worked was hidden from view—until, that is, Tuft & Needle and Casper, having emerged among the top-selling new brands, each decided it perhaps didn't need to pay affiliate fees to review sites. Before ending payments, Marino recalls, "We took screen shots [of the reviews of Tuft & Needle mattresses] because I knew what the hell was about to happen. As soon as we cut them, then boom, we were knocked way down. And the same thing with Casper."

In April 2016, as the review sites started rating other mattresses above its products, Casper sued several of them, including Sleepopolis, alleging false advertising and deceptive practices, as recounted by *Fast Company* magazine. Sleepopolis was "part of a surreptitious economy of affiliate scam operators who have become the online versions of the same commission-hungry mattress salesmen that online mattress shoppers have sought to avoid," its lawsuit asserted.

In his response, Derek Hales said Casper's ranking fell simply because newer mattresses had come out that he liked more. Moreover, he alleged in court filings that "immediately after Casper announced this termination [of the affiliate arrangement], Casper approached Hales and offered to resume the relationship, on terms considerably more favorable to Hales, if Hales would agree to state a more positive opinion of Casper's mattress on Sleepopolis. Hales refused."

After more legal back-and-forth, the suit was settled in July 2017, and that same month, another online mattress review site bought Sleepopolis with "financial support" from none other than Casper itself. Soon after, Sleepopolis gave an updated, "very positive" review of Casper.

Sleepopolis now discloses that it earns "a commission from the sale" of mattresses when a visitor to its site clicks on a "referral" link and buys a mattress. Its reviewers recommend the top several mattresses in more than a dozen different categories—best for pressure relief, best for side sleepers, best memory foam, best latex, best for couples, best cooling etc.—resulting in top ratings for around fifty different models. The fact that it gets paid a commission by so many mattress makers, it says in its disclosures, "helps us maintain our own personal integrity and reduce financial bias."

To break through the noise, the new entrants have had to pour more and more money into advertising. Casper raised successive new rounds of funding, bringing its venture capital participation to nearly $240 million by 2017, part of it going to fund its own R&D lab, to keep improving its mattresses and to expand its product line, but much of it going toward advertising.

Most of the mattress companies are private and don't disclose detailed financial information. But an inkling of how much the table stakes had risen can be seen in the documents of Purple Innovation, the one online mattress company whose stock is publicly traded and which thus has to file financial statements. Once named WonderGel, the company was founded by Tony and Terry Pearce, two brothers in Utah who for a couple of decades had made foam used in wheelchairs and hospital beds to help prevent pressure sores. When the online mattress business took off, they started selling mattresses using their foam with a marketing boost from a video that went viral, much like Michael Dubin's self-made video.

The "Raw Egg Test" video showed four eggs attached to a sheet of glass being dropped several feet onto a Purple mattress—and sinking safely into the foam without breaking. "Yes, these eggs are raw. And no, we didn't fake it," says the woman dressed as Goldilocks narrating the video. Within six months, the video had more than 5.8 million views on YouTube and more than 50 million on Facebook.

Despite being a relative latecomer, Purple quickly emerged as one of the top online mattress firms. Its sales rose to $197 million in 2017, below Casper's estimated $250 million but ahead of Tuft & Needle's $170 million. But as Purple's sales rose, its marketing and sales costs skyrocketed as well, quadrupling to $79 million in a single year, mirroring that for the rest of the big bed-in-a-box players. The higher spending was needed, the company explained, "to expand brand awareness and drive consumer demand."

As the advertising arms race heated up, Tomorrow Sleep fell farther behind. A few months after it began selling its mattresses, Murphy had expressed confidence about taking on the fast-growing newcomers. "Right now, Serta Simmons has thirty to forty percent of the mattress market overall. So, we aim to have thirty to forty percent of the direct-to-consumer market," he declared.

But six months later, in the spring of 2018, Murphy's tone was decidedly more downbeat. "It's the most competitive space I've ever seen, let alone been in," he said. "Initially, Casper was spending about twenty million dollars a year on marketing. By the time we launched, they were spending eighty million a year. We thought eight million a year would be enough for us to get a foothold, but that turned out to be a drop in the bucket."

With sales falling short of expectations, Serta Simmons considered pulling the plug. After intense discussions, Michael Traub gave Tomorrow Sleep a temporary reprieve. "We were challenging ourselves: 'Is this a dead horse we need to get off of?' No, we decided, it's more like a cold," Traub says. "We had to reset our growth expectations. I look at it as a marathon and not a sprint."

Tomorrow Sleep's sales finally began picking up later in 2018, reaching an annual rate of about $30 million. That year, it also introduced a lower-priced, foam-only bed, in addition to its more expensive spring-and-foam hybrid, but it was still far behind Casper, Purple, and Tuft & Needle. Trying to narrow the gap would require Tomorrow Sleep to increase its ad spending dramatically—and even then, there was no assurance that sales would grow faster, as the competition kept expanding. New Chinese imports, led by the brands Nectar and Zinus, collectively were selling hundreds of millions of dollars of mattresses annually. Amazon introduced Rivet, its own private-label bed-in-a-box foam mattress brand, and Walmart launched a new brand called Allswell.

No industry, in fact, has been more disrupted by direct-to-consumer start-ups than mattresses. By the end of 2018, the new entrants would collectively have sales approaching $2 billion, with Casper (more than $400 million), Purple ($286 million), and Tuft & Needle ($250 million) accounting for nearly half that total.

Despite the impressive growth in online sales, however, making a profit has been more elusive for some players because of fierce competition. Tuft & Needle has been profitable since its early days, Marino claims, because it had to be, without venture capital backing to finance things like a big marketing budget. Casper, laden with cash from VC firms, put a priority on rapid sales growth, which meant losses in its early years, although Casper anticipated posting a small profit in 2019. But with an eye on making an initial public stock offering at some point (and the need to show higher profits and make its stock attractive to investors), Casper made a strategic decision to be something more than just a mattress manufacturer.

It started by expanding its product line beyond mattresses and offering pillows, sheets, and bed frames. Even more, Casper is trying to position itself as a sleep and health company—becoming the "Nike of sleep," in the words of its executives—to differentiate itself from other online mattress start-ups. It began selling a $129 Glow Light, a bedside lamp with a built-in gyroscope that lets you adjust the lighting; it "gradually dims so you can doze off without interruptions" at night and "fills the room with soft light for an easy morning rise." And it has partnered with another company to sell gummies infused with CBD, one of the active ingredients in marijuana; Casper says the product, which costs $35 for a small tin of fourteen gummies, has calming qualities meant to help you relax when you go to bed.

The increasingly cutthroat competition in the direct-to-consumer mattress market prompted Traub and his private equity bosses at Advent International to reconsider how best to compete: Should Serta Simmons pour a lot more money into Tomorrow Sleep to match the competition? Or should it go back to the idea he initially had rejected: buying one of the successful start-ups? In early 2018, Advent executives reached out to JT Marino at a trade show in Las Vegas. The timing was propitious. With Tuft & Needle's rivals upping the ante with ad spending, Marino and Park were exploring options: raising outside capital (something they had long resisted) to test and ramp up their marketing, or perhaps selling the company. Asked by the Advent executives what he thought of Serta Simmons, Marino says, "I just went on a diatribe, what I thought about how to reload those brands and save them."

To his surprise, rather than try to shoot down his ideas, they suggested a follow-up conversation with Traub, the first of several meetings. The two men hit it off. "He's not from the industry, and he's talking about the future and saying things that we say," Marino recalls. To succeed, he told Traub, Serta Simmons couldn't just disrupt a little. It had to consider major changes, including simplifying its mattress offerings, making returns easier, and improving how its mattresses were displayed at retail locations—more like, well, Tuft & Needle. Along with Casper, Tuft & Needle was extending its reach by testing out physical retail stores that would sell its brands in light, airy spaces, more akin to Apple stores than traditional mattress stores. Tuft & Needle's stores are uncluttered, with display models screened off for privacy for customers who want to give them a try. And its salespeople are salaried, rather than on commission.

Marino and Traub quickly reached an agreement for the sale of Tuft & Needle, which included the appointment of Marino as chief strategy officer and Park as chief growth officer for all of Serta Simmons. Though neither side would say how much Serta Simmons paid for Tuft & Needle, people in the know say it was in the range of $400 million to $500 million, or about two times Tuft & Needle's annual sales. Because they never raised money from VC firms, Marino and Park owned nearly 90 percent of the company, pocketing $200 million each, give or take, with the rest owned by employees who had been given stock. Based on its higher sales, Casper is valued at $1.1 billion, but because it had raised about $340 million from investors by mid-2019, its founders retain significantly lower stakes than Marino and Park.

Tuft & Needle did make one concession to its new owner. Shortly after the merger, it changed the wording on the hundreds of billboards it had plastered in cities around the nation, many of which had a simple message: "Mattress stores are greedy. Learn the truth." Those mattress stores that Marino and Park had long derided, that indeed had been the inspiration for Tuft & Needle, accounted for most of the mattress sales of its new owner, Serta Simmons. The new billboard messages— "We Hate Your Mattress, Too" and "Solving the National Sleep Debt Crisis"—were much less edgy.

Tomorrow Sleep was soon permanently put to rest. Michael Traub, who had championed its creation, left Serta Simmons six months after the Tuft & Needle merger, with no explanation beyond a terse press release quoting an Advent partner saying, "We believe the time is right for this transition." Not long after Traub's departure, a decision was made to discontinue the Tomorrow Sleep brand, a signal that his bosses felt his strategy had gone awry.

Bryan Murphy concedes that Tomorrow Sleep didn't accomplish what he had hoped. While it did force Serta Simmons to become more digital and customer-focused, in the end, buying Tuft & Needle made more sense. "We were late to the party," Murphy explains, a problem compounded by the tsunami of competitors. If Tomorrow Sleep does become a Harvard Business School case study, it won't be for the reason he once had hoped. "Big enterprises are better suited by acquiring or investing in disruptors," concludes Murphy, who left the company not long after his bosses decided to buy Tuft & Needle. "Before I took this job, I couldn't think of any company that had successfully disrupted itself from within. That's still the case."

10

Breaking the Sound Barrier

Christian Gormsen's hearing is perfectly good, but he wears hearing aids from time to time anyway. He likes to pluck them from inside his ear canal and then show them to the person he's talking to. It's his way of saying, "See, you had no idea I was wearing these, did you?"

It's a good conversation starter. He's right, you didn't notice them, because the hearing aids are about the size of a peanut. Thanks to advances in technology, they aren't just tiny and nearly invisible; they are powerful as well, packed with a miniature speaker, microphone, and computer chip that can amplify sound to different levels to adjust to your degree of hearing loss.

Many people who need hearing aids don't wear them, Gormsen points out. In part, that's because of the stigma: if you are hard of hearing, you must be old. And in part it's because they are so expensive. Though the components cost only several hundred dollars, patients typically pay $4,500 to $7,000 for a pair of hearing aids.

The hearing aids that Gormsen doesn't need but occasionally wears are meant to solve both these issues. They are made by Eargo, the

Silicon Valley start-up he runs, and are sold directly to the consumer. By cutting out the middleman, Eargo offers a pair of hearing aids for about one-third to one-half the price of comparable hearing aids made by its established rivals.

Elegantly designed and packaged, the Eargo might be described as the iPhone of hearing aids. *Time* and *Popular Science* have both put Eargo on their Best New Product lists. Engadget called it a "favorite"; and Interesting Engineering anointed it one of its "most exciting products." One of Eargo's early customers, the billionaire financier Charles Schwab, liked his Eargo hearing aids so much that he became one of the biggest investors in the fledgling company.

For all the buzz, a big question looms: Can Eargo do for hearing aids what Warby Parker did for eyeglasses, Dollar Shave Club did for razors, and Tuft & Needle and Casper did for mattresses? "We're testing the boundaries of classic e-commerce," Gormsen acknowledges. "Eargo is a medical product as well as a consumer product. Can you sell direct to consumer?"

In many ways, hearing aids seem ideal for (and in need of) disruption. Like other products targeted by insurgent brands, hearing aids are a multibillion-dollar-a-year business dominated by a classic oligopoly. Five hearing aid companies account for more than 90 percent of sales in the United States. The industry leaders don't compete on price, but instead, like Gillette and Serta Simmons, have churned out an array of models, seemingly offering distinctions without much difference, making the experience of buying a hearing aid befuddling.

This frustrates consumer advocates and even some audiologists. "How can a smartphone do everything it can for less than $1,000, but the average price of hearing aids is more than $4,000?" wonders Kim Cavitt, an audiologist who is now a consultant to the health care industry and a vocal critic of the high cost of hearing aids.

The answer to Cavitt's question has nothing to do with what it costs to manufacture hearing aids and everything to do with how they traditionally have been sold. Like with mattresses and eyeglasses, the middleman takes a big cut (typically several thousand dollars, give or take), the middleman being audiology clinics. The consumer doesn't know about their steep fees because these are bundled into one price that includes the device and services, such as a hearing test and a fitting.

For patients with severe hearing loss, who can benefit from expert assistance in measuring their loss and selecting the right hearing aid, these costs can make sense. But for the tens of millions of people with mild to moderate hearing loss, the hidden fees are a steep price—especially considering that an audiogram, like a vision test, generally costs only around $100 to $200. Getting a test and then buying a hearing aid online would make sense economically for most patients, though even a test isn't required. And hearing aids have become so advanced that they can be easily programmed by the user, which means a visit to an audiologist can add little if any value for these patients. Millions more of them would buy hearing aids if only they were cheaper, health care advocates say.

All this has prompted investors to pour money into a half dozen hearing aid start-ups, with different strategies and a variety of products and prices. Some already have gone bust. Despite hundreds of millions of dollars in venture capital financing, entrepreneurs have found it confoundingly hard to crack the hearing aid market. If many product categories have been disrupted faster by direct-to-consumer start-ups than even their backers expected, hearing aids have been far slower, even though they have adopted the same business model: lower prices and free returns for a product that offers many of the key features of established brands.

For all the similarities, there are differences that have created obstacles. The most daunting: many potential buyers are in their sixties and older, and less comfortable with buying anything online, especially a sophisticated and expensive medical device. Even for Eargo, getting traction has proved challenging. As of early 2019, it had raised $135 million from various venture capital firms, an amount several times higher than its total sales over the three and a half years it had been selling hearing aids.

"It's been more expensive and harder than I would have predicted to succeed," confesses David Wu, a partner at the VC firm Maveron, Eargo's earliest backer. "We have seen so much disruption by direct-to-consumer brands that we felt hearing aids were a natural target, because there was so much pent-up demand and many people hate the existing devices. It turns out that age demographics and the stigma around the category has made it difficult."

To support their view that disruption in the medical world is possible, hearing aid investors point to the fast-growing teledentistry business. Not long ago, if you had crooked teeth and wanted to get them straightened, you had to visit an orthodontist and pay $5,000 or more and wear unsightly metal braces. A half dozen start-ups, led by Smile-DirectClub, have upended that business by offering to do the same for less than $2,000. It's all done with clear plastic aligners, custom-fit for your teeth, which can be made from a mold taken with an at-home impression kit or by getting your teeth scanned at a retail outlet. Wearing the aligners over a six-to eight-month period straightens your smile—and all your checkups can be done online, by a licensed dentist or orthodontist. "We're looking a lot at mirroring SmileDirectClub," says Gormsen, because it has used advances in technology to win over customers who couldn't afford braces or might be embarrassed to wear them.

In 2019, with more than seven hundred thousand customers and its revenue on an annualized basis soaring to about $900 million, Smile-DirectClub—though still unprofitable—made an initial public offering of stock in September that valued the company at about $4 billion even after its shares fell sharply over the next few weeks. So threatened are orthodontists that their trade group filed complaints with regulators in several dozen states.

It was frustration over persuading patients to wear hearing aids that was the inspiration for Eargo. Florent Michel, a French ear, nose, and throat surgeon, found that his patients often ignored his suggestion that they get hearing aids. They didn't want to wear a behind-the-ear hearing aid, which is the most common model, because other people could see it. Then Michel had an idea while tying flies for fly fishing, one of his passions: What if you could make a hearing aid about the same size and shape? It could be inserted in the ear using small fibers akin to the tiny feathers used to make fishing flies, which would hold the hearing aid in place but allow air and sound to go through and be amplified. It would nestle snugly and almost invisibly in the ear. Yes, there were in-the-ear hearing aids already on the market, but they were either bulky and noticeable or prohibitively expensive for most patients. The trick would be making one that was small, powerful, and reasonably priced.

Michel mentioned the idea to his son Raphael, who had moved to San Francisco in the early 2000s. After getting an advanced engineering degree at Stanford and an MBA at the University of California, Berkeley, Raphael then worked for a couple of health care start-ups. "Eargo started as an evening and weekend project, like a fun distraction," Raphael Michel recalls. In mid-2012, things became more serious. He quit his job and started working out of his garage in Palo Alto. He also recruited a friend, another health care entrepreneur who was a physician and had an electrical engineering degree. "That's really cool," Daniel Shen thought when Raphael Michel approached him. "That's something that could change the way that hearing aids fit and could really reduce the cost." Their research confirmed the market potential: of an estimated forty-eight million Americans with some level of hearing loss, only eight million wear hearing aids. "All these issues—stigma, comfort, cost, access, ease of use—these were big things staring us in the face. We thought, 'Wow, there's an opportunity,'" Shen says. He and Michel then began developing prototypes with a small team they recruited.

They weren't the only entrepreneurs sensing that the conditions were right for trying to disrupt the hearing aid market. Around the same time, iHear Medical, founded by a scientist who had invented an expensive high-end hearing aid, was trying to democratize the market by selling a lower-priced product online. Another start-up, Audicus, pursued a business model akin to that of Dollar Shave Club, reselling under its own brand a German-designed hearing aid. They both sold behind-the-ear hearing aids for $1,000 to $1,400 a pair.

But Eargo isn't trying to create the cheapest hearing aid, or to offer every feature that the most expensive hearing aids have. It wants to redefine the hearing aid and expand the market by making it feel like a consumer product rather than a medical device for the elderly. As

Shen puts it, the goal was, "How do you take it as far away as possible from the beige, behind-the-ear prosthesis that people remembered their grandparents or parents wearing?"

To succeed in this mission, the hearing aid had to be a nearly invisible, inside-the-ear device, and for ease of use, it needed to be rechargeable, like a smartphone, rather than requiring tiny batteries that had to be replaced every few days, as with most hearing aids. And it had to be reasonably priced, which meant it had to be sold directly to consumers. Only by doing that, and bypassing audiology clinics, could Eargo undercut the prices of the expensive in-the-ear devices.

With financing from some wealthy angel investors, Michel and Shen started tinkering with possible designs, even before they had working parts. Their small, jury-rigged mock-ups featured wires, plastic pieces, and pliable thin fibers on the end that would be inserted in the ear. "We used whatever we could find in arts and crafts stores and Home Depot," Michel says. "We made some out of wood, we made some out of metal and plastic, just really gluing and cutting things together to show what it might look like."

But they needed a working prototype to show VC investors to persuade them to finance the company. This proved so challenging that at times they wondered if it could be done at all. They searched fruitlessly for months for a supplier who would sell them a tiny in-ear amplifier, because they couldn't afford to build their own. Then, at an audiology conference in Boston in early 2013, they stumbled across a company that had exactly what they needed. "Now we can actually do this," a relieved Michel told colleagues at a dinner that evening to celebrate.

After nearly a year of work, they fashioned a basic working prototype, and Michel began making the rounds to meet with VC firms. It proved a hard sell. "When you talk to investors about a new hearing aid, it's like, 'There are a lot of dead bodies along the road.' The history of hearing aids is that people have tried and failed," he explains.

But Michel managed to pique the interest of some partners at Maveron, a VC firm cofounded in the late 1990s by Howard Schultz, the former chief executive of Starbucks. Maveron focuses on consumer

start-ups, and its prominent investments include eBay, the e-commerce
pioneer, and direct-to-consumer brands such as online clothing retailer
Everlane. The firm's website boasts that it has been "disrupting the
status quo for 20 years," adding a dig that "middlemen are so 20th
century."

Maveron had invested in only one other medical device start-up,
and it saw Eargo's vision of straddling the health care/consumer product worlds as a way to apply the principles of disruption to a new
category. "Our biggest question was 'Do you think you can sell a multi-
thousand-dollar hearing device direct to the consumer, unseen, on the
internet?" David Wu recalls. Still, despite that uncertainty, the firm
agreed to lead a $2.6 million seed investment round.

Another important connection was forged as well. Christian
Gormsen learned about Eargo from a former colleague of his at the
management consulting firm McKinsey who now worked for an investment firm in San Francisco. Gormsen had spent nearly a decade in the
hearing aid business, and he expressed skepticism at first. "I'll help you,
but you're wasting your time and money," he responded initially. "I've
seen the last twenty hearing aid start-up ideas, and they're not worth
the paper they're printed on."

But after meeting with the founders at Florent Michel's house in
France and seeing the prototype, Gormsen began thinking that this one
might work. "It was really comfortable, and the sound magnification
was good," he recalls. Plus, he believed that a reasonably priced in-the-
ear device for people with mild-to-moderate hearing loss might have a
better chance of success by overcoming the stigma of wearing hearing
aids. But Gormsen pointed out a major shortcoming in the early prototype: the rechargeable battery ran out of juice after about eight to ten
hours; it would need to last a full day, he advised, or the wearer would
have to take the hearing aid out and recharge it during the day, which
would discourage buyers.

Although the VC firm where Gormsen's former colleague worked
ended up not investing in Eargo, Raphael Michel recruited Gormsen
to become an adviser and join the start-up's board of directors. Rather
than being discouraged or turned off by Gormsen's initial skepticism,

Michel appreciated how frank he was. "When you want to transform an industry, you also have to surround yourself with people who are in that industry, who have a ton of knowledge," Michel says. "I knew nothing about the hearing aid industry. I needed a devil's advocate."

It took another couple of years to test and fine-tune the product. Solving the battery-life problem was hard, because batteries that would last all day were too big to fit inside the ear canal. The engineering team suggested giving up on a rechargeable battery for the first-generation Eargo, Michel recalls, and instead using a battery that would have to be replaced after a few days, as in most hearing aids. "No, because that hearing aid wouldn't do a good job at what people want," Michel told them. "It has to be rechargeable." Finally, the engineers came up with the idea of putting two batteries together in a configuration small enough to fit inside most ears. This meant the hearing aid would work sixteen to eighteen hours before needing to be recharged.

In keeping with Florent Michel's vision, at the tip of each hearing aid were several dozen short and thin medical-grade silicone "Flexi Fibers," which would allow sound and air to pass through and would hold the hearing aid in place. While the Eargo could not be custom-programmed, like expensive behind-the-ear hearing aids, it came pre-set with four volume settings to cover the most typical high-frequency sounds that the vast majority of people with mild to moderate hearing loss have a difficult time registering; to change the settings, all you had to do was gently tap your ear twice when the hearing aid was in place.

Even with an innovative product, Raphael Michel and Daniel Shen knew one of the biggest obstacles would be to convince customers to buy a sophisticated medical device online. To build trust, they got FDA approval of the Eargo hearing aid, certifying that its quality met federal standards. They also began recruiting a team of audiologists and hearing aid specialists to counsel prospective customers and provide advice if they did purchase an Eargo device. The goal was to replicate as closely as possible, over the phone or online, the type of personal advice and service they would normally get when visiting an audiologist at a clinic—and, not coincidentally, to deflect criticism from audiologist trade groups about the risks of buying online.

In June 2015, Eargo secured $13.6 million in new VC financing in another investment round led by Maveron and began selling what Raphael Michel calls a "minimum viable product"—a Silicon Valley term for a product with enough features to satisfy early customers—even as Eargo was working on a second-generation device. "It's not like we were a large company like Apple and we could take five years to get the perfect product, like the Apple Watch or iPad," he explains.

Using the playbook of other direct-to-consumer start-ups, Eargo offered free sixty-day trials. In addition, if a customer first wanted to find out if the hearing aid felt comfortable, Eargo would send a dummy pair, a replica without the working electronic components. The goal was to keep returns as low as possible. Throughout the industry, even for hearing aids fitted by an audiologist, return rates range from 10 to 30 percent, with higher rates for in-ear models and lower rates for behind-the-ear models.

The initial reviews of Eargo's hearing aids were positive. Tech-Crunch, a widely followed technology news site, proclaimed Eargo "the hearing aid of the future." A *PC Magazine* reviewer who wore them for a couple of weeks wrote, "They are tiny, lightweight, comfortable and nearly invisible. And more importantly, they sound great: very natural, light, and airy . . . During those two weeks, not a single person saw them. Many times I pointed them out and people still couldn't see them."

Publicity like this has helped many direct-to-consumer brands (Warby Parker, Hubble, Dollar Shave Club, Casper, and others) get off to a fast start. But unlike other start-ups, Eargo had the added burden of persuading customers to buy a product they needed but didn't really want.

Recognizing the challenge, Eargo tested a variety of advertising messages on the internet, Facebook, and television, where it bought inexpensive "remnant" spots that most advertisers didn't want, such as during reruns of classics that are mostly watched by older audiences. "We thought that TV would be the best way to convert [customers] and scale, but it ended up being Facebook," Raphael Michel says. "It was very shocking because we didn't expect our target customers to be so active on Facebook. So, actually, digital marketing ended up working super well."

To suggest that you don't have to be old to need hearing aids, and that you shouldn't be embarrassed to wear them, Eargo's marketing typically features people in their forties and fifties, not in their sixties or seventies or even older. One ad campaign featured comical misunderstandings: a puzzled husband working in a garden thinks his wife says, "Honey, remember to slaughter the tomatoes with the nun," when what she really says is, "Remember to water the tomatoes when you're done." Other ads depicted people totally missing what a family member says.

The marketing struck a chord. "Hearing loss is taboo, so if you can actually use humor to start a dialogue, you are removing the taboo and starting a conversation," Raphael Michel says. The number of people responding to Eargo's ads and inquiring about the new hearing aid rose rapidly from two thousand a month in the summer of 2015 to around one hundred thousand a month by the end of that year. As with many expensive products sold online, only a small percentage of those people ended up buying. But sales for the company's first six months totaled about $1 million, an encouraging start in a category that traditionally had been a hard sell.

Demand was so promising, in fact, that Eargo had no problem raising another round of money to increase its advertising budget and continue doing R&D. In December 2015, just six months after Eargo's previous fund-raising, New Enterprise Associates, one of the nation's largest VC firms, led a group that included Maveron in investing an additional $25 million in Eargo.

Raphael Michel was ecstatic. It had taken several years to develop the Eargo device, but he had managed to make his father's vision a reality. "Everyone was really excited," he recalls.

Then, slowly at first but in increasing numbers, customers started sending back their Eargos. What initially was a normal return rate soon became a "tsunami," Christian Gormsen recalls, even though customers credited Eargos with improving their hearing when they were working properly, while being nearly invisible. "Many customers loved them, and when they returned them, they wanted them back," Gormsen adds.

Raphael Michel scrambled to unravel the mystery of what was causing many of the devices to fail. "Troubleshooting is complicated, because you have to go all the way back to what's the source of the defect and how to resolve it," he notes. The ear canal—hot, humid, oily, and salty—can be an inhospitable environment for an electronic device like a hearing aid.

Even though Eargos had undergone elaborate testing, the flaws became clear only after they were worn for extended periods by people in real-life settings. One fundamental problem involved the "jacket" encasing the hearing aid's electronic components. It was made with a flexible silicone that was found to expand by tiny amounts over time, allowing humidity and salt from the ear to seep into the device and fry its electronics. "Everything was tested to an industry standard, but how long was it tested?" Gormsen explains. "There are advantages to being a newcomer to an industry, but there are disadvantages as well. The cash-burn rate was high. We were spending all our money putting out fires."

Things looked so bad that David Wu at Maveron remarked, "This is like a Shakespearean tragedy. In the first act, everyone is very excited. In the second act, everything goes wrong."

Wu and other investors turned to Gormsen, given his experience in the industry. "Can we salvage this?" they asked. Yes, Gormsen replied. "We've proven that this is a product that people want. We've proven that we can sell medical products online. These are all positives," he recalls telling them. "We need to stop the bleeding, fix the product, cut down the organization to save costs."

The investors agreed to continue backing Eargo, on one condition: that Gormsen replace Raphael Michel as chief executive officer, because they needed someone with more production know-how to redesign and fix the Eargo. It was a painful message for Michel, who had nurtured the company from the start, but he accepted the investors' verdict. He took a new job as head of strategy and remained on the board of directors. Stepping aside as chief executive, he says, "was very hard to do, unbelievably hard to do, because Eargo was one of my babies. . . . It was tough, but it was the right business decision."

Eargo stopped taking new orders while it reengineered its hearing aid. Gormsen used his contacts in the industry to recruit veterans with deep knowledge of hearing aid components and what can go wrong.

Fixing the flaws, while keeping the basic design, took most of 2016. "We played whack-a-mole, knocking down the big ones to start with," Gormsen says. The redesigned second generation Eargo, called "the Max," had a more durable shell encasing the electronic components to prevent leaks and protect the components from shorting out. Eargo also decided to contract out manufacturing, which had been done internally, to a Thai-based company with expertise in making and assembling small electronic products.

To help Eargo through its recovery, Gormsen recruited new backers, including the financier Charles Schwab, through his personal investment fund. Schwab himself had tried many different hearing aids, price not being a problem for him, but he was never satisfied. Then a friend recommended Eargo, and he liked the idea that the devices fit nearly hidden in his ears, had rechargeable batteries, and delivered good sound. Even better for Gormsen, Schwab was undeterred by the company's problems because he knew what it took to disrupt an industry. He saw the hearing aid industry as similar to Wall Street in the 1970s, when he founded the discount brokerage firm that bears his name: a clubby world that kept prices high and put the interests of established players ahead of customers'. Success wasn't assured and didn't come easily.

"Over forty years later, it seems almost instant, but it took a number of years to perfect," Schwab says of his own company's success. "We had difficulties. We had to make huge investments in technology, huge investments in people, huge investments in marketing. It was never a straight line. There were downturns, too." Gormsen recalls Schwab telling him, "I set out to change things with discount brokering. You have the same mission at Eargo."

In January 2017, Eargo resumed selling hearing aids, and spent heavily on advertising, figuring it had one chance to regain its lost momentum. "The industry overall spends only about 2 percent of revenue on marketing," Gormsen notes, because the established companies rely on audiology clinics to do their marketing. "We spend over 20 percent." That's the only way Eargo can succeed, he believes: "If you want to build a brand, which is ultimately our purpose, then you've got to invest money to make people aware of your presence."

Gormsen also brought in new marketing executives with experience in consumer advertising. Jurgen Pauquet, a former vice president of e-commerce at Warner Bros., signed on as chief commercial officer and cast a wider net with Eargo's marketing. Rather than targeting groups of people likely to have suffered hearing loss (musicians and military veterans, among others), Pauquet advised that Eargo could generate more "leads" at an efficient cost by directing its ads at a general audience aged forty-five and older with an income of at least $80,000. And he decided to focus the company's ads even more on the emotional aspects of hearing aids, and less on the technical details. "Initially, we had more product shots. Now we have more people in social settings, connecting with friends and family," Pauquet explains.

Hearing aids aren't an impulse purchase but rather one typically made after lots of contemplation and research. So, Eargo's digital advertising targets people who have indicated possible interest by clicking on news or advertising related to hearing aids. It also built up a staff of more than a hundred salespeople to reach out by phone and online to potential customers who expressed an interest in Eargo by responding to an ad. And to keep the return rate as low as possible, Gormsen pushed for more after-sales hand-holding. When someone buys a hearing aid, instead of waiting for the customer to call with questions, the company emails a link to a "pre-arrival" video; follows up with a link to another video on the third day, with tips on how to get the best use from the hearing aids; another video on how to clean the hearing aids on the tenth day; and a long-term-care video on the twenty-fourth day.

Two years after selling its first hearing aid, and a year after suspending sales to fix the design flaws, Eargo finally began getting momentum. Sales of its second-generation hearing aid rose steadily throughout 2017, reaching about $6.5 million for the year and then quadrupling to $24 million in 2018. About two-thirds of its customers are first-time hearing aid buyers, and on average they are four to five years younger than typical first-time users. This suggests that Eargo can expand the market of hearing aid users, Gormsen notes, and will not have to depend on stealing customers from established players.

In line with Raphael Michel's early vision of starting with a minimum viable product and then continually improving it, Eargo is also expanding its hearing aid options, to appeal to the broadest range of customers. In 2019, it introduced its third-generation hearing aid, the Neo, which added features that higher-end competitors already had, such as Bluetooth connectivity so that the Eargo's settings can be programmed by the user with a smartphone or from afar by a technician. The Neo also has improved sound amplification and feedback reduction. All this comes at a higher price—$2,550 to $2,750 a pair—but Eargo lowered the prices as much as 25 percent on its first two models, with the first model now selling for $1,650.

To speed its growth, in late 2018 Eargo, like many digital-first brands that once were sold only online, started partnering with retail stores. The stores don't sell its hearing aids but have samples for potential customers to try on. "You can play with them, you can plug them in your ears, and you can experience them," Gormsen explains. "We can meet the customer and build that comfort and trust" with people who might initially be reluctant to buy a pricey medical device online.

The turnaround helped the company win a vote of confidence from investors. It raised $45 million in late 2017 from several VC funds and another $52 million in early 2019, mostly from existing investors, including Charles Schwab, who has put in more than $10 million overall and now owns about 10 percent of the company. "Something like this will win. I hope Eargo is the one," Schwab says of his decision to keep backing the company.

Eargo's market share remains tiny. In contrast to the razor and mattress businesses, where new digitally native brands have grabbed 15 to 20 percent of the market in just a few years, hearing aid start-ups remain under 5 percent. For Eargo to justify the large VC investment it has received, it will need to persuade a lot more people who need hearing aids to buy them—to make hearing aids socially acceptable as well as financially affordable. After all the early travails, Gormsen predicts that it will. "Can we become a triple-digit million- to one-billion-dollar company?" he asks, and then answers, "Absolutely. I believe it."

Flying High, Then Crashing to Earth

In May 2016, Josh Udashkin got the call he had been anxiously awaiting. A few months earlier, he had launched his "smart" luggage start-up, Raden. The elegantly designed hard-shell suitcases retailed for about one-half to two-thirds the price of better-known brands.

Raden's main selling point was its suitcase's nifty electronics: a built-in battery to recharge your phone and other gadgets, a scale to avoid overweight charges when checking it in, and a Bluetooth locator that tracked your case and let you know when it was coming down the baggage carousel.

Udashkin wasn't the only entrepreneur to spot the opportunity to shake up the staid luggage business. Direct-to-consumer start-ups such as Away (founded by two former employees of Warby Parker) and Bluesmart were also vying for the attention of travelers in their twenties and thirties who couldn't afford luxury brands and were shopping for a hip alternative to Samsonite and American Tourister.

To keep up its early momentum, Raden needed a good holiday season, when many shoppers buy new luggage for vacation or as gifts.

Then came the news Udashkin was hoping for: Oprah Winfrey had selected his company's luggage for "Oprah's Favorite Things 2016," an endorsement that he had begun working to win even before Raden sold its first suitcase. Udashkin and his small team of about two dozen employees were ecstatic. When the news became official that fall, Raden posted on Instagram that "@oprah and @oprahmagazine have named us one of their Favorite Things, 2016!" Even better, embedded in the Instagram post was a nine-second video of Oprah herself, dressed in red-and-white candy cane stripes, high-fiving a smiling Udashkin while loudly crying out, "THIS IS THE SMARTEST LUGGAGE EVERRR-RRRRR." On the Oprah.com website, she wrote, "My mind is blown: These suitcases have a built-in charging station, tracking capability and a weight sensor (buh-bye, overage fees!). They practically come with a college degree—smartest luggage ever. And the apple green shade was created exclusively for me."

It was the ultimate marketing coup for a start-up.

With the Oprah endorsement, Raden's sales exploded. After selling many thousands of suitcases, the company quickly ran out of inventory and had a waiting list exceeding ten thousand. Raden's customers, the company let it be known, included Golden State Warriors basketball all-star Draymond Green, fashion designer Tory Burch, and actress Jessica Alba. First-year sales were about $6 million, and Udashkin predicted that sales for 2017 would reach $12 million.

The race was on to become the luggage brand of choice for Millennials, and Raden seemed poised to grab the early lead. Away and Bluesmart had raised more money from VC investors than Raden, but that meant that success would be even sweeter and more lucrative for Udashkin and his colleagues, as they had retained a larger ownership stake in their company. Building on the Oprah surge would help Udashkin achieve his goal of growing Raden's sales quickly and selling the company to a bigger rival for a giant payday.

"It was a big turning point," recalls Justin Seidenfeld, the chief product officer and one of Udashkin's first hires.

* * *

The direct-to-consumer revolution has spawned many success stories, enriching company founders. Kellogg's paid $600 million for Rxbar, an all-natural "energy bar." The online watch company MVMT ("movement," get it?), financed with a Kickstarter fund-raising campaign, was purchased by Movado for $100 million, with the potential for another $100 million in payments to the founders, depending on sales growth. Procter & Gamble acquired Native deodorant for $100 million, and Amazon bought the digital doorbell start-up Ring for about $1 billion. Stitch Fix, the online fashion subscription service, made an initial public stock offering in 2017, six years after its founding, and its market value in late 2019 exceeded $2 billion. And as we've seen, Unilever bought Dollar Shave Club for $1 billion, and Edgewell Personal Care (the owner of the Schick brand) bought Harry's for $1.37 billion.

But because the barriers to entry are so low, many direct-to-consumer categories have become especially crowded, leading to fierce competition. Getting VC funding is one thing. Getting enough customers when you are competing against a handful of look-alike rivals is another. How many new luggage or bra or vitamin or pet food brands does the world really need? More than one start-up might survive in a category, but typically a big winner will emerge, with the rest also-rans, along with some losers.

In the electric toothbrush market, there are more than a half dozen new entrants: Quip, Goby, Boka, Burst, Bruush, Shyn, Gleam—and Gleem, a copycat from Procter & Gamble. Most share a similar business model: short names, automatic timers, and some with two versions (plastic at a lower price, metal at a higher price), a subscription that includes a new brush and toothpaste every one to three months, and free returns, typically for forty-five to sixty days. Even their websites feature remarkably similar wording:

> The built-in timer ensures you brush for a dentist-
> recommended two minutes, with 30-second
> prompts to tell you when it's time to switch
> quadrants. *(Goby)*

Every 30 seconds you'll feel a momentary pause
to remind you to move on to another part of your
mouth. After brushing for the dentist approved 2
minutes, your brush will automatically switch off.
(Burst)

Just what the dentist ordered for a wholesome two
minute clean . . . 30-second quadrant timer. *(Quip)*

Quip, the earliest entrant, which began selling its toothbrushes in 2015, has emerged as the leader, with one million toothbrushes sold as of mid-2018. Cofounder Simon Enever believes that this number is ten times higher than that for any of its start-up competitors, and estimated that Quip's annual sales would triple or more in 2019.

Being first mover gave Quip its early advantage, as did its elegant design. (Enever is an industrial designer.) Though it wasn't heavily funded early on, it bet heavily on Facebook advertising and got lots of attention. Helping was a Bloomberg News story in August 2015 headlined, "Is Quip the Tesla of Toothbrushes?"

As Quip gained traction, it was able to draw more investment, and it plowed that money back into marketing. As of late 2018, it had raised $62 million in financing, with a valuation in "the hundreds of millions of dollars," says Enever. To distinguish itself, it used some of that money to buy a dental insurance company. Goby, by contrast, which started around the same time, has raised just $4.1 million in funding.

Some winners have succeeded while raising little or no venture capital money, and instead financed themselves with sales revenue, such as Tuft & Needle and MVMT, but many successful start-ups have raised lots of money to fuel growth. Casper has raised nearly $340 million. Ditto for Warby Parker, with $290 million. Dollar Shave Club raised $163 million, and Harry's, $375 million. Glossier, the cosmetics company, has raised $186 million.

"It's a bit chicken-and-egg, but the most successful [direct-to-consumer] venture companies have raised a lot of money. Success begets capital, but capital also begets success," says Henry Davis, former president of Glossier. "It is not always a low-capital-intensive business, as it turns out. I don't think people knew that in the beginning."

But there is a potential downside: The more money you raise, the bigger price you have to fetch to deliver a good return to investors. Bonobos sold for $310 million to Walmart, after having raised about $128 million. While that was certainly better than losing money, the returns were modest for VC firms, which typically hope to make five to ten times or more on the early-stage investments from their winners.

Of course, raising a lot of money doesn't guarantee success. Birchbox, founded in 2010, was one of the early direct-to-consumer subscription start-ups. It didn't make its own products but rather sent customers samples of a handful of beauty products for $10 a month. Birchbox quickly became a VC darling, attracting investments from Kirsten Green's Forerunner Ventures, Lerer Hippeau, and others. By 2016, it had received a total of nearly $90 million in financing and was valued at around $500 million.

But its growth stalled as the novelty wore off, and it resorted to layoffs to cut costs. Eventually, Viking Global Investors, one of its earliest backers, bailed it out by investing another $15 million to take a majority stake—meaning the company's estimated overall value had fallen to about $30 million, less than one-third of the total amount invested in it.

* * *

Josh Udashkin of Raden, like many other founders of new digital brands, knew next to nothing about the product he had decided to launch. A Canadian with law and MBA degrees, he was working as an attorney at a New York firm when he realized that he was miserable practicing law. He went to work in international development for Aldo Group, a Canadian footwear company, and noticed on his many travels that suitcases were boring and hadn't changed much in decades.

He quit that job in the summer of 2014, soon after turning thirty, and spent months studying the luggage market, often working out of hotel lobbies, where he could get a Wi-Fi connection, because he couldn't yet afford office space. "My original thesis was looking at luggage like a consumer electronic product, like going into an Apple store," says Udashkin. "There is a ton of luggage, but the customer gets confused about warranty and quality and price and design. It was hard to imagine a brand that a twenty-eight-year-old guy or girl would want to travel with." Or, as he would later tell a reporter for the website the Verge, "The truth is, and I don't want to say this arrogantly, luggage is such a fucked category."

The last major innovation in luggage had, in fact, come decades earlier. In 1970, Bernard Sadow, an executive at a Massachusetts luggage company, came up with the idea of putting four wheels on the long, narrow side of a suitcase and attaching a strap to one corner to pull it horizontally. Sadow applied for a patent for "rolling luggage" that stated, "With the enormous recent growth in travel, a number of problems have arisen in the handling of luggage. Whereas formerly luggage would be handled by porters and be loaded or unloaded at points convenient to the street, the large terminals of today, particularly air terminals, have increased the difficulty of baggage handling . . . One object of the present invention is to provide an article of luggage which can be readily handled with a minimum of effort and time by the traveler." In 1972, Sadow was granted a U.S. patent. "It was one of my best ideas," he told the *New York Times* years later, without saying what other ideas might have rivaled this one.

Robert Plath, a pilot for Northwest Airlines, came up with a better and easier way to roll luggage in 1987. He attached two wheels to the bottom of a suitcase and added a retractable handle, so the suitcase could be rolled upright. He dubbed his brainchild the Rollaboard, a name he trademarked. After initially operating out of his garage and selling suitcases on the side to pilots and flight attendants, Plath retired and founded a company named Travelpro. Eventually, two wheels became four on most suitcases, but that was the extent of rethinking the suitcase for several decades.

Then came the smartphone and tablets and laptop PCs, which uncannily seemed to run out of power just before you got on a flight. For a long time, most planes didn't have electrical outlets or charging ports, which meant that when you landed and really needed your phone to make calls or check email, the battery was kaput.

That's when Udashkin and bunch of other entrepreneurs came up with roughly the same idea around the same time: Why not build a charger into the suitcase, and maybe even throw in other electronics? Sure, you could separately buy a portable power pack for your devices, but this way, you would never forget it because it would travel with you, in your luggage. Customers most likely to want this feature were gadget-obsessed Millennials—who, as it happens, were also most likely to be shopping for their first nice piece of luggage.

Even better, it was a new twist (like wheeled suitcases) that the major luggage companies were slow to recognize. The newcomers arrived when the business needed fresh thinking, says David Sebens, who had worked for several major luggage brands before becoming a consultant to a number of companies, including Raden. "Luggage is very staid. Luggage departments in department stores are on the third floor, in the far back corner. They could use some excitement."

Udashkin knew he needed help to develop a prototype. So, he sought advice from people who had worked with the luggage makers Tumi and Samsonite, and recruited an industrial designer for Beats, the earphone company now owned by Apple. "One of the key inspirations for him was Beats," recalls George Koulouris, who worked briefly at Raden during the development stage. "He said they took the head-phones market, which was rather big, but there was no big brand in the space. He wanted to do something similar with suitcases."

The Raden team started working on a design that included a bat-tery charger, which could be removed, although only when the suitcase was opened and its contents were set aside or out of the way. It also featured a sensor for weighing the contents and a Bluetooth locator that would pair the suitcase with your smartphone.

In 2015, Udashkin used an early version of the prototype to secure initial venture capital funding of $2.1 million. Then his team raced to commercialize the product as quickly as possible, to avoid falling behind other VC-backed smart suitcase start-ups.

The luggage market was already crowded, of course, with every-thing from luxury brands such as Louis Vuitton and Rimowa, costing more than $1,000, to no-name Chinese imports selling for $100 or less.

The sweet spot for Raden, Udashkin and his colleagues concluded, would be to sell a premium product at a mid-range price. With the electronics packed inside, that would be a great value, they figured, and enable Raden to make a profit.

For durability and stylish looks, Raden's shell was made from a high-grade polycarbonate that could take a beating and was scratch-resistant. For the wheels, the team chose Japanese-made Hinomoto spinner wheels, which are known for swiveling and gliding easily and for not breaking when the bag is tossed around by airport baggage handlers, says Justin Seidenfeld, who was hired as head of product because he was an outsourcing expert.

The Raden team decided to price the carry-on size at $295 and the larger check-in size at $395—or $590 (a $100 discount) if you bought them as a pair—which they calculated was one-third to one-half less than comparable-quality luggage on the market. At that price, there was little margin for error, says Seidenfeld. Raden paid its Taiwanese manufacturer about $100 for each suitcase. Shipping and warehousing added $40 to $50, and marketing costs were budgeted at $100 per order; on top of these costs were expenses such as salaries and other overhead.

Raden had hoped to begin selling its luggage toward the end of 2015, but that proved too ambitious. The manufacturer it chose already produced suitcases for well-known brands, but it hadn't worked with electronics, so it took time for it to learn how to efficiently make Raden luggage with all the gadgets inside.

Raden and its rivals Bluesmart and Away all went to market within months of each other in late 2015 and early 2016, with Raden's suitcases priced in the middle. Leading up to the launch, Udashkin and other senior managers were more focused on competing with Bluesmart than Away, Koulouris says. Bluesmart had similar electronics, while Away had only a battery for recharging devices. "I distinctly remember conversations around Away, and the team at Raden dismissing Away for just including a battery" [but no other electronics] "and saying, 'They don't know what they're doing,'" Koulouris says.

Initially, Raden's plan had been to sell online only, but Udashkin eventually decided on a multichannel strategy, opening a pop-up store on Prince Street in Manhattan's trendy SoHo neighborhood and offering its bags at a few retailers such as Bloomingdale's and Macy's.

Even without spending a lot of money on advertising, Raden got off to a strong start, thanks to press coverage. A glowing *New York Times* story featured a photo of Udashkin, wearing sunglasses, a tropical shirt, and jeans, posing like a hipster next to a wall of white Raden suitcases at the pop-up store. "We sold ten thousand units in the first sixty days. There was a lot of novelty," says Udashkin.

The outlook was so promising that Raden raised a second round of VC financing in March 2016, albeit the relatively small amount of just $3.5 million. That was in keeping with Udashkin's vow to avoid raising so much VC money that investors could end up driving his decision-making strategy. "They want to earn returns of ten times their money, and they're not going to let you out until that happens," he explains. "As a founder, your ownership can get diluted. I've read more stories about founders who built a business but ended up with a tiny share of the upside."

Udashkin, in fact, had made clear to his team that he wanted to ramp up sales and then, ideally, quickly sell Raden to a bigger luggage maker. "One of the good outcomes that was talked about was 'Samsonite buys Raden,'" Koulouris says. The more money you took from VC investors, the higher price you would need to get from a buyer to make those investors happy, which could make it harder to interest a buyer.

Udashkin's strategy was looking smart as Raden's sales shot up later in 2016, after it got the highly coveted spot on the Oprah list. "It was just incredible. In two or three days we blew through all of the inventory we had. That's a great problem to have," recalls Bryan Alston, a marketing consultant at a firm Raden hired to handle its digital marketing. But there was a downside as well. In the luggage business, it can take several months from the time an order is placed with a manufacturer to the time the product is delivered and available for sale. "There were a lot of people who wanted a suitcase, but they were sold out literally for months. And in those months, you could just go to Away or go to Bluesmart or go to another competitor," Alston says. "The fact that they sold out of all inventory at the peak of the travel season, when everyone is traveling, that just led them to ceding business to others."

Away in particular seemed to benefit. Its founders had met while working at Warby Parker, Jen Rubio as head of social media and Steph Korey overseeing the supply chain, where she had learned about sourcing quality materials. Away also used premium parts (high-grade polycarbonate, Hinomoto wheels, and YKK zippers, generally regarded as among the best on the market) and offered a lifetime guarantee. And Away's prices were even lower than Raden's, initially $245 for a carry-on, $295 for its larger suitcase, and $475 for the pair, cleverly conveyed with a snappy slogan: "First-Class Luggage at a Coach Price." And the company often offered $20 discounts, widening its price advantage.

Seeking to establish Raden as more of a premium brand, Udashkin opposed discounts. Bryan Alston, the marketing consultant, says he presented a case that Raden was losing lots of sales because it wouldn't offer incentives. "Discounting was one of the most frustrating arguments we'd get into," Alston says. "There was no discounting. Period."

Another difference in approach: While Raden marketed its luggage as a tech product, Away positioned itself more as a lifestyle brand. As part of the strategy, it launched a monthly travel magazine, where customers could get advice on destinations they liked. "Some of the brands that launched at a similar time to us were very focused on wheels and trolleys," says Selena Kalvaria, Away's senior vice president of brand marketing. "We love those things, but that's not what's going to make your brand have an emotional connection that you want to talk about at the dinner table."

And Away, in the summer of 2017, began offering a line of lower-ticket accessories in addition to its suitcases, which eventually included everything from smaller bags and backpacks to shaving and cosmetics kits to garment bags and leather luggage tags, all ranging in price from $30 to $195. "It also allows us to build overall share of closet, which extends to share of mind," Kalvaria explains. "How do we try to keep building out with that circle of products so that we continue to become synonymous with travel? Luggage is just the start. Everything else extends from that."

Raden took a different tack. "At the time, our opinion was that it was more a lack of focus than strategy" to offer accessories, says Thibault Le Conte, Raden's chief technology officer. But Away's move proved to be savvier, says Bryan Alston. Most of Raden's customers, he notes, were one-and-done shoppers; after buying a suitcase they never came back because few needed another one and Raden didn't sell anything else. That meant its marketing cost per order was high; it often spent more than the $100 it had budgeted for advertising to bring in each customer, at times even as much as $200, Alston says. By selling accessories, Away could bring in more revenue per customer and effectively lower the marketing cost of each dollar in sales. "Away found a way to generate additional purchases. They were able to get more lifetime value out of people than us having one expensive product," he says. "If you have to keep replacing your customers every month, or every day, that's expensive."

Away's focus on creating a lifestyle brand rather than just selling a tech-laden product was a key reason Kirsten Green of Forerunner Ventures had agreed to lead its first VC funding round. "They're tapping into the zeitgeist of a generation and their nomadic lifestyle," Green explains. "The customers are buying into an identity: 'I'm an explorer.'"

In that way, Green's investment in Away was much like her earlier bet on Dollar Shave Club, where the razor was less important to her than Michael Dubin's vision for reimagining men's grooming. The strategy was serving Away well. In May 2017, with its sales increasing, it raised another $20 million in VC funding, bringing its total at that point to $31 million, or more than five times what Raden had raised.

By that fall, Raden, Bluesmart, and Away were all jockeying for position and hoping for a good holiday season. Udashkin and his team were determined not to repeat their mistake of the year before, when they sold out and lost business to their rivals. So Raden increased its orders to make sure that it would have plenty of inventory on hand.

Then, on December 1, 2017, came ominous news. Delta Airlines declared that starting in mid-January, it would "no longer accept as checked or carry-on luggage so-called 'smart bags' or smart luggage with non-removable lithium-ion batteries, due to the potential for the powerful batteries to overheat and pose a fire hazard risk during flight." American Airlines made a similar announcement.

It was effectively a deathblow for Bluesmart, which was already slumping after a fast start. It had positioned itself as a luxury brand, with suitcases priced at $499 and $599, similar to the lower end of upscale luggage makers Tumi and Rimowa. "The leaders of the company always thought they could rely on the product being the best smart suitcase product in the market, and that customers would see that and latch on to that," says Chris Fulton, who was the head of business development at Bluesmart. But the company's sales had fallen behind Away and Raden, whose suitcases were less expensive. Many customers either couldn't tell the difference, Fulton says, or didn't think Bluesmart's bags were worth the higher price.

An even bigger problem for Bluesmart was that its battery charger couldn't be removed. This meant you now couldn't use the luggage when traveling on an airline.

David Sebens, the luggage industry consultant, says Bluesmart should have foreseen this problem. As early as 2015, he notes, people traveling with battery chargers at China's airports were being told to remove them from suitcases. "When a major air terminal like Pudong, in Shanghai, starts doing that, you ought to really pay attention," he adds. "People who disregarded that heads-up paid a price."

The airline edicts posed a challenge for Raden as well. Unlike with Bluesmart, the batteries in its suitcases could be removed, but only from the inside, when the bag was opened, which was a headache when your bag was fully packed. On social media, people began moaning about being stopped while going through airport security and having to open and unpack their luggage to take out the battery. In a few cases, travelers posted messages about missing their flights because of the delay caused by unpacking, removing the battery, and then repacking their suitcases.

"When I was traveling with my Raden bag, it was a concern," says Bryan Alston. "I would always get stopped, and people would have to inspect my suitcase to see what was in it, because they thought the battery was a bomb. A lot of the comments we were getting [at Raden] were saying the same thing. They were like, 'I love the suitcase, it's great, but the convenience of charging my phone is not outweighing the inconvenience of being stopped by security.'" Compounding the problem for Raden was its advertising message, which had always emphasized its tech features. "When we tested a lot of different messages, the messages that mattered most were tech," Alston notes.

Of the three smart luggage start-ups, Away was best positioned to deal with the issue. Because it had marketed itself as a lifestyle brand, it wasn't identified primarily as a tech-laden suitcase. Even more important, it had reengineered its suitcases months before. Like Raden, Away's initial design allowed the battery to be removed only from the inside of the case, with a tiny screwdriver it supplied with its suitcases. But early customers told Away that it really should be easier to remove the battery, and Away listened. In August 2017, it changed the design so the battery could be easily ejected from the outside, without users opening the suitcase; you just pressed down on the battery, and it popped out.

For customers who had bought the first version, Away assigned a team of engineers to develop a quick-fix kit to retrofit those bags so their batteries, too, could be ejected without the suitcase's being opened. And it made these repairs free of charge, at significant expense to the company—it won't say how much—which it could afford, thanks to the cushion of $20 million in additional VC money it had raised in mid-2017. That wasn't an option for Raden, which was running low on cash as sales declined. "They ate the cost," recalls Thibault Le Conte. "We couldn't do that."

Raden found itself in a downward spiral. "Our returns doubled, and our sales dropped by half. We hadn't raised enough capital to pivot our product," Udashkin acknowledges.

As at Away, his team had spent months working on a redesign so the battery could be popped out without users having to open the suitcase. But because Udashkin had kept VC investment to a minimum, Raden needed to sell enough of its existing inventory to generate the cash to place an order for its redesigned suitcases with its Asian manufacturer, and it was having a hard time making those sales after the airline alert.

Raden had always spent less on marketing than Away, and now it didn't have the money to ratchet up advertising to sell its old inventory. It tried to conserve its dwindling cash on hand by cutting salaries as much as 50 percent and laying off workers. Udashkin, who himself took no pay for most of 2017, belatedly tried to raise more financing, but he couldn't pull it off at a time when sales were slumping.

"We had prototypes, but the problem was securing production," laments Le Conte. "You're not going to order ten thousand new bags of the new generation when you have thousands of the old generation unsold." All the while, the old luggage was running up storage fees, draining Raden's dwindling reserves. In February 2018, in an attempt to raise cash, Le Conte says, Raden held discussions to sell its entire inventory of warehoused luggage for around $80 a bag, even less than the cost of having them built and shipped to the United States. But the deal didn't go through. In addition to pay cuts, Raden's staff, once a couple of dozen, was reduced to fewer than ten. Morale plummeted. "One year before, you are on Oprah," Le Conte notes. "And then one year later, you are so far away. You are like, really? Wow."

In March, *Wired* magazine featured Raden as its top pick of "Tech-Packed Suitcases" for savvy travelers. By then, however, the company was struggling to stay afloat, as was Bluesmart. On May 1, Bluesmart posted "bittersweet news" on its website: "After exploring all the possible options for pivoting and moving forward, the company was finally forced to wind down its operations." Bluesmart's intellectual property and technology were being sold to Travelpro, the company founded thirty years earlier by Robert Plath, the retired airline pilot who invented the Rollaboard suitcase. The investors who put more than $20 million into Bluesmart went away empty-handed.

Just over two weeks later, Raden announced that it, too, was going out of business. "It's an unfortunate thing that happened that, believe me, I wish it had not," Udashkin told BuzzFeed News. "Smart luggage is not a viable business given the uncertainty of regulations and past liability of these bags."

That wasn't precisely right. Raden and Bluesmart may not have been viable, but Away was thriving. Shortly after its rivals went out of business, Away disclosed that it would create about 250 jobs over the next five years, in addition to the 150 people it already employed, in return for $4 million in government tax breaks. By May 2019, it had raised a total of $156 million in VC equity funding, which gave it a valuation of $1.4 billion. It projected that its sales for the year would double to about $300 million, as it further expanded its offerings to include Away apparel and wellness goods.

"The people at Away understood that there's a real difference between a product idea and a brand," says David Sebens, the luggage industry consultant, when asked why this company succeeded but its competitors failed. "Brands survive. Product ideas come and go. Those two women [Away's founders] are really, really smart."

Not that Udashkin has given up on the luggage business. He took a job as an executive at Rimowa, the luxury suitcase brand owned by LVMH.

As for Raden itself, a Denver private equity firm, the Stage Fund, is trying to see if the brand can be revived. The Stage Fund specializes in buying distressed companies, and it acquired the assets of Raden (including around four thousand unsold suitcases) for about $100,000, with all the money going to Raden's lenders. Raden's backers, including Lerer Hippeau and the founders of Casper (who had personally invested in the start-up), wrote off the $5.6 million they had put into the company.

The Stage Fund then turned around and disposed of the suitcases to a liquidation company for less than it cost Raden to manufacture them. The twenty-two-inch carry-on size, which Raden once sold for $295, could be found for $79.99 online.

But the brand still may have a future. Daniel Frydenlund, founder and chief executive of the Stage Fund (whose father worked for Samsonite and American Tourister), says that his company is seeking to partner with a luggage maker to relaunch Raden. With one difference: "It's a cool, great-looking bag, but we redesigned it so the battery can be popped out easily. That was the Achilles' heel."

Back to the Future?

A few weeks before Christmas 2018, the display windows at Lord & Taylor's flagship store on Fifth Avenue in Midtown Manhattan were all decked out. But this holiday season, they weren't showcasing the elaborate animated creations that have long wowed New Yorkers and tourists alike, who would gawk and stare in amazement as they passed by.

Instead, the windows were plastered with garish red-and-yellow signs. One window's sign blared, ENTIRE STORE ON SALE! Another window punctuated the point: CLOSING. EVERYTHING MUST GO! Inside the Italian Renaissance–style building, once one of the world's grandest emporiums, signs were plastered on every massive pillar. Display cases of jewelry declared "50% OFF" and "70% OFF." The sale signs outnumbered the shoppers, and the few who strolled the aisles gave the building the feel of a dated and tattered museum, a sad monument to a glorious age.

Quincy, a saleswoman at a cosmetics counter, recalled magical visits to the store as a child. "I remember my grandma coming here. It was a big deal to get something from Lord & Taylor. When my daughter was born, I remember my aunt would buy her gifts from Lord & Taylor," she said wistfully. "She must have spent a small fortune. I remember the window displays. They were so iconic. Then, when I came here to work, I was so happy."

But she wouldn't be working there for much longer. The Fifth Avenue location, which drew more than seventy-five thousand visitors when it opened in February 1914—they were serenaded by music from a pipe organ in the store's seventh-floor concert hall—had been sold for $850 million to WeWork, the start-up specializing in offering modular office space to tech companies and entrepreneurs. Lord & Taylor was planning to shutter the store in January, leading employees such as Quincy to worry about their futures. "As long as I find a job, that's my main concern," she said glumly.

She might have considered heading south about two miles, to what might be dubbed the Shopping Republic of Direct-to-Consumer. In less than one square mile, centered on Manhattan's SoHo district, at least fifteen direct-to-consumer brands—the very brands that proclaimed that physical retail is so last century—have opened physical retail stores.

Start at Away luggage, at 366 Lafayette Street, and meander around the neighborhood until you arrive at Glossier cosmetics, just ten blocks to the south. Along the way—without having to leave the 10012 or 10013 zip codes—you will pass Showfields, a showroom start-up that features once-digital-only brands such as Made In cookware and the Farmer's Dog pet food. Just a few minutes away is Casper. A couple of blocks farther are Warby Parker and Burrow furniture, virtually next door to each other. From there, it's a quick walk to Leesa, another mattress start-up; One Kings Lane home décor; and Everlane clothing, whose founder, Michael Preysman, told the *New York Times* in 2012, "We are going to shut the company down before we go physical retail."

Next, it's on to Lively intimate apparel and, just around the corner, Allbirds shoes. Then ModCloth women's clothing, Indochino and Bonobos menswear, and Outdoor Voices workout apparel. By the time you arrive at Glossier's flagship store (with a giant Glossier flag draped from the front façade), at 123 Lafayette Street, it is almost certain to be crowded, often with more shoppers in its three thousand square feet than there were on an entire floor of Lord & Taylor, with tens of thousands of square feet, in its last, sad holiday season.

Just as Lord & Taylor once helped inaugurate a grand era of department store retailing by making shopping an experience, with four restaurants, live music, and "Red Rose Personal Shopping Service," Glossier and other digitally native brands seek to do the same in the era of e-commerce. For almost all of them, the vast majority of their customers still buy online, but even with the rapid growth of e-commerce, about 90 percent of all retail goods are sold the old-fashioned way: a shopper walks into a store and picks an item off a shelf. It's fine to be an online brand, but many start-ups are finding that if they want to grow bigger and grow faster, they eventually have to go where the people are.

Before you even walk into the Glossier store, you are likely to be greeted by an unusual scene: clusters of Glossier groupies in their teens and twenties standing on the sidewalk outside, taking selfies and then promptly posting the photos on Instagram. Only then do they proceed up the wide Glossier-pink staircase to the store on the second floor, where they are greeted by the pulsing beat of hit songs such as Flume's "Never Be Like You" or Clear's "Pusher"—over and over and over. Shoppers crowd around displays to try on samples, then head to communal sinks where they can wash off the Boy Brow eyebrow filler, Lidstar eye shadow, Cloud Paint blush, or Wowder face powder.

But to many visitors, and even to Glossier's management, buying something is almost beside the point. Just as outside, nearly everyone inside seems to be clicking photos with their smartphones: photos of the sales clerks in pink suits (gals and guys); photos of the boyfriends they've dragged along (hence the popular Instagram account @glossierboyfriends); even photos of their pets inside the store, looking bored or bewildered (@dogsofglossier). The Instagram accounts started by Glossier customers are obsessively followed by hundreds of thousands—as is the official Glossier account, with nearly two million followers, and the account of founder Emily Weiss, with about five hundred thousand followers.

Most retail stores use every available square foot to show off their wares. Not Glossier. To cater to the nonstop selfie taking, it constructed a room specifically for taking photos and posting them on social media. In New York, visitors take selfies in the mirrored "Experiential Boy Brow Room," with its collection of a half dozen six-and-a-half-foot-tall replica tubes of one of Glossier's most popular products. At the company's second store, on Melrose Place in Los Angeles, it created "Glossier Canyon," a rendition of the undulating, etched brown-red walls of Antelope Canyon in Arizona, replete with an audio recording of desert sounds. The room would feel right at home in an art gallery. There's often a line to get in to the 1,500-square-foot store and, once you're inside, yet another line to get into the canyon room; a sales clerk monitors the times to ensure that no one lingers too long. "It's aesthetic AF," one reviewer, Rodrigo C., wrote on Yelp (using Millennials' social media shorthand for "as fuck"). "The canyon room was so tranquil and the smells of the air were heavenly. Currently I'm all about vibes and this was a 10/10 in that criteria [sic]."

Veteran retail experts are taken aback by the passion generated by Glossier stores. Marla Goodman, a former Glossier vice president, recalls inviting a Manhattan real estate developer who had built Brookfield Place, a major shopping destination, to an early iteration of the New York City showroom, which was then located in a cramped space on the sixth floor of Glossier's old headquarters. When the guest arrived, Goodman had second thoughts. "I was thinking that he's probably going to be like, Why the hell is she taking me up this decrepit elevator?" she says. "Then we got into the crowded store, and he stood absolutely stock still and dead silent—for, like, a solid three or four minutes. He turned and said to me, 'This is a billion-dollar business,' based on the foot traffic he saw. He was fascinated."

Henry Davis, Glossier's president for its first four years, smiles when he talks about how the stores have become must-see destinations. "We approached it more like building a film set or theater design set than building a store in the traditional sense," he explains. Glossier didn't initially plan to open a brick-and-mortar store, but when loyal fans began making pilgrimages to Glossier's corporate office on Lafayette Street, the company set aside space to welcome them and let them buy cosmetics. The makeshift store proved so popular that when Glossier moved to fancier digs, it decided to maintain a permanent store at the old location.

"This isn't about selling anything," Davis says. "It turned out to be wildly successful from a sales point of view, mostly because people, when they're there, are like, 'Okay, I'll buy something.' We sell thousands, even tens of thousands of items a day at the store. But the whole point is about connection, connection between the company and you, between you as people."

But why are Glossier and other digitally native brands opening retail stores at all? Didn't the direct-to-consumer brand revolution mean that start-ups didn't need physical stores any longer and, in fact, that the economics were better if the retail middlemen were cut out? "DTC is not really about distribution. It's about connection," Davis says, repeating a word he uses frequently.

* * *

CAC: "customer acquisition cost." Talk to anyone at any direct-to-consumer start-up, and it doesn't take long before the term comes up. In the early years, 2010 to 2016, the cheapest way for most new brands to acquire customers was through Facebook, Instagram, and other social media platforms that could narrowly target their most likely customers. But over time, two things happened.

First, after targeting and persuading the most likely customers to buy their new products, start-ups invariably found they had to target other groups of potential customers, who took more persuading. This meant that, over time, it cost a bit more to lure in each additional customer. Depending on the product category, once a direct-to-consumer start-up's sales reach an inflection point (usually somewhere between $20 million and $100 million), the advertising needed to generate every additional $1 million in sales requires more spending than the previous $1 million.

Second, once the early direct-to-consumer brands such as Dollar Shave Club proved that advertising on Facebook was an inexpensive way to bring in customers, just about every other company started doing it. And given that Facebook limits the supply of advertising—it typically allows only about every fifth item in a user's "News Feed" to be an ad, lest people tune out—the price of a Facebook ad increased as more companies advertised.

So, around 2017, with more new brands advertising on Facebook and more existing brands advertising as well, everyone had to spend more to keep growing, especially since many of them were chasing the same demographic. By some estimates, social media advertising costs had risen 25 to 50 percent. This was offset in part by Facebook tweaking its algorithm to make it ever more sophisticated in targeting likely customers and in part by companies using more effective video advertising on social media to catch a customer's attention. So, while Facebook and Instagram remain the advertising channel of choice for many start-up brands, social media channels rarely command 80 percent or more of their marketing budgets. The current ratio is generally 40 to 60 percent, or even less for some brands.

As the costs of advertising on Facebook were going up, the costs of brick-and-mortar retail were going down in many cities. Again, it was a matter of supply and demand. In the decades when retailers were thriving and opening more stores, real estate developers, mall owners, and landlords kept raising rents. But with e-commerce growing rapidly and taking sales away from traditional stores, retailers closed thousands of locations. Anxious landlords had little choice but to lower rents—or see their real estate sit vacant, earning nothing.

"Walk along Canal Street when you're down in SoHo," Henry Davis points out. "There's a huge amount of empty buildings. Walk down where all the luxury stores used to be, on Bleecker Street. Bleecker Street is empty." By 2017, rents on that Greenwich Village street had fallen in half from a peak of $500 to $600 per square foot. "They're desperate for people who bring people, destination stores. And DTC does that because they're unique and different and quirky."

Parts of SoHo, the shopping destination of choice for many Millennials, have seen prices fall, too. "On a square footage basis, the rental price of retail space on Broadway used to be about $1,200 a month. The most recent deal [in 2019] was for $250 a square foot," says Karen Bellantoni, a real estate broker there. Though the rents on some neighboring streets are a bit higher, landlords who once insisted on five- to ten-year leases are willing to rent space for as short as three to six months, which makes it relatively cheap for a new brand to test whether a brick-and-mortar store will work economically. And this phenomenon isn't limited to New York. Macy's, Abercrombie and Fitch, J.Crew, Foot Locker, Henri Bendel, Victoria's Secret, Gap, Payless, Guess, Michael Kors, and others have closed stores around the United States, leaving gaping spaces with empty shelves.

Like Glossier, many digitally native brands are trying to reinvent rather than replicate the traditional retail experience. "We put fitting rooms in the lobby of our headquarters in 2011 because people wanted to see the clothes," recalls Bonobos cofounder Andy Dunn. "People tried pants on and walked out without anything in hand, but then placed orders online. That's when we realized we could make clothing stores with no clothing"—or no clothing to purchase, anyway. "It was a happy accident."

The next year, Bonobos opened a "Guideshop" in seven hundred square feet of its fifth-floor office in Manhattan. Dunn reports that the average order placed by customers who visited the shop was double what first-time online customers ordered—and they came back more frequently. By 2019, Bonobos had about sixty shops. To hold down costs, all are small (generally a couple thousand square feet or less) and carry little inventory, just enough of a selection for a customer to get a fit and feel for the fabric. "Try on anything you like and have a cold one from the fridge . . ." its Guideshop website beckons. "A Guide will place your order and it will be shipped directly to your home or office. Walk out with your hands free."

The minimalist approach is a feature of many of these new stores. Walk into the Tuft & Needle mattress store in an airy, loftlike building on First Avenue in Seattle, a couple of blocks from Pike Place Market, and you might well wonder, Where are the mattresses? Traditional mattress stores are jammed with dozens or even more than one hundred mattresses. But at Tuft & Needle's store, there are only four, taking only about 5 to 10 percent of the floor space, and by design they are largely hidden from view, surrounded by mesh white fabric that stretches from the floor most of the way to the high ceiling. (The material is a variation of the breathable fabric used on the bottom of a Tuft & Needle mattress.) You might say that it is, to borrow a phrase, aesthetic AF. The cloudlike mesh simulates the privacy of a bedroom, so you can lie on the mattress out of view of other shoppers—and salespeople.

Not that you need to worry about the salespeople following you around and badgering you from the minute you walk in, as at most mattress stores. They are paid a salary, not a commission, another feature of most direct-to-consumer brands' stores. You have questions about the mattresses? Sure, they'll answer them. But many customers prefer to grab the tablet PCs stationed around the showroom.

With the space kept simple and uncluttered, the cost of outfitting the Tuft & Needle store was only around $70 a square foot, compared with several hundred dollars or more spent by most retailers, says Chris Evans, the company's head architect. Each of its half dozen stores uses slightly different natural materials (in some cases, wood lattice or concrete), but they share the principle of creating privacy barriers in an uncluttered space. "There is a physical quality of existing mattress stores—a sea of mattresses, the drop ceilings with gross lighting fixtures—that makes traditional mattress stores feel like warehouses," Evans explains. "I was really nervous at first that some of our designs would turn people off and might be a little much, that maybe we've gone too far, but people like the daylight and the artistic look, the use of different materials."

By keeping store costs down, Tuft & Needle found that it could deliver sales as economically as other marketing methods. "It might cost $9,000 a month to lease a store, but a billboard can cost up to $4,000 a month," explains Evan Maridou, Tuft & Needle's former chief operating officer. And the company found that its stores had a multiplier effect: in addition to orders placed by people who visited the stores, online orders in the areas where it opened stores rose as well.

"Does having a store make some people feel more confident in their online purchase? Yes," he says. "Sales were higher online because people saw we had a store. It's almost like some people are thinking, 'I don't know if you're a sketchy online company and if I try to return it you're going to be there. But if there's a store, I can march right in.' It gives the consumer more conviction that your company is real." To further test this hypothesis, Tuft & Needle showed some visitors to its website its store locations and hid the links from others. Sure enough, he notes, "Conversion was higher online when people saw we had stores."

This confirms studies by the Wharton professor David Bell, working alongside colleagues from Dartmouth and Harvard. Using detailed sales data for Warby Parker's first few years in business, they conducted extensive research on what happened to sales as the company started to expand, gingerly at first, into physical retail.

In its early days, in addition to setting up a makeshift showroom in Neil Blumenthal's Philadelphia apartment, Warby Parker managed to get some apparel retailers in the city to carry its frames so people could try them on, though not buy them. "First, and perhaps not too surprising, total sales increased about 9% in the locations within the trading area of the showrooms . . . Next, we found that website sales that had their origin in the showroom trading area (as measured by zip code) increased significantly, too, by about 3.5%," Bell and his colleagues concluded. Even a temporary physical presence boosted sales, they discovered. In 2012, to increase its profile and get publicity, Warby Parker outfitted a school bus as a rolling showroom that traveled around the country. "We found that in locations where the bus stopped, sales increased, both in total and through the website, implying that pop-up stores boost both sales and awareness," the researchers determined.

Warby Parker opened its first permanent store in SoHo in April 2013, and had nearly one hundred stores by the end of 2018; retail stores and online sales each account for about half its overall revenue. "We were never dogmatic that it had to be only digital," says Blumenthal. "If ninety-five percent of glasses in America are sold in brick-and-mortar stores and you want to be the biggest optical brand in America, it would be difficult not to have stores." Similarly, Away luggage opened its first store in New York City in 2017 and added six more in other cities over the next couple of years; online sales rose 40 percent in cities where it opened stores early on, which was "meaningfully" higher than in cities where the company didn't have a physical retail presence.

Even ThirdLove, whose cofounder Heidi Zak has said she would rather empty the dishwasher than go bra shopping, began testing physical retail by opening a boutique, two-thousand-square-foot "concept" pop-up store in SoHo in the summer of 2019. To make the experience more pleasant (or at least less uncomfortable) for women, ThirdLove is trying to reinvent the in-store experience, as Tuft & Needle and Casper are doing with mattresses. "To get you the help you need without having to call out in your underwear, each fitting room has a 'support' button that calls a Fit Stylist to your room," notes Ra'el Cohen, chief creative officer. For added privacy, some fitting rooms also are equipped with a "pass-through tray" so customers can try on different styles and sizes without dealing face-to-face with a sales person. To hold down inventory costs, the store carries a limited selection of key bra styles for purchase, while other styles can be tried on but need to be purchased online.

The electric toothbrush start-up Quip doesn't have its own store. With just two products, an electric toothbrush and toothpaste, that wouldn't make sense. But it is trying to keep growing the old-fashioned way, offering its products on retail shelves. In Target stores, Quip toothbrushes often have prime end-of-aisle shelf space, as do a few other direct-to-consumer brands, such as Harry's razors, Native deodorant, and Casper pillows, sheets, and low-end mattresses. The combined sales of these new brands themselves won't make much of a difference to a retailer like Target, with annual revenues of around $75 billion, but they help bring in shoppers who might otherwise stay at home and order goods online. Indeed, even as many physical retail stores have suffered from lower foot traffic, Target in 2018 said the number of shoppers entering its stores rose at the fastest pace ever.

For digitally native brands, unaccustomed to sharing revenue from each sale with a store, the economics can be tricky. When Quip sells a toothbrush online and Harry's sells razors online, they keep all the revenue. When Target sells something, it typically pockets 20 to 50 percent of the retail price. For a brand, the lower profit margin of selling through a retailer can be somewhat offset by lower costs in other areas: even though it is cheaper than ever to ship a product directly to a buyer's home, it is much less expensive per unit to ship a pallet of the same goods to a retailer. And a well-done display in a retail store gets eyeballs from shoppers passing by that a brand otherwise would have to spend more to get on Facebook or Instagram. "Thirty million people walk through a Target every week, which is insane," says Quip cofounder Simon Enever. "And they are walking through the oral care aisle and seeing Oral B and Sonicare. There's an opportunity to become the one new brand, to enter the zeitgeist. We wanted that."

As part of its deal, Quip also insisted that Target sell its toothbrush only, and not replacement brush heads. To subscribe for regular brush head replacements, Enever notes, "you are pointed to getquip.com," which enables Quip to maintain a direct connection with the customer.

Wooing digital-first brands to its store shelves is just one of Target's strategies for fending off the disruption caused by e-commerce. In 2017, Target paid $550 million to buy Shipt, a same-day delivery company, and an undisclosed sum to acquire Grand Junction, a "transportation technology" start-up whose software is aimed at making faster and more efficient home deliveries. That same year, it invested $75 million in Casper, after making an inquiry about buying the company outright. And it has copied the marketing strategy of online clothing subscription start-ups such as Stitch Fix and Rockets of Awesome. Target customers can now sign up for a monthly delivery to their homes of a box of children's clothing from its Cat & Jack private label, which was once available only in its stores.

With the emergence of direct-to-consumer brands, traditional retailers such as Target have to adapt to the changing landscape, by copying them and working with them—or else. "Legacy retailers are trying to come up with something truly transformative, by placing a range of bets," says Chris Walton, a retail consultant and former vice president of Target's Store of the Future project.

* * *

Shoppers almost certainly don't notice it, but from the moment they walk into a Neighborhood Goods store in Plano, Texas, an eye in the

sky is tracking them—or, more precisely, multidirectional cameras suspended from the high ceiling over the entrances, as well as more than a
dozen other cameras and tracking devices mounted around the store,
are watching them. The cameras use facial recognition software to
estimate each visitor's age, though not identify them individually. The
cameras calculate how much time each person walks around the store,
and even how much time is spent browsing each brand on display:
MeUndies underwear, Allswell mattresses, Hims hair-loss treatments
and vitamins, Hubble contact lenses, Primary children's clothing, and
products from a dozen or so other digital start-ups. They will also
know which brands are skipped altogether.

Neighborhood Goods wants to be the retail showroom of the
future for direct-to-consumer brands. Taking a page from Glossier, it
aims not so much to sell goods on display but to let customers touch
and feel the new brands they have been hearing about but maybe have
shied away from buying until they could see them in person. And to lure
the brands, Neighborhood Goods collects and shares the type of data
that start-up brands gather online and use as a competitive advantage.

The first Neighborhood Goods opened in Plano in November 2018,
and cofounder Mark Masinter envisions it becoming a national chain—
sort of a cross between a pop-up and a traditional store that will reinvent
the concept of a department store. In many ways, Neighborhood Goods
takes an old idea and makes it new again. No matter how hard they try,
most old-line department stores feel dated, with the same old displays
of the same old goods. But what if you constantly rotated several dozen
hip new brands, switching them out every few months so that shoppers
found a different mix, got a bit of a surprise, every time they came in?
By displaying only cool products, you could attract other cool products
that want to be next to them, creating a curated collection. With the right
mix, the store could become like a popular nightclub, where the cool kids
want to go because, well, other cool kids are going there.

Put a casual restaurant and a bar in the middle. Add events (barre
workout classes; floral arrangement workshops; block parties with
games, speakers, live music), and you can become a fun destination,
like Lord & Taylor of a century ago, when people went to dine and

attend concerts and also to shop. "I never believed that physical retail would lose its relevance," says Masinter, "but that it would have to become different."

Little known outside the world of retail real estate, Masinter started his rise in 1999, when he answered what he thought was a prank call while on a ski lift in Vail, Colorado. "Is this Mark Masinter?" the person on the other end of the line asked. "I'm calling for Steve Jobs." Masinter, a Dallas real estate developer then in his mid-thirties, replied with a swear word and hung up. Later that day, he got a call from Stephen Gordon, the founder of Restoration Hardware, a fast-growing retailer Masinter had invested in and advised on its retail strategy. "Hey, by chance did Steve Jobs call you, or someone from Steve's office?" Gordon asked. Masinter responded with the same swear word and added, "Come on, man, that's not even funny."

Told that indeed it was Jobs trying to reach him, and that the Apple CEO wanted to set up a meeting, Masinter wondered aloud, "Why would he want to meet with me? I know nothing about computers. I have a Mac, but I can barely operate one." But Gordon persisted: "It's an interesting idea. You should talk to him."

Jobs's idea was something he hadn't yet told the world about: the Apple Store. Jobs himself, of course, would conceive and direct the design, but he wanted a real estate expert to help determine the best locations for these new retail outlets. Masinter and a couple of colleagues made a presentation and recommended, among other things, high-traffic areas such as shopping malls. They thought the hour-long meeting went well, but Jobs didn't. "He was adamant that an Apple Store would never appear in a mall. At the end of the discussion, he basically told me it was the worst presentation he'd ever seen," Masinter recalls. But Jobs added, "I'll give you a second chance. I'm not encouraging you to do it, but if you want, we're going to give you another shot."

In retrospect, Masinter suspects, it was classic Steve Jobs: "I think he was truly measuring us. And we stood our ground." Masinter returned for a follow-up meeting with a slightly tweaked proposal that still included malls as the best location for many of Apple's new stores.

Jobs didn't bother attending the meeting himself and instead dispatched underlings, but afterward he made the mission clear, Masinter recalls: "Go find amazing real estate in the right places, but it must without compromise be able to afford us the opportunity to build something on brand and very special, and don't dare bring back anything that wouldn't pass that test."

Masinter's involvement with the rollout of the wildly successful Apple Stores quickly became known among retailing cognoscenti and established his reputation as a savant when it came to helping brands launch brick-and-mortar strategies. He would become an adviser to Warby Parker and Bonobos—in both cases after being introduced to their founders by Kirsten Green of Forerunner Ventures, and investing in them as well—and to Tuft & Needle, among others.

Advising digital brands reinforced Masinter's belief that they would benefit from selling "offline" as well as online. But he also recognized that many new brands knew little about physical retail and that many couldn't afford to open stores on their own. He was mulling this thought in late 2016, while taking his regular fifty-mile weekend bike ride from his home in central Dallas to White Rock Lake, which he then circles several times. "I had an epiphany," he recalls. "By the time I got off the bike ride, I thought there needs to be a new definition of a department store, where first and foremost these newer brands can physically manifest themselves and do something playful."

Many digital brands have experimented with pop-up stores to let consumers touch and feel their products, but pop-ups generally cost a lot to set up, especially given that they often are open for only a week to a few months. Masinter's idea was that new brands could rent and share space with other new brands for two to twelve months, in an uncluttered, minimalist store with a stylish design sensibility, staffed by trained sales associates carrying iPads to help customers out—much like, well, Apple Stores. "I learned so much about design and design execution from Steve Jobs," Masinter explains. "I adapted it in everything I do today. Don't think that I didn't hearken back to all the lessons I learned from him when I was thinking about Neighborhood Goods."

After getting home from his bike ride and jumping into his pool to cool off, he called Andy Dunn, the cofounder of Bonobos, who responded, "Wow, that's a pretty good idea! Have you talked to Kirsten?" So, Masinter's next call was to Kirsten Green, who encouraged him to flesh out the concept and come back to her. In a follow-up conversation, Green told him, "You've got a lot more work to do, but I want to be your lead investor." Figuring that her involvement gave him the "USDA seal of approval," Masinter went searching for someone to sharpen his idea and run the business.

Rather than hiring a seasoned retail executive, Masinter zeroed in on a twenty-nine-year-old entrepreneur named Matt Alexander, who had started an online clothing company in Dallas but sold it after failing to get much traction. But it was a different venture that caught Masinter's eye: Alexander had also cofounded a nonprofit project called Unbranded that in 2014 had converted empty commercial space in a gentrifying part of downtown Dallas into a holiday pop-up store for local artisanal products. It created some buzz and eventually was taken over by the downtown Dallas business association. Though less sophisticated and smaller in scale, it was along the lines Masinter envisioned for Neighborhood Goods. "I was inspired by your creation Unbranded and I believe there is crazy white space for that concept . . . and would love the opportunity to muse with you on it," he wrote Alexander in an email.

They met over lunch in March 2017, and a couple of weeks later, Alexander sent Masinter what they now call "the manifesto," a six-page memo outlining his vision. Masinter liked it so much that, without telling Alexander, he forwarded it to Kirsten Green.

Alexander's memo emphasized using technology to gather information about visitors, knowing from his experience running a clothing start-up how online brands crave data on their customers. In addition to cameras collecting demographic information, there would be a Neighborhood Goods app for shoppers to download, which they could use to learn about the rotating brands in the store, to find out about events (such as when bands might be playing or wine tastings would be held), and to place orders. Some existing retailers have begun testing similar technology, but retrofitting stores can be more expensive than starting from scratch.

"It's not personally identifiable, but within a margin of error, we can tell you the typical age and gender of people coming into the store, and their trajectory and direction, which brands they are looking at," Alexander explains. "We'll know that men in their fifties come in and tend to turn right, and women in their twenties tend to turn left, and brands will have a heat map of how people are interacting with their area. And you'll know if three other brands are getting triple the traffic that you are, so you can start remerchandising."

But beyond the technology, the pitch to digital-first brands is that Neighborhood Goods would offer a low-cost way of testing brick-and-mortar retail, at a time when it has become more expensive for new brands to attract customers with digital advertising. Each of the brands carried by the store at a given time gets its own boutique-type display of up to about five hundred square feet. It's akin to renting a furnished apartment in a luxury building with other like-minded tenants, rather than buying a house that needs even more money for decoration and repairs. "We allow for really rapid iteration and experimentation in a relatively low-risk way," Alexander explains. "If you're opening your own store, you're spending a huge amount on rent on a longer-term lease, on staff, on technology. You have to build out the whole thing."

Thanks to Kirsten Green's interest, Masinter and Alexander had little trouble raising $5.7 million in early financing rounds. Among the investors was Michael Dubin of Dollar Shave Club. In the cozy world of digitally native brands, Green years earlier had introduced Dubin to Masinter (who became an early investor in Dollar Shave Club), and Masinter introduced him to Alexander. About a year and a half after Masinter hatched the idea, the first Neighborhood Goods store was opened at Legacy West, a real estate complex in Plano with a new outdoor shopping mall amid office and residential buildings developed by a group that includes Masinter. (Other stores in the mall are Warby Parker and Bonobos.)

At fourteen thousand square feet, the Neighborhood Goods store is about one-tenth the typical size of a department store like Nordstrom. It resembles a spruced-up converted loft space, with concrete floors and a twenty-three-foot-high ceiling with suspended track lighting and exposed duct work. Some first-time shoppers walk around with a puzzled look on their faces, and the Neighborhood Goods founders recognize that visitors may need a bit of educating. "If we're a carbon copy, smaller version of Neiman Marcus or Macy's or Bloomingdale's, who's going to care?" says Masinter. "What we are is a discovery mechanism for emerging brands."

Among the nearly two dozen initial tenants was the contact lens start-up Hubble, which until then had been online only. "At first, we weren't thinking about retail space. But ninety percent of all stuff isn't bought online," says Jesse Horwitz. "We're testing this for prescription sign-ups." A couple of months after the store opened, Hubble was experiencing a good rate of sign-ups, but the foot traffic wasn't as high as the company had hoped. One challenge is helping shoppers understand the concept. Having a collection of different, unrelated brands under one roof is so new, Horwitz notes, "It's still a bit confusing to consumers what exactly the thing is."

Even Dollar Shave Club, one of the last holdouts among the early direct-to-consumer brands—Dubin says he turned down an opportunity to sell the company's razors at Target, before Harry's did—decided to test brick and mortar by joining the second wave of brands at Neighborhood Goods in Plano. "What I like about Neighborhood Goods is that they will give us the opportunity to bring the brand to life," Dubin explains. "It can give a lot of space versus a traditional retailer, where you're confined, the shelves are cluttered, and the salespeople don't know your product. 'Where's the Red Bull?' 'Aisle Five.' 'Where's the shampoo?' 'Aisle Two.' They're sort of born from the same DNA of a lot of the younger brands, in the sense that they want to give your customer an experience, versus only trying to hawk a product."

It remains an open question whether Neighborhood Goods can successfully reinvent the department store and become the next Nordstrom or Macy's or Target. But it is racing ahead. Less than a year after its first store opened, investors put in another $20 million to finance the rapid rollout of new stores, starting with its second location, at Chelsea Market in Manhattan, and a third in Austin, Texas. It may have plenty of company. Several others—Showfields (which boasts that it is "the most interesting store in the world"), Fourpost, B8ta (pronounced beta), and BrandBox—are pursuing the same strategy of creating the department store of the future by offering a collection of new brands. Recognizing that competition could become fierce, Alexander says Neighborhood Goods' financial backers told him, "We think you are the McDonald's in the space, and we want to give you sufficient capital to fend off the prospective Burger Kings."

But none of the rivals should have a hard time finding locations for their stores. "One of the things that's going to be quite poetic for us," notes Alexander, "is that a lot of the places that we are going to be looking at and moving into are old department stores."

13

Building a Digital Brand Factory

Yaniv Sarig was not moved to create the hOmeLabs portable ice maker because he thought portable ice makers were overpriced and customers were being gouged by a dominant player, the way that the founders of Warby Parker felt about the eyeglass business.

Sarig didn't launch the product with a clever video that went viral, as Michael Dubin did with Dollar Shave Cub, or by first building up a large following with a popular blog, as Emily Weiss did with Glossier. Nor do ads for the hOmeLabs ice maker show up constantly on Facebook or Instagram, the way they do for ThirdLove bras and Hubble contact lenses.

Sarig decided to sell ice makers because Aimee told him it was a good idea. "Everything we do is Aimee and what she recommends," he explains. Aimee isn't a person, even though Sarig frequently refers to Aimee as "she" or to "her" uncanny skill in launching new products. AIMEE is a computer program, short for "Artificial Intelligence Mohawk E-commerce Engine," designed to identify products with the potential to become top sellers on Amazon, a platform that many start-ups have deliberately avoided.

Instead of following the established playbook of most digitally native brands and pursuing the passions or trusting the intuition of their founders, the entrepreneurs behind Mohawk Group, the company that Sarig cofounded and runs, are aiming to create brands by focusing exclusively and obsessively on data gleaned by computers. In the spring of 2019, Mohawk had five products ranked among the top fifty bestsellers on Amazon in the "appliances" category alone: a beverage fridge, a minifridge, and a countertop dishwasher, in addition to two ice maker models.

Mohawk Group is bigger than most direct-to-consumer start-ups, with sales of $73.3 million in 2018 and the goal of doubling that in 2019 (for the fifth consecutive year), though most people have never heard of its brands: hOmeLabs small home appliances, which include dehumidifiers, beverage fridges, compact countertop dishwashers, and ice makers; Xtava beauty products, such as curling irons, blow dryers, hair spray, and styling cream; and Vremi small appliances and kitchenware, such as single-cup coffeemakers, pot-and-pan and knife sets, and salad spinners.

Sarig's goal is nothing less than to build a brand factory, an assembly line powered by technology to analyze data about what shoppers are searching for online and what they don't like about existing brands, and then churn out products tailored specifically to meet those desires. "We're trying to build not just a consumer product company but more of a group that can create and repeat the creation of consumer product brands," he explains. "I take my hat off every day to the guys at Casper and Warby Parker. They've built amazing companies. But for good or for bad, we want to try to build something that will be a repeatable model, where it's not like you go and disrupt one particular category, almost like a conveyor belt that takes trends and turns them into a brand very quickly, faster and more efficiently."

Mohawk, which occupies the same spartan office space in downtown Manhattan that was once the headquarters of Casper and which describes itself as a technology and e-commerce holding company, isn't the only start-up using data science as the building block for creating new brands targeted at Amazon customers, and it isn't the first. In 2011, a Google engineer quit his job and moved back to his native China, where he started a company called Hunan Ocean Wing E-commerce. It makes Anker brand computer accessories and other electronic products (cables, power banks, plugs, chargers, earphones, Bluetooth speakers), which are sold primarily on Amazon. The company's sales reached nearly $600 million in 2017. In addition, other technology companies that don't make their own goods have created software similar to Mohawk's, aimed at helping consumer product makers unlock the code to successfully selling on Amazon.

But Mohawk may be the most ambitious of these start-ups. While Anker focuses almost exclusively on electronic products, Mohawk aims to be the Everything Brand for the Everything Store. If the metrics are right, Sarig says, Mohawk will make anything it thinks it can sell enough of. It has built a team of about two dozen outsourcing, engineering, and logistics experts in Shenzhen, China, so it can create a product in as little as three to four months, once its software engine spots an opportunity. "If tomorrow the data shows that a ukulele is a great product, we'll make a ukulele," he says, "all based on the data of what the consumers are telling us they want, right?"

Sarig, an Israeli-born software engineer in his early forties, knows that his plans could be viewed as outlandish. "It's like jumping out of a plane and building a parachute on the way down," he quips. Despite its rapid sales growth, the company lost nearly $32 million in 2018. While most direct-to-consumer start-ups lose money in their early years, Mohawk acknowledges that its success is far from assured. In a filing with the Securities and Exchange Commission in 2019 for an initial public stock offering, the company stated bluntly that there is "substantial doubt about our ability to continue as a going concern. We will require significant additional funding to fund our growth strategy." And investors were less than enthusiastic when Mohawk's stock began trading in June, with the shares falling about 30 percent in the first week from the offering price, which had valued the company at about $175 million.

Sarig shrugs at the skepticism. While he concedes that investing in Mohawk is a "high-risk, high-reward play," he also points to the staggering volume of overall sales on Amazon.com—$277 billion in 2018, much of it by entrepreneurs—as support for his belief that it's not an impossible dream.

Mohawk's ability to generate sales quickly with a slew of new brands raises some obvious questions: In the digital age, how much is creating a new brand science, and how much is it art? To what extent is a brand dependent on establishing an emotional connection with consumers, and to what extent is it enough to rely largely on data to decipher and then satisfy consumers' unspoken desires? Is selling a lot of products (as Mohawk is doing with hOmeLabs, Vremi, Xtava, and countless other brands still in its future) the same as creating an enduring brand? In the end, does it matter if a brand is recognizable if you can create an endless series of products that sell well?

None of Mohawk's early backers had any experience, or even particular interest, in consumer products. The venture was conceived as a side project to generate revenue that would help finance a loftier endeavor, called Titan Aerospace, a venture to build large, solar-powered drones that could travel twelve miles high and fly continuously for several years. The drones were designed to cruise just below the edge of Earth's atmosphere, where they would create a network of satellites to blanket remote parts of the globe with inexpensive internet service. "It was a very pie-in-the-sky project," says Sarig, who didn't work for Titan but was a friend of the founders.

While the Mohawk idea was still in the conceptual stages, Titan's management concluded that making the drone venture commercially viable would require a huge investment beyond their means, and beyond whatever cash Mohawk might yield in the short term. So, in April 2014, they sold Titan to Google for about $150 million. Two of Titan's main investors, Asher Delug and Maximus Yaney, decided to plow some of their profits into Mohawk and focus on growing it in its own right.

Delug had started several mobile advertising companies and recognized how technology was upending that business by automating the ability to target customers cheaply with marketing messages. The idea behind Mohawk was similar: What if technology could also be used to make it cheaper to target customers with new products? "I felt this is definitely going to happen in e-commerce. It's like I'm living the same movie again," says Delug. "I was smitten by the business model right out of the gate." Mohawk subsequently raised additional VC funding, bringing total investment to $72.6 million by 2018. One of its lead investors is GV (the venture capital arm of Alphabet Inc., Google's parent company), which came to own a 7.6 percent stake in Mohawk.

While most direct-to-consumer brands initially steer clear of Amazon because they want to control the customer relationship, Mohawk has embraced Amazon. Why spend marketing money finding customers and trying to funnel them to your own website? Why not go where you know hundreds of millions of customers are already going every day to search for products and spending hundreds of billions of dollars?

Central to Mohawk's thinking is the soaring growth of Amazon Marketplace, and of other online marketplaces such as Walmart .com and eBay. The biggest traditional retail stores have limited shelf space, with room for perhaps thousands of items, which means it is the retailer who decides which products to carry, and which aisle and shelf to put them on. Amazon Marketplace, in contrast, carries millions of items, and anybody can place a product on its unlimited digital shelf space. "As we started tinkering around, we realized, 'Wow, we're looking at one of the biggest transitions of wealth in the history of modern economies,'" Sarig says. "You've got all these companies like Amazon reinventing retail, but no one has reinvented the CPG company"—retailspeak for consumer packaged goods companies with many different brands, such as Procter & Gamble and Unilever—"that would be a fit for this new retail model."

With so many other products on Amazon, the challenge is to crack the code for which products to offer and, even more important, how to get prime digital shelf space on the opening screen when a shopper enters a search term on the site. Typically, 70 percent of shoppers never go past the first screen when searching for something they want to buy. Both of these are math problems, the Mohawk founders realized, problems that can be solved by collecting and crunching enough data. It turns out that Amazon provides all sorts of basic data to anyone who wants to sell something on its site, including the sales ranking of every product on Amazon Marketplace and the one million most frequently searched keywords.

Amazon makes this data available because it encourages companies to sell more things on its site, collecting a fee (typically 15 percent) on each sale. Amazon also pockets money from companies advertising their wares on the site and in exchange for handling the warehousing and shipping for sellers who don't want to bother going through a third-party logistics company.

"The availability of the sales rank and the availability of the top keywords pretty much tells you 90 percent of what you need to know about the demand for products," explains Juozas Kaziukenas, the founder of Marketplace Pulse, one of the legions of consultancies that have sprouted up to advise companies that sell on Amazon. "Of course, then it's up to you to figure out: Can you make something cheaper, can you make it better, can you make something different?"

That's where AIMEE comes in. Sarig spent several months writing its software. To save money, nearly all the furniture in Mohawk's office (desks, tables, even some of the chairs for lounging around) are fashioned out of wooden shipping pallets. But no expense is spared when it comes to AIMEE. Mohawk employs fifty computer engineers, one-third of its staff, to work on AIMEE. Tucked in a corner are four high-tech sleeping pods to accommodate people working around the clock. These engineers are constantly focusing on ways to improve AIMEE's ability not only to spot new product opportunities, but also to automatically raise and lower prices depending on inventory and sales at any given moment. "Comparing the first version of AIMEE to now is like comparing one of the first airplanes to the latest Airbus jetliner," says Sarig.

To demonstrate, Sarig fires up AIMEE on his laptop. Displayed on its screen are reams of data and charts for teeth-whitening products sold on Amazon—thousands of them. (You get more than seven thousand results if you search for "teeth whitening" on Amazon, though many of these will be different sizes or variations of the same product.) Mohawk doesn't yet sell teeth whiteners, but AIMEE is constantly scraping Amazon's data for every product category to look for frequently sold or searched items that Mohawk might consider making. About

70 percent of the searches on Amazon aren't for a brand name, such as "Crest Whitestrips" or even "Crest teeth whitener," rather, they are descriptive. This fact is critical to creating an opening for new products, because it enables start-up brands to get noticed.

"We basically survey millions of consumer paths, meaning we automate the searches that consumers would do on a big scale and we look at what they see on the shelf"—the screen—"when they do that, and we compare that to the day before, and to the day before, and to the day before. We see how the shelf is evolving," Sarig explains.

He points to a graph on the screen, where one axis plots sales over-all as well as sales by each existing brand. "We estimate the current run rate of teeth-whitening products to be about $160 million in rev-enue annually on Amazon," he says. "And all these little dots you see here on the graph are products contributing to this revenue." The sales estimates are extrapolations of a variety of data points, based on cor-relations from what AIMEE has "learned" over time from the number of searches, advertising rates for search terms, the historic percentage of searches resulting in sales ("conversion rates"), and the average esti-mated sale price.

Crest Whitestrips, made by Procter & Gamble, is the top-selling product in the category. But some lesser-known brands also are among the better-selling products, such as AuraGlow, with annual sales of about $7 million, based on AIMEE's calculations. Another brand, Active Wow Activated Coconut Charcoal Powder, has annual sales of about $2 million. There are dozens of other teeth-whitening products, each with estimated sales of $100,000 or less annually.

The other axis on the graph plots how many times a particular brand shows up in related search terms, and thus how many digital shelves, or screens, it shows up on. It would be like a brand getting shelf space on many different aisles in a retail store. The more times a brand shows up, the more opportunities to make a sale. This is where things get especially interesting, if you are looking for product gaps to fill. To determine which brands are doing best, AIMEE tracks all the related searches and estimates the sales volume generated by each. "Teeth whit-ening," naturally, is the most searched term, with "teeth whitening kit" second and "charcoal teeth whitening" third, but there are dozens of variations of searches that include "teeth whitening."

AIMEE estimates that product sales related to the search term "charcoal teeth whitening" amount to $22 million a year on Amazon. So, is this a potential opportunity for Mohawk? Drilling down deeper into the historical data, Sarig says probably not. Searches for "charcoal teeth whitening" actually are declining, AIMEE calculates, which indicates that sales for that term might be peaking. "It is starting to lose its steam," he notes. "But what's interesting is if you look at 'teeth whitening pen.' It's going up. It's a new trend, a ten-million-dollar-a-year business that is increasing. If you have the supply chain in place to really react quickly, you could potentially get a piece of that." It's something he will ask his sales and manufacturing people to look into.

The other valuable X factor that AIMEE measures, by automatically browsing buyer reviews, is what customers are saying about existing products. Accurate reviews are a constant challenge for Amazon, as some sellers, especially Chinese companies, try to skew results by generating fake five-star reviews. But AIMEE focuses more on bad reviews. If shoppers complain about the quality, or don't like the features, or even express an interest in different colors or sizes, that presents a potential opportunity for a new brand. "We use natural language processing to parse through thousands of reviews to identify any pain points customers have," Sarig explains.

If not for AIMEE, it wouldn't have occurred to Mohawk to consider a line of small home appliances. The category surfaced in a "top product model" feature Mohawk software engineers added to AIMEE to spotlight bigger-ticket items worth looking at. As Sarig and his colleagues began studying the data, they quickly noted that AIMEE had identified a high rate of bad reviews for existing products. Comments like this:

> Just a few months after purchasing, it randomly
> stopped working.

> Sometimes the light is on saying ice full when there
> is no ice.

My advice is to run the other way on this product.
Run...do not stop. Do you have $135 or so you want
to throw in the trash? If you do, go ahead and buy
this piece of junk!

Within a year and a half it stopped working. It
wouldn't suck up the water anymore to make ice.

These were all reviews on Amazon for a Frigidaire countertop ice maker. Of all the reviews for this Frigidaire model, 25 percent were the lowest possible, one star, and another 9 percent were just two stars, compared with 49 percent of reviewers rating it five stars; its overall rating was just 3.3 stars, based on more than fifteen hundred reviews.

While some Frigidaire models and other brands fared a bit better, none had off-the-charts good ratings. Delving deeper into the data, Mohawk's team found what they believed was the source of the customers' dissatisfaction. This step, done by human beings rather than AIMEE, is critical, because Mohawk will pursue an idea only if it can engineer a product that addresses the problem at the right price and thus attract shoppers. "Basically, there was a fundamental functional problem where the pump that was pumping water had a tendency to break down after a few months," Sarig says.

A couple of other factors made the market attractive. AIMEE estimated that portable ice makers, which sell for $100 to $150, are about a $35 million-a-year business on Amazon. (If that sounds like a lot, it's because built-in ice makers on refrigerators are prone to break down and cost several hundred dollars to repair, so some people buy a cheaper countertop ice maker because it costs less.) And as with many small home appliances, there is relatively little innovation, so if you can crack the market, you don't have to invest in R&D. "It's not just how big a category is, but how long you think you can be the market leader," Sarig notes. "Let's say you can sell five million to ten million dollars of a product a year, but it's going to be five to ten million a year for ten years. It's on autopilot."

After finding a manufacturer in China to make the hOmeLabs ice maker, fixing the problem that was causing its competitors' break-downs, Mohawk introduced the product on Amazon in June 2017.

The next challenge: getting attention for the new product. Search for "portable ice makers" or "countertop ice makers" on Amazon, and more than one thousand results pop up: different makes and models, different sizes, different colors, different features, along with accessories and related ice-making products. Because so few shoppers bother going past the first screen, the chances of a new brand's success drop dramatically if it doesn't make it onto that prime digital shelf space, as Sarig calls it. And so, it is critical to understand how Amazon determines which products get the highest rankings and thus will appear on the opening screen.

Amazon's algorithm is a black box, its metrics generally give the most prominence to brands that customers are most likely to purchase, because Amazon makes money when shoppers buy what they are looking for. And they're more likely to buy if they see something they like—with the right features and price and with positive reviews overall. For every search, every product gets a score. "The higher the score, the higher you're going to show up in the search," Sarig explains. "The beauty of what Amazon did is they put the customer in charge. If you're the best choice of the customer, you will get the best place on the shelf."

If you're selling a new product, however, you have no sales and no reviews. So how can you achieve a high ranking that will propel your product onto the opening page when a shopper searches for "countertop ice maker"? To build sales and encourage reviews, Mohawk advertised aggressively for several months on Google and Facebook, and on Amazon itself, which lists "Sponsored" (advertised) products at the top of each page, above all other ranked items. This can be a major expense early on, Sarig concedes. "We lose money at first, but we're betting that if we did our job well, at the research level, at the manufacturing level, at the quality-control level," he says, "then we have a chance to outperform the incumbents, take market share from them, and get a higher ranking."

And that's exactly what happened. It took less than a year for hOme-Labs to become the bestselling portable ice maker on Amazon, and AIMEE estimated that Mohawk had grabbed about one-fourth of all ice maker sales on Amazon. A search for "countertop ice makers" on Amazon in April 2019 found that hOmeLabs had the top spot on the page, after the sponsored products, along with the coveted label "Best Seller," highlighted in orange, which Amazon bestows on the highest-selling product for that search term. It had 1,548 customer reviews—69 percent of them five-star reviews, another 11 percent of them four-star, and only 12 percent one-star, a stark contrast with the poorly rated Frigidaire model. Ditto for a search for "portable ice makers" or, simply, "ice makers." The hOmeLabs model would be edged aside as the top-selling countertop ice maker on Amazon in the second half of 2019—by yet another Mohawk countertop ice maker sold under its Vremi brand, which became number one, with hOmeLabs still ranking high at number four.

Using the same playbook, Mohawk repeated the success with the hOmeLabs Beverage Refrigerator and Cooler, a 120-can-capacity mini-fridge with a glass door. hOmeLabs became the top-ranked and "Best Seller" product when anyone searched for "beverage fridge" or similar terms, and when they searched for "dehumidifier." For "window air conditioner," hOmeLabs has ranked a respectable fourth at times. And its "Sunrise Alarm Clock" has ranked in the top ten for its category, and has garnered an "Amazon's Choice" label, a seal of approval Amazon gives to "highly rated, well-priced products available to ship immediately."

"The whole appliance category is basically up for grabs because all the companies that have been leaders in appliances in retail are unsophisticated when it comes to online," says Sarig. "And consumers are just now getting used to buying more and more of the bigger items online, so it's a nascent category."

In just their second year on the market, the various appliances accounted for nearly $49 million in sales, or about two-thirds of Mohawk's 2018 revenue. The company's other brands have high-ranking products on Amazon, too. The Xtava 5-in-1 Professional Curling Iron and Wand Set, at $39.99, with nearly three thousand reviews (69 percent of them five-star), pops up on the first screen for "curling iron" searches. The Vremi Colorful Knife Set, Single Cup Coffee Maker, and 15 Piece Nonstick Cookware Set also show up on the first search page in those categories.

But not all Mohawk's products have done well. The problem wasn't

AIMEE, Sarig says, but mediocre quality. "The data was there, and we brought out the right product, and it was at the right price," he says. "We were able to get a good market share position. But consumers were just not happy with them, and over time, the reviews they gave us degraded." Its Vremi Olive Oil Dispenser, introduced in 2015, got off to a good start before fading. Its overall rating on Amazon fell to three stars—anything less than a four-star rating hurts sales—and 26 percent of reviewers gave it just one star. "Leaks all over the place after a week of use. Total waste of money," wrote one unsatisfied customer.

But Sarig says the early miscues validated Mohawk's approach—if it got the product right. That's when it decided to build an outsourcing team in Shenzhen to vet the manufacturers' quality controls more closely. "The good news is that we learned on small products, not on giant fridges," Sarig adds. Even now, out of every fifteen ideas that Mohawk considers, it pursues only a couple. In some cases where AIMEE finds a market worth exploring, either because it spots a nascent trend or registers that an existing brand is getting mixed or bad reviews, Mohawk's team in China finds that it can't build a better product at a reasonable price that will enable it to take sales from the incumbent brands. And Sarig acknowledges that some product categories lend themselves to a data-driven approach more than others. So far, Mohawk has avoided clothing, even though it is a huge category on Amazon. "Fashion is harder because it has more elements of subjectivity than functionality," he notes. "And luxury is the least meaningful for us. When you buy luxury, you buy the brand image, not functionality of product features." Technology also is a low priority, in part because Anker already dominates the accessories market on Amazon and in part because product cycles are so fast that a company needs to spend a lot on R&D to constantly update features.

But that leaves a whole field of potential products. Mohawk envisions dozens of brands under its umbrella, each independent in case some of them prove so valuable that Mohawk decides to sell them to other companies. And Mohawk plans to accelerate its efforts to allow other consumer product companies to pay to use AIMEE to create new brands, or even just to improve the sales of their existing brands.

Though this venture accounted for only about $500,000 in sales in 2018, that figure could increase if Mohawk kept growing and demonstrated how effective AIMEE was.

One potential obstacle to Mohawk's grand design is that Amazon has adjusted its rules regarding user reviews. It once allowed people who had received freebies to post reviews—Mohawk did this when introducing new products—but has since curtailed that practice. Mohawk says that, like other companies, some of its reviews were purged "because Amazon believed they were questionable or not authentic." Now companies have to rely on actual customers to post reviews, which the companies encourage by reaching out to customers after a purchase. So, it can take longer for new products to build up enough positive reviews to make their way onto a search term's opening screen.

As long as the playing field is level, Sarig thinks Mohawk will continue to do well on Amazon. "Time will tell if it actually works," says Juozas Kaziukenas, the Amazon consultant. "In theory, it all makes sense. In practice, it's still a challenge to replicate. It's still challenging to launch products repeatedly and successfully. As much data as you can find, can you scale that with capital and still remain successful?" He notes that Mohawk is "burning a crazy amount of money" on marketing new products to boost sales. "I'm unconvinced they can achieve profitability any time soon." Others are even more skeptical. Pointing to Mohawk's losses, the financial website Seeking Alpha wrote, "While the idea of having technology-enabled consumer goods sounds nice, the market is way too diversified and dominated by much more resourceful competitors."

Indeed, Mohawk isn't alone in having ambitions to churn out a steady flow of new online brands over a variety of categories, using data gleaned from Amazon to determine what to make. Another company has launched nearly two hundred brands, far more than Mohawk—brands such as Rivet, Ravenna Home, Stone & Beam (furniture), Belei (skincare), OWN PWR (nutritional supplements), Revly (vitamins), Mama Bear (diapers and baby wipes), Presto! (paper towels and cleaning products), Pinzon (sheets and towels), Solimo (razors and personal care and household products), Wag (pet food), Happy Belly (coffee and nuts), and literally dozens of brands of all types of men's and women's clothing.

The name of the company that has introduced all these brands? Amazon.

It's a topic that, like just about everything else Amazon does, the company won't discuss in detail. But a clue about its ambitions can be found online, in dozens of Amazon job postings: for product designers, marketing managers, private-label category managers, product leaders. "Private Brands is a highly-visible, fast-growing business within Amazon," states one posting. "We have a unique business and obsess over quality and building global brands our customers love. We aspire to be part of our customers' everyday lives by offering them unique products at compelling prices backed by Amazon's strong customer obsessed reputation." And another: "Do you want to create new brands from scratch? Do you want to invent and Think Big . . . You must possess strong analytical acumen and be comfortable drawing metric-based conclusions by managing an extensive amount of data."

The company introduced its first house brand, AmazonBasics, in 2009. It started with commodity electronic products such as batteries, computer cables, chargers, and headsets, but has since expanded to luggage, cookware, patio lights, screwdriver sets—you name it. Batteries show the power of Amazon to sell commodity goods with the Amazon name. The Energizer Bunny—it keeps "going and going"—may be one of the most iconic advertising symbols ever, but in the years since Amazon introduced its private-label batteries, the company has taken anywhere from 67 to 90 percent of online sales, and it often has as many as six to eight of the top fifteen brands on the site's "household battery" bestseller list.

Amazon began selling a handful of its stealth private-label brands without its name—like Pinzon, in 2007—but it started to ramp up this business in earnest in 2016. Few of these lines gained much traction in their first couple of years, leading some Amazon watchers to say that the company doesn't have the right sensibility to create the kind of emotional connection associated with the most popular brands, including fast-growing direct-to-consumer brands such as Warby Parker, Dollar Shave Club, and Casper.

Amazon has created more than sixty women's private-label clothing brands, with names, including Camp Moonlight, Daisy Drive, Ella Moon, Lark & Ro, and Painted Heart. But one of the hottest clothing items on all of Amazon in 2019, what many buyers referred to as the "Amazon coat," wasn't made by any of the company's new brands. It was the Orolay down jacket, produced by Jiaxing Zichi Trade Co., a small Chinese company. Utilitarian, even drab, in design, it sold for $120 to $150, a fraction of the cost of high-end brands such as Canada Goose, whose down jackets typically retail for upward of $1,000 at department stores such as Nordstrom and Neiman Marcus.

The Orolay jacket became a top seller—as fashion items often do—thanks to serendipity. On March 27, 2018, *New York* magazine ran a story headlined, "The Unlikely Tale of a $140 Amazon Coat That's Taken Over the Upper East Side." Other publications picked up the story, and more women started buying the coat and posting Instagram selfies boasting about the great deal they got on their down jacket on Amazon. This prompted more shoppers to go to Amazon.com and search not for Orolay, because nobody knew the brand, but simply for "Amazon coat." And because sales were picking up, the Orolay jacket was tabbed as an "Amazon's Choice" item on the opening screen.

Company founder Kevin Chiu told Reuters that monthly sales in January 2019 had reached $5 million—as much as its sales for all of 2017—and that he expected sales to total $30 million to $40 million for the year. "They don't sell to stores. They don't sell through their own website. They don't use social media. They don't do any of these things," says Juozas Kaziukenas, the marketing consultant. "They're just utilizing the massive reach that Amazon itself has. [The coat is] receiving the same attention as DTC brands would, but all of it is happening on Amazon. It's the golden dream of everyone doing this, of course. Funny enough, it's more successful than any clothing brand that Amazon has built."

Even Amazon founder Jeff Bezos conceded in his 2018 letter to shareholders that "third-party sellers" (jargon for entrepreneurs and others that sell their products on Amazon) "are kicking our first party butt. Badly." But it is far too early to dismiss Amazon's brand-creation machine. That's what skeptics did after Amazon's Fire Phone failed miserably in 2014, but late that same year, Amazon began selling its Echo smart speaker, powered by the Alexa voice-recognition personal assistant, and it quickly became one of the fastest-growing new electronics brands ever.

In 2018, Amazon's sales of its own products totaled an estimated $7.5 billion, with more than $1 billion coming from AmazonBasics and the new private-label Amazon brands. And the company is just getting started. The financial firm SunTrust Robinson Humphrey predicts that sales of Amazon's own brands will grow to $25 billion by 2022, with the private-label brands contributing significantly to the growth. "I would be nervous if Amazon entered my category," says James Thomson, a consultant who previously worked at Amazon for six years helping other companies sell their brands on the site. "Amazon itself is the biggest long-term threat to the thousands and thousands of private-label sellers, because it knows how to play the Amazon launch game even better."

Even if none of Amazon's new brands becomes as well known as traditional brands, the company doesn't much care, as long as online shoppers buy them. In this, it shares the same philosophy as Mohawk. "Amazon fundamentally is trying to reverse how you buy things," explains Kaziukenas. "Amazon is saying, 'Instead of you trusting brands, how about if you just search for what you want, and we will show you what's the best.' So, they're saying, 'Forget brand building. Let's just use reviews and ratings.' Which is a terrible deal for brands because, fundamentally, it downplays everything you used to build yourself on."

Even worse, some sellers complain, Amazon has an unfair advantage. Though it shares some data with all would-be sellers, the company has access to more detailed data (actual sales figures of everything sold on Amazon, for example), which it can use to target products sold by others. And to the chagrin of some sellers, Amazon at times advertises its own brand on their pages. "This isn't very nice," a boutique olive oil maker wrote on an online forum for Amazon sellers. "Look at my listing on the search results page. Amazon tags onto MY listing diverting you over to the Amazon Branded Olive Oil."

For his part, Yaniv Sarig professes not to be worried. Retailers have long made private-label brands that copy and compete with successful brands they carry, he notes, adding that hundreds of billions of dollars of product are sold annually on Amazon.com. "Is Amazon going to win a piece of that? Yeah, for sure. How big a piece will it get? Not enough for me to worry that it's not going to leave room for anyone else." Besides, he adds, "Essentially what Amazon is doing is very similar to what we're doing, which to me is a great indicator that we're on the right track."

14

The Brand Is Dead, Long Live the Brand

It's a crisp Friday morning. Your hOmeLabs alarm clock wakes you at 6:15 sharp. You get out of your Tuft & Needle bed made with Brooklinen sheets, put on your Birdies slippers, and head to the bathroom. You shave your legs with a Dollar Shave Club razor and wash your hair with Prose shampoo. You swipe Native deodorant under your arms. Then you put on your Warby Parker glasses or put in your Hubble contact lenses.

You slip on your MeUndies briefs and your ThirdLove bra, Everlane jeans, Allbirds sneakers, and MVMT watch. You're going out of town for the weekend, so you pack your Away carry-on suitcase with a couple of pairs of Outdoor Voices leggings, a supply of Lola tampons, and your Coastal Blue private-label swimsuit from Amazon.

You head to the kitchen, where you make a cup of Brandless Organic Fair Trade Dark Roast Coffee with your Vremi Single Cup Coffee Maker and cook a couple of eggs over easy on your Great Jones skillet. You pop some Ritual vitamins in your mouth. You pour some Farmer's Dog pet food for your dachshund, who is wearing his Fi GPS Smart Dog Collar. (Short for "Fido," get it?) Then you brush your teeth with your

Quip toothbrush and apply your Glossier makeup. You put the baby in her Mockingbird stroller and toss a package of Mama Bear diapers in a bag, and use your smartphone on the way out the door to set your Kangaroo Home Security alarm.

You bought all these brands, and many more, online, and they were delivered a day or two after you ordered them (or, if you live in a big city, maybe even the same day). A few of these products have already joined the list of billion dollar brands, and others will attain "unicorn" status in the coming years. Some will remain small companies, and a few will go out of business.

The direct-to-consumer brand revolution began with a handful of start-ups, then grew to dozens, then hundreds, and now thousands, counting the brands filling the endless digital aisles and shelves of Amazon Marketplace. But it will take time before it is clear how many truly enduring brands will emerge from this revolution. Can Dollar Shave Club and Bonobos survive a century or longer, like Gillette and Levi Strauss? Will Casper be around as long as Sealy and Serta, and can Glossier become the Estée Lauder of the twenty-first century?

Or will the same forces that have led to a democratization of brands make it harder for new brands to become dominant themselves? We may not know for years or even decades, but without doubt, we are at another inflection point in the history of brands—the way brands are created, how many are being created, and what ultimately prompts us to buy a new brand and stay loyal to it, or not.

"I don't have a crystal ball," says Jeffrey Raider. "But in every decade, in every period of time, there have been enduring brands that have gotten built, and I think there definitely will be enduring brands that get built today." Raider has observed the new brand revolution from a front-row seat. He is the only entrepreneur who started not one, but *two* direct-to-consumer unicorns before he reached his mid-thirties. In 2013 he cofounded Harry's (which was bought by Edgewell for $1.37 billion in 2019), only a few years after having cofounded Warby Parker (worth $1.75 billion based on its latest 2019 VC funding round).

Harry's and Warby Parker sell different products (razors versus eyeglasses) at different price points (a few dollars for a razor versus $95 and up for eyeglasses) and have different purchase patterns (every week or month versus every year or two), but they share a strategy: Each saw an opening to challenge entrenched market leaders (Gillette and Luxottica) with quality products at a much lower price. In Raider's view, however, what catapulted each to become a billion dollar brand is an obsession with constantly connecting with the customer.

"We're making them feel very much like they're on this journey with us, they're part of the company, and we're not some monolithic brand out in the world but a group of people who are there to talk to them," he says. "Being a direct-to-consumer company enables you the opportunity to really get to know your customer." Everyone who joins the staff of Harry's, no matter what the job, has to spend a day working in the call center as part of the customer experience team. Raider and his cofounder Andy Katz-Mayfield themselves spend several hours each month listening to customers' complaints or suggestions.

Among these was an odd inquiry that they heard from about a hundred customers in Harry's first year. "People were calling us all the time, saying, 'Hey, can I get one of those little plastic covers that go over the blade?'" Raider recalls. "And we're like, why?" From the start, Harry's had included a blade cover (a small, rigid plastic piece that snaps snugly over the razor cartridge) when it shipped a customer's first order, to protect the blade from getting dull. Many people threw the cover out or lost it, only to decide later that it might have been nice to use while traveling, not just to shield the blade but also to protect their fingers from getting nicked when they reached into their toiletry kit and accidentally grabbed the razor at the wrong end. "Since I travel a lot, and the razor goes into my travel kit, I would like to get another. I don't need another handle/blade set. Is the blade guard alone available?" one customer wrote in an email.

So, in 2015, Harry's began selling a replacement Travel Blade Cover for $1. It may seem insignificant, and indeed it brings in only a tiny amount of revenue, but Raider points to it as something that signals to customers that Harry's cares about what they have to say. "We're like, okay, here's an opportunity to do something better for you. We identified a need that customers had." And that helps to build loyalty that will last for a long time, which is one of the things that makes for a successful and enduring brand.

Raider also acknowledges that it may be harder than ever to create mass brands in the mold of Gillette or Serta or Victoria's Secret. The ease of launching a new product also has led to fragmentation, which likely will make it harder for new brands to achieve the dominance of the great twentieth-century brands.

In 2010, it would have been difficult to imagine a start-up razor company taking significant sales from Gillette. Astonishingly, it happened with not just one but two companies, Dollar Shave Club and Harry's. By 2018, they together had grabbed nearly 14 percent of U.S. razor blade sales. But it is equally hard to imagine either of them individually achieving a market share of even 25 percent, much less the market share of 70 percent once controlled by Gillette. It is equally hard to imagine Gillette ever returning to that level. If anything, with more razors (such as Amazon's Solimo brand) jumping into the market all the time, the long-term challenge for everyone, not just Gillette but also Dollar Shave Club and Harry's, will be to fend off new players.

In the old world, once a popular mass-market brand was established, it could count on a long reign. In the new world of brands, this is no longer true. Brand loyalty is declining as never before. One report on the one hundred top consumer product brands found that 90 percent had lost market share in recent years. A study by Accenture in 2015 found that more than half of all consumers consider significantly more brands when they buy something than they did a decade earlier. And a survey focusing on luxury brands by British market research firm YouGov and *Time* magazine found that fewer shoppers identified favorite brands. The reason: a plethora of choices they can find online. "Single-brand loyalists are nearing extinction as people use their digital resources to bring a pocketful of brands to the same marketplace," said Jim Taylor, a brand and marketing consultant who was a senior adviser to the study. "This doesn't mean that brands don't matter, but rather that the consumer is more empowered to make richer, more enlightened choices, spurred primarily by technology in the form of comparison shopping via smartphones and online reviews."

The decline in brand loyalty, of course, has helped power the rise of the new direct-to-consumer brands. Between 2013 and 2017, some $17 billion in sales shifted from big consumer brands to small brands—and that was before many of the latest start-ups began getting traction. This trend is likely to strengthen in the coming years, thanks in large part to the continued rapid growth of sales on Amazon. In 2018, small- and medium-size companies sold $160 billion in goods on Amazon, up from just $100 million in 1999, a 1,600-fold increase. While some of those companies are reselling products made by others, many of them (such as Mohawk Group, as well as Amazon itself) are creating their own new brands.

This development hasn't gone unnoticed by Neil Blumenthal of Warby Parker. "It's never been cheaper to start a business, although I think it's never been harder to scale a business," he says. Warby Parker is the most prominent new eyewear brand, but its market share is still less than 5 percent. And in the years since it sold its first pair of eyeglasses, in 2010, other start-ups have launched well over a dozen new online eyeglass brands.

Many of the newcomers are copycats with essentially the same business model as Warby Parker, but others are niche players, such as Lensabl, which will make prescription lenses for your favorite frames so you don't have to buy new ones—"Our Lenses, Your Specs"—or Pixel, which sells eyeglasses with a pigment in the lenses, so they filter out "blue light" from computer screens, which can cause eye strain; or Topology, which makes frames custom-fitted to your face using an iPhone's 3-D scan technology.

How many of these start-ups will succeed? To some, the constant influx of new entrants offering eyeglasses and other products under-scores that the direct-to-consumer frenzy has elements of a bubble—much like the dot-com boom of the 1990s, with VC firms financing rival brands that are chasing the same customers. But while not all will survive, it's possible that many will—some, like Warby Parker, as megabrands perhaps; others, as microbrands.

That's why Kirsten Green of Forerunner Ventures, a decade after making her first direct-to-consumer investments, is raising ever-bigger

VC funds to finance e-commerce start-ups. It's why David Bell, the early adviser to Bonobos and Warby Parker, quit his tenured professorship at the Wharton School in 2018 to try his hand at starting digitally native brands at his new company, Idea Farm Ventures. It's why Henry Davis left his job as the president of Glossier to start a direct-to-consumer personal-care products company named Arfa Inc. (financed by Forerunner Ventures, among others), which will endeavor to create a "house of brands."

The revolution, as they see it, has just begun.

The good news for brands, new and old, is that the market for consumer products isn't just tens of billions or even hundreds of billions of dollars a year, but several trillion dollars a year in the United States alone. That leaves plenty of room for start-ups, with the most successful ones joining the billion dollar brand club. After all, they could be a $1 razor blade and a one-minute, thirty-three-second video away from making it happen.

Notes

NOTE: *Unless otherwise indicated, all quotations are from interviews conducted by the author.*

Chapter 1: Our Blades Are F**king Great

1 He was turned down: Email correspondence with Michael Dubin, Dollar Shave Club founder, May 13, 2019.

2 "My basement has": "The Brave Ones: How One Man Changed the Face of Shaving," CNBC, May 25, 2017, https://www.cnbc.com/2017/06/21/michael-dubin -shaving-america.html.

3 "Can you please come to our office right now?": Email sent by Peter Pham, Science Inc. cofounder and adviser to Dollar Shave Club, to Steve Lackenby, cofounder, TulaCo technology firm, March 6, 2012.

4 he submitted a patent application: U.S. Patent number 775,134, application filed December 3, 1901, patent granted November 15, 1904.

4 when the Gillette razor went into production: "K.C. Gillette Dead; Made Safety Razor," *New York Times* obituary, July 11, 1932.

5 Out of work, Dubin was looking: Author interview with Michael Dubin, Dollar Shave Club founder, March 14, 2017.

5 investing $25,000 (most of his life savings): Ibid.

6 he had to pay $800: Ibid.

7 "I remember Mike's face": John Patrick Pullen, "How a Dollar Shave Club's Ad Went Viral," *Entrepreneur*, September 2012, https://www.entrepreneur.com /article/224282

8 the check had been mistakenly written for only $100: Author interview with Peter Pham, Science Inc. cofounder and adviser to Dollar Shave Club, April 18, 2018,

with details confirmed in email correspondence with Tom Dare, Science's chief financial officer, June 18, 2019.

10   After nearly seven weeks of pleading and cajoling: Author interview with Peter Pham, April 18, 2018.

11   "I don't shave often, but": In their order of appearance in the text, the tweets were posted by: Benoit Lafontaine, @joel1di1, March 6, 2012; Gordon Fraser, @blnd-swmr, March 6, 2012; John Caron, @jcaron2, March 7, 2012; and Chris Barth, @BarthDoesThings, March 6, 2012.

12   "Their blades are not fucking great": Author interviews with former Gillette executives who didn't wish to be named, to avoid offending their former employer.

12   Founded in 1955 as a knife maker: Author interview with Ken Hill, DorcoUSA president, May 15, 2018; "Capturing the World One Razor at a Time: Dorco," Korea.net, January 19, 2015, http://www.korea.net/NewsFocus/Business/view ?articleId=124994.

13   was a minuscule 1 percent: Author interview with Ken Hill, May 15, 2018.

13   advertising rights to the World Series: "The Gillette Company Advertising Fact Sheet," Business Wire, January 26, 2004, https://www.businesswire.com/news /home/20040126006099/en/INSERTING REPLACING-FEATUREThe-Gillette -Company-Debuts-New.

14   virtually monopolistic 70 percent: Ciara Linnane, "Procter & Gamble's Gillette Razor Business Dinged by Online Shave Clubs," *MarketWatch*, April 27, 2017, citing data from Euromonitor International, a market research provider, https:// www.marketwatch.com/story/procter-gambles-gillette-razor-business-dinged-by -online-shave-clubs-2017-04-26.

16   "We'll just ride them out": Author interview with unnamed former Gillette executives.

17   for an additional $9.8 million: Author interview with Peter Pham, April 18, 2018; Crunchbase.com, https://www.crunchbase.com/organization/dollar-shave -club#section-funding-rounds.

17   eventually total about $163 million: Email correspondence with Michael Dubin, May 13, 2019.

17   "Would you buy our shares?": Pakman says, "I got a phone call from them after we sold [Dollar Shave Club] for $1 billion, and they said, 'Boy, were we wrong.'" Author interview with David Pakman, Dollar Shave Club investor and director, April 5, 2017.

17   One potential investor that turned Pham down: Gillette declined requests to discuss Dollar Shave Club.

18   asked for—well, insisted on—getting shares in Dollar Shave Club: Author interview with Ken Hill, May 15, 2018.

18   has more than 26 million views on YouTube: "DollarShaveClub.com—Our Blades Are F**king Great," YouTube.com video, 1:33, posted by Dollar Shave Club, March 6, 2012, https://www.youtube.com/watch?v=ZUG9qYTJMsI.

19   Dollar Shave Club's annual sales: "Dollar Shave Club Makes Surprise Super Bowl Entry," *AdAge*, February 7, 2016, https://adage.com/article/about-us/dollar-shave -club-makes-surprise-super-bowl-entry/302582.

19   Gillette's market share had plummeted: Data provided to the author by Euromonitor International, a market research firm.

20   asserted that its blades were up to 50 percent cheaper: Gillette Shave Club TV commercial, "Save Money," 0:30, 2015, https://www.ispot.tv/ad/73Xe/gillette-shave -club-save-money.

20 "Gillette's product is significantly consumer preferred": Procter & Gamble Company earnings call, October 23, 2015, https://www.bamsec.com/companies/80424/the -procter-gamble-company/transcripts.

20 including independent testers: "Which Shave Club Has the Best Razor?" *Consumer Reports*, April 25, 2016, https://www.consumerreports.org/razors/which -shave-club-has-the-best-razor/.

20 Gillette filed a lawsuit: Gillette, "Gillette Files Patent Infringement Lawsuit Against Dollar Shave Club," press release, December 17, 2015, https://news.gillette.com /press-release/product-news/gillette-files-patent-infringement-lawsuit-against-dollar -shave-club.

21 As Dollar Shave Club's sales reached: Michael Dubin, speaking at Shoptalk retail conference, Las Vegas, quoted in Phil Wahba, "Dollar Shave Club Says Butt Wipes Will Help Lead It to Profit This Year," *Fortune*, May 16, 2016, http://fortune.com /2016/05/16/dollar-shave-club-2/.

21 Dubin began talking with suitors: Author interview with David Pakman, April 5, 2017.

21 Harry's, which had a lower market: Edgewell Personal Care, "Edgewell Personal Care to Combine with Harry's, Inc. to Create a Next-Generation Consumer Products Platform," press release, May 9, 2019, https://www.prnewswire.com/news -releases/edgewell-personal-care-to-combine-with-harrys-inc-to-create-a-next -generation-consumer-products-platform-300847130.html.

21 3.7 times the total investment in the company of $375 million: Total equity financing, according to Harry's, which says that other sources indicating total financing of $460 million were inaccurate.

21 he still owned about 9 to 10 percent of the company: People with knowledge of Dollar Shave Club's finances; Michael Dubin declined to comment.

21 Science, for its early bet: Author interview with Peter Pham, April 18, 2018.

22 Dorco's earnings have soared: Author interview with Ken Hill, May 15, 2018.

22 walked away with several million dollars: Author interview with Michael Dubin, May 14, 2018.

22 it cut prices by an average of 12 percent: Sharon Terlep, "Gillette, Bleeding Market Share, Cuts Prices of Razors," *Wall Street Journal*, April 4, 2017, https://www.wsj .com/articles/gillette-bleeding-market-share-cuts-prices-of-razors-1491303601.

Chapter 2: The Pied Pipers of Disruption

24 *Time* magazine's 100 Most Influential People: "The 100 Most Influential People in the World 2017," *Time*, April 20, 2017.

24 *Vanity Fair*'s International Best-Dressed List: *Vanity Fair*, "The International Best-Dressed List," https://www.vanityfair.com/international-best-dressed-list-2017/photos.

24 "I mean, who ever aspires to be an auditor?": Emily Note, "Career/Kirsten Green," Atelier Doré, https://www.atelierdore.com/photos/career-kirsten-green/.

24 in a Safeway grocery freezer counting inventory: Leena Rao, "Meet the Woman Funding the Valley's Hottest Shopping Startups," *Fortune*, June 25, 2017, http:// fortune.com/2017/06/25/kirsten-green-forerunner-ventures-women-vc-fund/.

26 at an initial cost as low as $29 a month: Shopify.com website, "Basic Shopify" price, https://www.shopify.com/pricing.

30 lamented losing a $700 pair of eyeglasses: Warby Parker cofounders David Gilboa and Neil Blumenthal have both related this origin story, including in an interview the author had with Blumenthal on November 2, 2018.

30   In another version of the story: Michelsonmedical.org, "Wharton BPC Semifinalists 2009," video, 3:24, https://michelsonmedical.org/initiatives/nir-diagnostics-2009/.

30   owns or produces on license many popular brands: Luxottica.com, http://www.luxottica.com/en/retail-brands and http://www.luxottica.com/en/eyewear-brands.

32   "It's sort of an absurd idea": "Professor David Bell on Digital Marketing: Wharton Lifelong Learning Tour," video presentation, November 8, 2012, https://www.youtube.com/watch?v=m9zowHS79xM.

32   They made it to the semifinals: Wharton article on the eight business plan competition finalists in 2009, "Rowing, Robots and Roommates: And the Best Business Plan Is . . ." Knowledge@Wharton, May 13, 2009, https://knowledge.wharton.upenn.edu/article/rowing-robots-and-roommates-and-the-best-business-plan-is/.

33   "Guys, I don't know": David Gelles, "Jeff Raider on Founding Warby Parker and Harry's," *New York Times*, November 2, 2018, https://www.nytimes.com/2018/11/02/business/jeff-raider-warby-parker-harrys-corner-office.html.

33   One of Warby Parker's early backers: Author interview with Ben Lerer, managing partner at Lerer Hippeau venture capital, October 26, 2018.

34   "The large urban centers always predominate": "To Boost Online Sales, Focus on Close-Knit Communities," podcast, Mack Institute for Innovation Management, https://mackinstitute.wharton.upenn.edu/2017/community-ties-drive-online-sales/.

36   attended a dinner . . . hosted by Alpha Club: Author interview with Kirsten Green, Forerunner Ventures, August 14, 2018, with details of the event confirmed by Emily Judson Gonsenheim, Alpha Club director.

36   By coincidence, she found herself: Author interview with Peter Pham, April 18, 2018.

37   He made what's called a "warehouse loan": Author interview with Sandy Colen, founder and chief investment officer, SCP Investment, June 15, 2018.

38   Forerunner earned many multiples: Author interview with Kirsten Green, December 7, 2018. She declined to be more specific.

38   with investments in nearly ninety e-commerce companies: Forerunner Ventures listing of portfolio companies on its website, https://forerunnerventures.com/portfolio/.

39   had little luck—until she talked to Forerunner: Author interviews with Kirsten Green, November 21, 2017, and Henry Davis, former president of Glossier, March 15, 2019.

40   Glossier has turned into a big winner: Katie Roof and Yuliya Chernova, "Glossier Tops Billion-Dollar Valuation with Latest Funding," *Wall Street Journal*, March 19, 2019, https://www.wsj.com/articles/glossier-tops-billion-dollar-valuation-with-latest-funding-11552993200.

41   Venrock's investment in Nest Labs: Pakman said in email correspondence on May 16, 2019, that Nest "was the first consumer products company for Venrock—as long as you don't count Apple."

41   By that time, Nest was so successful: "Google to Acquire Nest," press release issued by Alphabet Inc., parent company of Google, January 13, 2014.

42   founded by several former Apple executives: Pearl cofounders Bryson Gardner, Brian Sander, and Joseph Fisher all worked at Apple just prior to starting Pearl Automation, according to their LinkedIn profiles.

Chapter 3: Making It in the World Bazaar

45   Hubble's second full year in business: The sales, customer, and market share figures were confirmed in email correspondence with Jesse Horwitz, Hubble cofounder, on May 22, 2019.

45 St.Shine now gets 10 percent: Author interview with Jason Ong, international business director, St.Shine Optical, October 3, 2018.

48 Bloomberg News journalist Sam Grobart: Sam Grobart, "I Used Alibaba to Make 280 Pairs of Brightly Colored Pants," *Bloomberg News*, September 17, 2014, https://www.bloomberg.com/news/articles/2014-09-16/what-is-alibaba-one-man-s-path-to-custom-made-bright-colored-pants.

49 the fastest-growing part: GfK market research firm report, May 15, 2017, https://www.gfk.com/en-us/insights/press-release/daily-contact-lenses-surpass-monthlies-in-us-sales-account-for-38-of-market/.

50 a former chief medical officer: Bausch & Lomb, "Bausch & Lomb Appoints Brian Levy Corporate Vice President and Chief Medical Officer," press release, March 5, 2004, https://www.businesswire.com/news/home/20040305005216/en/Bausch-Lomb-Appoints-Brian-Levy-Corporate-Vice.

51 one-day disposable contacts were used by: Hubble market share estimates in email correspondence from Hubble cofounder Jesse Horwitz, July 24, 2019.

51 at the time called Clarity Contacts: Emails sent by Hubble cofounder Ben Cogan to prospective contact lenses suppliers in Taiwan, December 2015.

52 a 2018 study found: Jennie Diec, Tilia Daniel, and Thomas Varghese, "Comparison of Silicone Hydrogel and Hydrogel Daily Disposable Contact Lenses," *Eye & Contact Lens: Science and Clinical Practice* 267 (September 2018), https://journals.lww.com/claojournal/Citation/2018/09001/Comparison_of_Silicone_Hydrogel_and_Hydrogel_Daily.30.aspx.

54 After some back-and-forth over price: Author interview with Jesse Horwitz, Hubble cofounder, on May 10, 2018.

56 Game 2 of the 2017 World Series: Hubble television commercial, "Why We Started Hubble," video, 0:15, October 25, 2017, https://www.ispot.tv/ad/wlR4/hubble-daily-contacts-why-we-started-hubble.

56 a Wall Street analyst for HSBC bank: HSBC Global Research report on St.Shine Optical, November 9, 2017.

56 About a year after Hubble: Alison Griswold, "Contact Lens Startup Hubble Sold Lenses with a Fake Prescription from a Made-up Doctor," *Quartz*, December 14, 2017, https://qz.com/1154306/hubble-sold-contact-lenses-with-a-fake-prescription-from-a-made-up-doctor/.

57 *New York Times* subsequently reported: Sapna Maheshwari, "Contact Lens Startup, Big on Social Media, May Be Bad for Eyes," *New York Times*, July 21, 2019, https://www.nytimes.com/2019/07/21/business/media/hubble-contact-lens.html

57 proposed tightening the rules: "Contact Lens Rule: A Proposed Rule by the Federal Trade Commission on 05/28/2019," https://www.federalregister.gov/documents/2019/05/28/2019-09627/contact-lens-rule.

57 Hubble had raised nearly $74 million: Author interview with Jesse Horwitz, August 2, 2018.

Chapter 4: Survival of the Fittest

59 hovering around 33 percent: "Victoria's Secret Gets Ready for a Makeover," *Economist*, December 8, 2018, citing data from Euromonitor International market research firm, https://www.economist.com/business/2018/12/08/victorias-secret-gets-ready-for-a-makeover.

59 failed for "myriad reasons": LinkedIn profile of David Spector, ThirdLove cofounder, https://www.linkedin.com/in/dspec/.

60 "No woman likes to bra shop": "ThirdLove CEO on Disrupting the Bra Space," video interview with Heidi Zak, ThirdLove cofounder, CNBC, October 10, 2018, https://www.cnbc.com/2018/10/09/thirdloves-secret-to-designing-the-perfect-fitting-bra.html.

61 In early 2013: Author interview with David Spector, ThirdLove cofounder, April 1, 2019.

61 has since received two patents: U.S. Patent numbers 9,489,743, issued November 8, 2016, and 10,055,851, issued August 21, 2018.

62 In 2004, Playtex had offered "Nearly" sizes: "'New' ThirdLove Half Cup Bra Sizes Are Nothing New," *Tomima's Blog*, August 29, 2018, https://www.herroom.com/blog/new-thirdlove-half-cup-bra-sizes-are-nothing-new/.

62 about double what Victoria's Secret offers: Victoria's Secret "Shop Bras by Size" website, https://ww.victoriassecret.com/bras/shop-by-size, lists about three dozen sizes.

66 "Would you try a boob selfie fitting app?": Ty Alexander, "The App That Uses Boob Selfies to Find Your Perfect Bra Size," HelloBeautiful.com, March 10, 2014, https://hellobeautiful.com/2709691/third-love-iphone-bra-fitting-app/.

68 the company's sales, which increased: Author interview with David Spector, December 7, 2018.

69 Thanks to the strategy's success: Author interview with ThirdLove cofounders David Spector and Heidi Zak, April 1, 2019.

Chapter 5: From Mad Men to Math Men

72 earning several hundred thousand dollars a year: Author interview with Jesse Pujji, Ampush cofounder, Mixergy, May 19, 2011.

72 "I didn't think it was a smart move": Author interview with Sandy Pujji, Jesse's father, July 13, 2018.

76 Pham had a small ownership stake in Ampush: Author interview with Jesse Pujji, June 7, 2019.

77 The payback was so good: Author interviews with Brian John Kim, Dollar Shave Club former vice president, October 2, 2018, and Cameron House, Ampush marketing director, March 23, 2018.

77 was signing up 55,000 new subscribers: Email correspondence from Kushal Kadakia, senior director of growth at Ampush, October 10, 2018.

77 sales for the year rose to $65 million: Interview with Michael Dubin in Adam Lashinsky, "The Cutting Edge of Care," *Fortune*, March 9, 2015, http://fortune.com/2015/03/09/dollar-shave-club/.

78 Ampush ranked number 61 on the "Inc. 5000": "Inc. 5000 2015: The Full List," https://www.inc.com/inc5000/list/2015.

78 Red Ventures paid $15 million: Author interview with Jesse Pujji, September 11, 2018.

78 "When you create a Lookalike Audience": Facebook.com, "About Lookalike Audiences," https://www.facebook.com/business/help/164749007013531?helpref=faq_content.

80 During the fourteen-day period: Data from ThirdLove "Weekly Paid Video Testing" presentation, reviewed at December 7, 2018, marketing staff meeting.

81 On a warm mid-September afternoon: The photo shoot took place at Studio Shotwell, a rental studio at 577 Shotwell Street, San Francisco, the week of September 17, 2018.

81 more than six million advertisers: Facebook.com, https://www.facebook.com/iq/insights-to-go/6m-there-are-more-than-6-million-active-advertisers-on-facebook.

81 Nisho Cherison, ThirdLove's head of growth marketing: After two and a half years at ThirdLove, Cherison left to join Facebook in 2019.

82 a polished TV commercial costing about $950,000: Author interview with David Spector, September 7, 2018.

83 its U.S. market share fell: "Victoria's Secret Gets Ready for a Makeover," *Economist.*

83 around 2 percent of the U.S. market: Calculation based on estimated ThirdLove sales of more than $130 million in 2018, from cofounder David Spector, and over- all U.S. bra sales of about $7.2 billion, from report by NPD Group data research firm, February 27, 2019, https://www.npd.com/wps/portal/npd/us/news/press -releases/2019/millennials-and-boomers-behind-three-areas-of-growth-in-bras -reports-npd/.

83 "The show is a fantasy": "We're Nobody's Third Love—We're Their First Love," *Vogue,* November 8, 2018, https://www.vogue.com/article/victorias-secret-ed -razek-monica-mitro-interview?verso=true.

83 In a full-page ad: ThirdLove ad in *New York Times,* November 18, 2018.

83 This got more media coverage: Paige Gawley, "Valentina Sampaio Is Victoria's Secret's First Transgender Model," August 5, 2019, ETonline.com, https://www .etonline.com/valentina-sampaio-is-victorias-secrets-first-transgender-model-129838.

Chapter 6: The Algorithm Is Always Right

87 a team won by writing an algorithm: Steve Lohr, "A $1 Million Research Bar- gain for Netflix, and Maybe a Model for Others," *New York Times,* September 21, 2009, https://www.nytimes.com/2009/09/22/technology/internet/22netflix .html.

88 to post on its website an "Algorithms Tour": "Algorithms Tour: How Data Science Is Woven into the Fabric of Stitch Fix," https://algorithms-tour.stitchfix.com/.

88 "Each attribute that describes": Eric Colson, "Machine and Expert-Human Resources: A Synthesis of Art and Science for Recommendations," *Multi- Threaded,* July 21, 2014, https://multithreaded.stitchfix.com/blog/2014/07/21 /machine-and-expert-human-resources/.

88 "We have our machines look": "Algorithms Tour," Stitchfix.com

89 total investment of $1.5 million: Author interview with Tamim Mourad, cofounder of eSalon and PriceGrabber, September 12, 2018.

95 "It just makes more sense": Productparamour.com, "eSalon Hair Color at Home, Salon Quality Results," May 16, 2017, http://productparamour.com/2017/05/16 /esalon-hair-color-at-home-salon-quality-results/#comments.

95 "When I was working full time": Trustpilot.com review, April 30, 2019, https:// www.trustpilot.com/review/esalon.com.

96 L'Oreal introduced a new brand: L'Oreal, "L'Oreal Transforms the At-Home Hair Color Experience with Launch of Color&Co, a New Direct-to-Consumer Brand Specializing in Personalized Hair Color, Powered by Professional Colorists," press release, May 8, 2019, https://www.lorealusa.com/media/press-releases/2019/may /color-and-co and https://www.colorandco.com/personalized-color.

96 Facing increased competition from a much bigger rival, eSalon: Henkel, "Henkel to Enter Into Joint Venture with Personalized Hair Coloration Provider eSalon .com," press release, July 26, 2019, https://www.businesswire.com/news/home /20190726005282/en/Henkel-Enter-Joint-Venture-Personalized-Hair-Coloration. Terms of Henkel's investment in eSalon were not disclosed.

Chapter 7: Eyes on the Customers

98 fifteen of the twenty-seven styles: Author interview with Neil Blumenthal, Warby Parker co–chief executive and cofounder, November 2, 2018.

99 it wasn't the cheapest, either: While Warby Parker glasses with single-vision lenses start at $95, it charges more than $400 for prescriptions with progressive lenses or stronger corrections that work best with the thinnest "ultra-high-index" lenses. Comparable frames and lenses typically cost $700 or more at traditional eyeglass retailers.

99 Well before it came along: Damon Darlin, "Do-It-Yourself Eyeglass Shopping on the Internet," *New York Times*, May 5, 2007, https://www.nytimes.com/2007/05 /05/technology/05money.html; Farhad Manjoo, "How to Get an Unbelievable, Amazing, Fantastic, Thrilling Deal on New Glasses," Slate.com, August 27, 2008, https://slate.com/technology/2008/08/how-to-get-an-unbelievable-thrilling-deal -on-new-glasses.html.

100 can cost as little as $42: "Zenni vs. the Other Guys: How We Stack Up," zenni optical.com, https://www.zennioptical.com/c/about-us#price-comparison.

100 Zenni has sold more than twenty million pairs of glasses: Zenni Optical, "Zenni Optical Marks 15th Anniversary by Selling 20 Millionth Pair of Glasses," press release, April 19, 2018; author interviews with Warby Parker executives, March 22, 2019.

100 has raised about $290 million: Email correspondence with Kaki Read, senior communications manager, Warby Parker, June 23, 2019.

100 estimated annual sales between $400 million and $500 million: Alfred Lee and Serena Saitto, "Can Warby Parker Sustain Investors' High Expectations?" TheInformation.com, March 26, 2018, estimated Warby Parker's sales at $320 million to $340 million in 2017, with a revenue growth target for 2018 of about 40 percent, https://www.theinformation.com/articles/can-warby-parker-sustain-investors -high-expectations.

100 valued at around $1.75 billion: Michael J. de la Merced, "Warby Parker, the Eyewear Seller, Raises $75 Million," *New York Times*, March 14, 2019, https://www .nytimes.com/2018/03/14/business/dealbook/warby-parker-fundraising.html.

100 a 2015 headline on the *Huffington Post*: Kenny Kline, "4 Industries Currently Getting Warby Parkered," *Huffington Post*, August 10, 2015, https://www.huffpost.com /entry/4-industries-currently-ge_b_7957872?guccounter=1&guce_referrer=aHR0c HM6Ly93d3cuZ29vZ2xlLmNvbS8&guce_referrer_sig=AQAAADD5KIa6NjD _w9vo96uzvRjCca66I0kiILlmeBrTrAVHPNAVkU_jb7YCh5QWROl7rq -TL3Iwqyv1xV_N5oERqSTcN2ocFKV1KpfskQLma_D2A7Sd64bQxr5NykwGYb _RqdwjKD6IrvCuwMSGasLz8-FwGfTIEvRiKP7SVhuOmOJp.

101 Glossier selected the soft pink color: "How a Beauty Blog Turned Instagram Comments into a Product Line," Wired.com, November 26, 2014, https://www.wired .com/2014/11/beauty-startup-turned-instagram-comments-product-line/.

101 McGhee started a popular Instagram account: #glossierbrown on Instagram.

104 @WarbyParker customer service: From @WarbyParker Twitter feed.

107 had a valuation of more than $1 billion: Away, "Away Is Valued at $1.4 Billion After a Series D Investment of $100 Million," press release, May 14, 2019, https:// www.prnewswire.com/news-releases/away-is-valued-at-1-4-billion-after-a-series -d-investment-of-100-million-300850285.html.

107 only a few hundred a year: Email correspondence with Kaki Read, senior communications manager, Warby Parker, April 16, 2019.

108 about 240 styles: Ibid.

109 ended up with just seven questions: https://www.warbyparker.com/quiz.

Chapter 8: Delivering the Goods

114 They arrive on his doorstep the next day: Quiet Logistics order tracking report, July 2, 2018, provided to the author by Nick Saunders, senior vice president, sales and marketing, Quiet Logistics.

116 In 2019, roughly eighteen billion e-commerce packages: In its "Statement Regarding FedEx Corporation's Relationship with Amazon.com, Inc.," June 7, 2019, FedEx said that e-commerce "is expected to grow from 50 million to 100 million packages a day in the U.S. by 2026." Fifty million packages a day equals 18.25 billion a year. http://investors.fedex.com/news-and-events/investor-news/news -release-details/2019/Statement-Regarding-FedEx-Corporations-Relationship -with-Amazoncom-Inc-/default.aspx.

116 generating more than $180 billion: Third-Party Logistics, "Third-Party Logistics Market Results and Trends for 2018," press release, June 7, 2018, https://www .3plogistics.com/bulls-lead-third-party-logistics-market-results-and-trends-for -2018-including-estimates-for-190-countries/.

118 it did secure a contract: AllPoints Systems, "Drugstore.com Prescribes AllPoints Systems for Advanced e-Fulfillment Management System," press release, June 13, 2000, https://www.logisticsonline.com/doc/drugstorecom-prescribes-allpoints -systems-for-0001.

118 sold AllPoints in 2001 for $30 million: Sales price confirmed in email correspondence with Bruce Welty, chairman and CEO cofounder of AllPoints, and cofounder of Quiet Logistics and Locus Robotics, May 23, 2019.

119 Kiva robots had been installed: Robert Malone, "Staples Fastens onto Kiva," December 19, 2005, Forbes, https://www.forbes.com/2005/12/19/staples-kiva -robots-cx_rm_1219robots.html#4fc29c502584.

119 customers received a product they didn't order: "The Big Send-Off," Internet Retailer, May 29, 2009, https://www.digitalcommerce360.com/2009/05/29/the-big -send-off/.

121 "We got the bad news": Amazon, "Amazon.com to Acquire Kiva Systems Inc.," press release, March 19, 2012, https://press.aboutamazon.com/news-releases/news -release-details/amazoncom-acquire-kiva-systems-inc/.

122 shipped five billion packages in 2017: Amazon, "Amazon's Best of Prime 2017 Reveals the Year's Biggest Trends—More than 5 Billion Items Shipped with Prime in 2017," press release, January 2, 2018.

122 By 2019, it operated: MWPVL International, "Amazon Global Fulfillment Center Network," May 2019, http://www.mwpvl.com/html/amazon_com.html. Amazon puts the figure at 270, but that doesn't include some facilities, such as distribution centers operated by Amazon's Whole Foods subsidiary.

122 With more than two hundred thousand robots: Lauren Feiner, "Amazon Shows Off Its New Warehouse Robots That Can Automatically Sort Packages," CNBC, June 5, 2019, https://www.cnbc.com/2019/06/05/amazon-shows-off-its -new-warehouse-robots.html; Nick Wingfield, "As Amazon Pushes Forward with Robots, Workers Find New Roles," New York Times, September 10, 2017, https://www.nytimes.com/2017/09/10/technology/amazon-robots-workers .html.

122 testing new warehouse automation equipment: Jeffrey Dastin, "Amazon Rolls Out Machines That Pack Orders and Replace Jobs," Reuters, May 13, 2019, https://www .reuters.com/article/us-amazon-com-automation-exclusive/exclusive-amazon-rolls -out-machines-that-pack-orders-and-replace-jobs-idUSKCN1SJ0X1.

122   delivered to secure lockers: Other companies also offer lockers, including start-ups such as Parcel Post, Luxer One, and Package Concierge.

123   Amazon would spend $800 million: Brian Olsavsky, chief financial officer, Amazon earnings call, April 25, 2019.

123   in a sign that it views Amazon: FedEx, "Statement Regarding FedEx Corporation's Relationship with Amazon.com, Inc.," June 7, 2019, http://investors .fedex.com/news-and-events/investor-news/news-release-details/2019/Statement -Regarding-FedEx-Corporations-Relationship-with-Amazoncom-Inc-/default .aspx; Thomas Black, "FedEx Ends Ground-Delivery Deal With Amazon," Bloomberg News, August 7, 2019, https://www.bloomberg.com/news/articles /2019-08-07/fedex-deepens-pullback-from-amazon-as-ground-delivery-deal -ends?srnd=premium.

123   Amazon sued Valdez: Amazon.com v. Arthur Valdez, Superior Court, King County, Washington State, March 21, 2016, https://www.scribd.com/doc /305577959/Amazon-vs-Valdez-Target-case. The lawsuit was subsequently settled, though the terms weren't disclosed, according to Kavita Kumar, "Target Hires Another Former Amazon Employee to Work on Supply Chain," *Star Tribune*, August 9, 2016, http://www.startribune.com/target-hires-another-former-amazon -employee-to-work-on-supply-chain/389626331/.

127   "We've been filing for so many patents": The list of Locus Robotics patents can be found in the U.S. Patent and Trademark Office's Patent Full-Text and Image Database, http://patft.uspto.gov/netahtml/PTO/search-bool.html.

127   By 2019, it had begun expanding: Email correspondence with Bruce Welty, cofounder and chief executive of Quiet Logistics, June 16, 2019; Quiet Logistics, "Quiet Logistics Eyes Global Expansion, Opening New Robot-Enabled Fulfillment Center in Los Angeles," press release, July 17, 2019, https://www.prnewswire.com /news-releases/quiet-logistics-eyes-global-expansion-opening-new-robot-enabled -fulfillment-center-in-los-angeles-300886350.html.

127   One of its main rivals, an autonomous mobile robot start-up: Shopify, "Shopify to Acquire 6 River Systems," press release, September 9, 2019, https://www.businesswire .com/news/home/20190909005924/en/Shopify-Acquire-6-River-Systems.

127   more than one hundred robots: Email correspondence with Rick Faulk, chief executive of Locus Robotics, May 30, 2019.

127   the company was bought for about $100 million: Related Companies, "Related Companies Announces Strategic Partnership with Greenfield Partners to Acquire Leading Omni-Channel E-commerce Fulfillment Provider Quiet Logistics," press release, March 13, 2019, https://www.related.com/press-releases/2019-03-13 /related-companies-announces-strategic-partnership-greenfield-partners. Sales price confirmed in email correspondence with Bruce Welty, cofounder of Quiet Logistics, May 23, 2019.

131   increasing its total funding to $64 million: Flexe, "Announcing Flexe's $43M Series B Funding," blogpost, May 7, 2019, https://www.flexe.com/blog/announcing-flexes -43m-series-b-funding; author interview with Karl Siebrecht, Flexe cofounder and chief executive, July 26, 2018.

Chapter 9: The Mattress Wars

133   only to exchange the mattress for a different one: Sit 'n Sleep's restocking fee is 20 percent, "not to exceed $500," https://www.sitnsleep.com/faqs.

133   "a Pinterest for shopping": JT Marino, appearing on "The Start-up That

Launched the Horse Race of Online Mattress Companies," *Mixergy*, August 15, 2018, https://mixergy.com/interviews/tuft-and-needle-with-jt-marino/.

135 tech luminaries: Marisa Kendall, "Coupa Café: Hot Spot for Silicon Valley Superstars," *San Jose Mercury News*, April 6, 2016, https://www.mercurynews .com/2016/04/06/coupa-cafe-hot-spot-for-silicon-valley-superstars/.

135 a Swedish company introduced: Tempur-Pedic foam mattress history from Tempursealy.com, https://www.tempursealy.com/brands/#!/, and Fundinguni-verse.com, http://www.fundinguniverse.com/company-histories/tempur-pedic-inc -history/.

136 about 30 percent of mattress sales: "Sleeper Cell," mattress industry report for Lerer Hippeau venture capital firm, May 2, 2013, citing 2011 data from the Inter-national Sleep Products Association.

136 Tempur-Pedic bought Sealy in 2013: Tempur-Pedic International Inc., "Tempur-Pedic Completes Acquisition of Sealy," press release, March 18, 2013, https://news .tempursealy.com/press-release/corporate/tempur-pedic-completes-acquisition-sealy.

136 Serta and Simmons became majority owned: Advent International, https://www .adventinternational.com/investments/.

136 Mattress Firm gobbled up rivals: Jef Feeley, Matthew appearing on Townsend, and Laurel Brubaker Calkins, "How a Frenzied Expansion Brought Down Amer-ica's No. 1 Mattress Seller," Bloomberg News, November 28, 2018, https://www .bloomberg.com/news/articles/2018-11-28/how-a-breakneck-buildout-brought -down-america-s-mattress-leader.

136 A shop vacuum cleaner sucked air: Marino, appearing on "The Start-up That Launched the Horse Race of Online Mattress Companies."

137 "We had to do quite a few returns": Hacker News online conversation, December 13, 2013, https://news.ycombinator.com/item?id=6900625.

137 "The mattress industry is rotten": "We Need a Warby Parker for Mattresses," Priceonomics, September 14, 2012, https://priceonomics.com/mattresses/.

138 reaching $15 million in 2017: "Sleeper Cell" mattress industry report for Lerer Hippeau venture capital firm, May 2, 2013.

138 Lerer Hippeau became the lead investor: Lerer Hippeau, "Lerer Ventures Leads Seed Round for Casper," press release, February 25, 2014, https://www.pehub.com /2014/02/lerer-ventures-leads-seed-round-for-casper/.

138 it started with just one foam mattress model: As of mid-2019, Casper offered five mattress variations: its highest-priced Wave model in all-foam or hybrid with foam and springs; its original Casper in all-foam or hybrid; and its lowest-priced Essential in all-foam only; https://casper.com/mattresses/. Tuft & Needle went from one to three models, its highest-priced Mint mattress and its Original, both in all-foam only, and its lowest-priced Nod mattress, sold exclusively on Amazon; https://www.tuftandneedle.com/ and https://www.amazon.com/Nod-Tuft-Needle -Amazon-Exclusive-CertiPUR-US/dp/B07J31T4NC.

138 the number of articles about Casper: "Casper Sleep Inc.: Marketing the 'One Perfect Mattress for Everyone,'" Harvard Business School case study, November 15, 2017, https://www.hbs.edu/faculty/Pages/item.aspx?num=51747.

139 sales rose to $9 million in 2014: Tuft & Needle, "Company Info," https://press.tn .com/company-info/timeline/.

139 A Hacker News post online: Miguel Helft, "Meet the Warby Parker of Mat-tresses," *Fortune*, January 22, 2014, http://fortune.com/2014/01/22/meet-the -warby-parker-of-mattresses/.

140 "Don't worry about them": Author interview with Michael Traub, former chief executive of Serta Simmons Bedding, June 29, 2018.

140 There's a machine that uses: Testing equipment explained by Chris Chunglo, Serta Simmons Bedding head of R&D, during a tour on June 29, 2018.

140 for which Chunglo received a patent: U.S. Patent number 9,645,063, issued May 9, 2017, http://patft.uspto.gov/netacgi/nph-Parser?Sect1=PTO2&Sect2 =HITOFF&p=1&u=%2Fnetahtml%2FPTO%2Fsearch-bool.html&r=7&f =G&l=50&co1=AND&d=PTXT&s1=chunglo&OS=chunglo&RS=chunglo.

145 The Tomorrow Sleep mattress didn't go on sale: Serta Simmons, "Tomorrow Sleep, Powered by Serta Simmons Bedding, Launches with Innovative Direct-to-Consumer Sleep System," press release, June 27, 2017, https://www.prnewswire.com/news -releases/tomorrow-sleep-powered-by-serta-simmons-bedding-launches-with -innovative-direct-to-consumer-sleep-system-300479973.html.

146 alleging false advertising and deceptive practices: David Zax, "The War to Sell You a Mattress Is an Internet Nightmare," *Fast Company*, October 16, 2017, https:// www.fastcompany.com/3065928/sleepopolis-casper-bloggers-lawsuits-underside -of-the-mattress-wars.

147 Sleepopolis gave an updated, "very positive" review: Ibid.

147 "helps us maintain our own personal integrity": Sleepopolis, "Disclosures," https://sleepopolis.com/disclosures/.

147 Casper raised successive new rounds of funding: Crunchbase.com, https://www .crunchbase.com/organization/casper.

147 founded by Tony and Terry Pearce, two brothers in Utah: Purple Innovation, https://purple.com/about-us.

148 "Yes, these eggs are raw": "Goldilocks and the Original Egg Drop Test," https:// purple.com/videos.

148 the video had more than 5.8 million views: "How This Purple Mattress 20 Years in the Making Became an Overnight Success," Shopify.com, July 15, 2016, https://www .shopify.com/enterprise/how-a-purple-mattress-20-years-in-the-making-became -an-overnight-success-with-shopify.

148 ahead of Tuft & Needle's $170 million: Tuft & Needle, https://press.tn.com /company-info/timeline/.

148 its marketing and sales costs skyrocketed: Purple Innovation LLC financial statement, March 15, 2018, www.sec.gov/archives/edgar/data/1643953 /000121390018003018/f8k020218a2ex99-1_purpleinn.htm.

148 "to expand brand awareness": Joe Megibow, Purple Innovation chief executive, earnings call transcript, November 14, 2018, Seeking Alpha, https://seekingalpha .com/article/4222345-purple-innovation-inc-prpl-ceo-joe-megibow-q3-2018 -results-earnings-call-transcript?page=2.

148 Tomorrow Sleep's sales finally began picking up: Ken Stauffer, Tomorrow Sleep head of operations and customer experience, LinkedIn.com profile, https://www .linkedin.com/in/ken-stauffer-b6b05895/; Serta Simmons declined to discuss Tomorrow Sleep sales figures.

149 sales approaching $2 billion: The estimate of U.S. online mattress sales in 2018 was provided to the author by Serta Simmons Bedding. Purple's estimate of its 2019 sales is contained in the company's Form 8-K filing with the Securities and Exchange Commission, August 13, 2019, http://www.snl.com/cache/c399169470.html.

149 Tuft & Needle has been profitable: Author interview with John-Thomas Marino, cofounder of Tuft & Needle, September 27, 2018.

149 Casper anticipated posting a small profit: Zoe Bernard, "Inside Casper's Financials," *The Information*, March 27, 2019, https://www.theinformation.com/articles/inside-caspers-financials.

149 becoming the "Nike of sleep," in the words of its executives: Jake Horowitz, "Inside Casper's Plan to Win Millennials by Tackling the Sleep Epidemic," *Mic*, May 14, 2016, https://www.mic.com/articles/137727/inside-casper-mattress-plan-to-win-millennials-by-tackling-the-sleep-epidemic.

149 selling a $129 Glow Light: Product prices and descriptions listed on Casper website, https://casper.com/glow-light/ and https://casper.com/cbd/.

150 Advent executives reached out to JT Marino: Author interview with John-Thomas Marino, September 27, 2018.

151 Marino and Park owned nearly 90 percent: Author interview with Daehee Park, cofounder Tuft & Needle, March 19, 2019.

151 Casper is valued at $1.1 billion: Casper, "Casper Raises $100 million and Adds Two New Independent Directors to Its Board," press release, March 27, 2019, https://www.prnewswire.com/news-releases/casper-raises-100-million-and-adds-two-new-independent-directors-to-its-board-300819857.html.

151 Michael Traub, who had championed: Serta Simmons, "Serta Simmons Bedding Announces CEO Transition," press release, April 10, 2019, https://www.sertasimmons.com/news/serta-simmons-bedding-announces-ceo-transition/.

Chapter 10: Breaking the Sound Barrier

153 *Time* and *Popular Science* have both put Eargo: "Best Inventions 2018: A Hearing Aid Meant for the Masses," *Time*, http://time.com/collection/best-inventions-2018/5454218/eargo-max/; "Best What's New," *Popular Science*, October 9, 2015, https://www.popsci.com/best-of-whats-new-2015/healthcare; James Trew, "Eargo Neo Is a Hearing Aid You Might Actually Want to Wear," Engadget.com, January 10, 2019, https://www.engadget.com/2019/01/10/eargo-neo-hearing-aid-hands-on/; Donovan Alexander, "15 Inventions That Will Make Your 2019 a Lot More Interesting," Interestingengineering.com, January 15, 2019, https://interestingengineering.com/15-inventions-that-will-make-your-2019-a-lot-more-interesting.

154 As of early 2019, it had raised $135 million: Author interview with David Wu, partner at Maveron venture capital firm, a major investor in Eargo, February 13, 2019.

155 In 2019, with more than seven hundred thousand: SmileDirectClub Inc.'s Amendment No. 1 to Form S-1 Registration Statement filing with the Securities and Exchange Commission, September 3, 2019, https://www.sec.gov/Archives/edgar/data/1775625/000104746919004925/a2239521zs-1a.htm. In the filing, the company reported revenue of $373.5 million in the first half of 2019, a 113 percent increase over the prior-year period. If that growth rate continued for the year as a whole, sales for 2019 would increase to $902 million from $423.2 million in 2018.

155 their trade group filed complaints with regulators: "Getting Your Teeth Straightened at a Strip Mall? Doctors Have a Warning," Bloomberg News, September 20, 2018, https://www.bloomberg.com/news/features/2018-09-20/orthodonists-aren-t-smiling-about-teeth-straightening-startups.

156 They both sold behind-the-ear hearing aids: iHearMedical.com hearing aids start at $499 per ear (https://www.ihearmedical.com/), and Audicus.com hearing aids start at $699 per ear (https://www.audicus.com/).

158 the firm agreed to lead a $2.6 million seed investment round: Author interview with Raphael Michel, Eargo cofounder, March 7, 2019.

160 Eargo offered free sixty-day trials: The free-trial period is now forty-five days, https://eargo.com/misc/warranty.

160 return rates range from 10 to 30 percent: Author interview with Christian Gormsen, chief executive of Eargo, August 7, 2018.

160 TechCrunch, a widely followed technology news site: Christine Magee, "With $13 Million from Maveron, Eargo Is the Hearing Aid of the Future," TechCrunch, June 25, 2015, https://techcrunch.com/2015/06/25/with-13-million-from-maveron -eargo-is-the-hearing-aid-of-the-future/.

160 "They are tiny, lightweight, comfortable": Matthew D. Sarrel, "Eargo Hearing Aids," PCMag.com, August 4, 2015, https://www.pcmag.com/article2/0,2817,2488793,00.asp.

161 The number of people responding: Author interview with Christian Gormsen, August 7, 2018.

161 just six months after Eargo's previous fund-raising: Eargo, "Eargo Raises $25 Million in Series B Funding from New Enterprise Associates," press release, December 9, 2015, https://www.eargo.com/assets/news/eargo-b27ea73b18f3bda2 df94bf51df908fa2.pdf.

162 "This is like a Shakespearean tragedy": Author interview with Christian Gormsen, August 7, 2018.

162 He took a new job as head of strategy: Raphael Michel left his job as Eargo's head of strategy in 2018 to become founder and chief executive of another VC-backed start-up, Onera Health, aimed at using diagnostic technology to help people sleep better. But he remained a member of Eargo's board of directors.

163 Schwab himself had tried many different hearing aids: Author interview with Charles Schwab, March 12, 2019.

164 reaching about $6.5 million for the year: Author interview with Christian Gormsen, June 20, 2019.

165 the first model now selling for $1,650: https://shop.eargo.com/eargo-plus.

165 now owns about 10 percent of the company: Author interview with Charles Schwab, March 12, 2019.

Chapter 11: Flying High, Then Crashing to Earth

167 "@oprah and @oprahmagazine have named": Instagram post, November 3, 2016, https://www.instagram.com/raden/p/BMXW2SoBq9_/.

167 "My mind is blown": "Oprah's Favorite Things 2016: Flights of Fancy, Raden Carry-on and Check-in Set," http://www.oprah.com/gift/oprahs-favorite-things -2016-full-list-carry-on-and-check-in-set?editors_pick_id=65969#ixzz5h3lSt1O1.

167 Raden's customers: Zachary Kussin, "This Suitcase Has a 10,000-Person Wait List," New York Post, February 7, 2017, https://nypost.com/2017/02/07/this -suitcase-has-a-10000-person-wait-list/.

167 First-year sales were about $6 million: Email correspondence with Josh Udashkin, Raden founder, June 12, 2019.

168 Kellogg's paid $600 million: Kellogg, "Kellogg Adds RXBAR, Fastest Growing U.S. Nutrition Bar, to Wholesome Snacks Portfolio," press release, October 6, 2017, http://newsroom.kelloggcompany.com/2017-10-06-Kellogg-adds-RXBAR -fastest-growing-U-S-nutrition-bar-brand-to-wholesome-snacks-portfolio.

168 The online watch company MVMT: Movado, "Movado Group Announces Agreement to Acquire MVMT," press release, August 15, 2018, https://www .businesswire.com/news/home/20180815005708/en/Movado-Group-Announces -Agreement-Acquire-MVMT.

168 Procter & Gamble acquired: "Procter & Gamble Just Bought This Venture-Backed Deodorant Start-up for $100 Million Cash," TechCrunch, November 15, 2017, https://techcrunch.com/2017/11/15/procter-gamble-just-bought-this-venture-backed-deodorant-startup-for-100-million-cash/.

168 Amazon bought the digital doorbell start-up: Jeffrey Dastin and Greg Roumeliotis, "Amazon Buys Start-up Ring in $1 Billion Deal to Run Your Home Security," Reuters, February 27, 2018, https://www.reuters.com/article/us-ring-m-a-amazon-com/amazon-buys-start-up-ring-in-1-billion-deal-to-run-your-home-security-idUSKCN1GB2VG.

168 bought Harry's: Edgewell, "Edgewell Personal Care to Combine with Harry's, Inc. to Create a Next-Generation Consumer Products Platform," press release, May 9, 2019, https://www.prnewswire.com/news-releases/edgewell-personal-care-to-combine-with-harrys-inc-to-create-a-next-generation-consumer-products-platform-300847130.html.

169 believes that this number is ten times higher: Author interviews with Simon Enever, Quip cofounder, November 2, 2018, and May 12, 2019.

169 Helping was a Bloomberg News story: Stephen Pulvirent, "Is Quip the Tesla of Toothbrushes?" Bloomberg News, August 5, 2016, https://www.bloomberg.com/news/articles/2015-08-06/is-quip-the-tesla-of-toothbrushes-.

169 Goby, by contrast: Pitchbook.com, https://pitchbook.com/profiles/company/166914-19.

169 Glossier . . . raised $186 million: According to Glossier communications department.

170 raised about $128 million: Crunchbase.com, https://www.crunchbase.com/organization/bonobos.

170 valued at around $500 million: Elizabeth Segran, "Here's Why Nobody Wants to Buy Birchbox, Even After VCs Spent $90M," Fast Company, May 4, 2018, https://www.fastcompany.com/40567670/heres-why-nobody-wants-to-buy-birchbox-even-after-vcs-spent-90m.

170 had fallen to about $30 million: Jason Del Ray, "Birchbox Has Sold Majority Ownership to One of Its Hedge Fund Investors After Sale Talks with QVC Fell Through," Recode.net, May 1, 2018, https://www.recode.net/2018/5/1/17305940/birchbox-recap-viking-global-qvc-merger-sale.

171 "The truth is, and I don't want to say this arrogantly": Sean O'Kane, "This Stylish Smart Suitcase Could Solve Some Big Travel Hassles," The Verge, March 29, 2016, https://www.theverge.com/2016/3/29/11321554/raden-smart-connected-luggage-gps-usb-power.

171 Sadow was granted a U.S. patent: U.S. Patent number 3,653,474, issued April 4, 1972.

171 "It was one of my best ideas": Joe Sharkey, "Reinventing the Suitcase by Adding the Wheel," New York Times, October 5, 2010, https://www.nytimes.com/2010/10/05/business/05road.html.

171 After initially operating out of his garage: Travelpro, "The History of Rolling Luggage," Problog, June 17, 2010, https://travelproluggageblog.com/2010/06/luggage/the-history-of-rolling-luggage/.

172 initial venture capital funding of $2.1 million: Author interview with Josh Udashkin, June 6, 2018.

173 Raden paid its Taiwanese manufacturer: Ibid.

174 A glowing New York Times story featured a photo of Udashkin: Matthew Schneier, "Your Suitcase Is Texting," New York Times, April 7, 2016, https://www.nytimes.com/2016/04/07/fashion/texting-raden-travel-suitcase.html.

174 Raden raised a second round of VC financing: Email correspondence with Josh Udashkin, June 12, 2019.

174 "One of the good outcomes": In a June 12, 2019, response to an email asking his view of this description, Raden founder Josh Udashkin wrote, "Maybe, but we were not entirely focused on exiting."

176 it raised another $20 million in VC funding: Crunchbase.com, https://www.crunchbase.com/organization/away-2.

177 "no longer accept as checked or carry-on luggage": Staff writer, "Delta Puts Limits on Select 'Smart Bags' Out of Safety Concerns," Delta Airlines, December 1, 2017, https://news.delta.com/delta-puts-limits-select-smart-bags-out-safety-concerns.

179 It tried to conserve its dwindling cash: Author interview with Thibault Le Conte, February 28, 2019.

179 featured Raden as its top pick: "Savvy Travelers Should Tote These Tech-Packed Suitcases," Wired, March 25, 2018, https://www.wired.com/story/smart-suitcases-rimowa-raden/.

180 "It's an unfortunate thing that happened": Leticia Miranda, "This Smart Luggage Company Is Going Out of Business," BuzzFeed News, May 17, 2018, https://www.buzzfeednews.com/article/leticiamiranda/this-smart-luggage-company-is-going-out-of-business.

180 It projected that its sales for the year: Away, "Away Is Valued at $1.4 Billion After a Series D Investment of $100 Million," press release, May 14, 2019, https://www.prnewswire.com/news-releases/away-is-valued-at-1-4-billion-after-a-series-d-investment-of-100-million-300850285.html.

180 it acquired the assets of Raden: Author interviews with Daniel Frydenlund, founder and chief executive, Stage Fund, March 12, 2019, and May 12, 2019.

180 including Lerer Hippeau and the founders of Casper: Email correspondence with Josh Udashkin, June 12, 2019.

Chapter 12: Back to the Future?

183 which drew more than seventy-five thousand visitors: "Lord & Taylor Open Fifth Avenue Store," New York Times, February 25, 1914.

183 had been sold for $850 million: Hudson's Bay Company, "HBC Closes Sale of the Lord & Taylor Fifth Avenue Building," press release, February 11, 2019, https://www.businesswire.com/news/home/20190211005142/en/HBC-Closes-Sale-Lord-Taylor-Avenue-Building.

183 "We are going to shut the company down": Lydia Dishman, "Site to Be Seen: Everlane.com," New York Times T Magazine, June 27, 2012, https://tmagazine.blogs.nytimes.com/2012/06/27/site-to-be-seen-everlane-com/.

184 Lord & Taylor once helped inaugurate: New York City Landmarks Preservation Commission, October 30, 2007, http://s-media.nyc.gov/agencies/lpc/lp/2271.pdf.

184 about 90 percent of all retail goods: U.S. Department of Commerce, "Quarterly Retail E-Commerce Sales, 1st Quarter 2019," U.S. Census Bureau News, May 17, 2019, https://www.census.gov/retail/mrts/www/data/pdf/ec_current.pdf.

185 In New York, visitors take selfies: Glossier closed the "Experiential Boy Brow Room" in 2019 and replaced it with a new "Into the Cloud Paint" room.

187 rents on that Greenwich Village street: Karin Nelson, "The Return of Bleecker Street," New York Times, December 4, 2018, https://www.nytimes.com/2018/12/04/style/bleecker-street-storefronts.html.

188 "Try on anything you like and have a cold one": https://bonobos.com/guideshop.

190 "First, and perhaps not too surprising": David Bell, Santiago Gallino, and Antonio Moreno, "How to Win in an Omnichannel World," *MIT Sloan Management Review* (Fall 2014), https://sloanreview.mit.edu/article/how-to-win-in-an-omnichannel-world/.

190 "We found that in locations where the bus stopped": Ibid.

190 retail stores and online sales . . . half of its overall revenue: Email correspondence with Kaki Read, April 16, 2019.

190 online sales rose 40 percent in cities: Ilyse Liffreing, "Shoppable Billboards: DTC Retailers Say Physical Stores Are Driving Online Sales," Digiday.com, September 18, 2018, https://digiday.com/marketing/shoppable-billboards-dtc-retailers-say-physical-stores-driving-online-sales/?utm_source=Sailthru&utm_medium=email&utm_campaign=Issue:%202018-09-19%20Retail%20Dive:%20Marketing%20%5Bissue:17191%5D&utm_term=Retail%20Dive:%20Marketing.

191 "To get you the help you need: Ra'el Cohen, ThirdLove chief creative officer, on ThirdLove blog, "ThirdLove's Concept Store Is Now Open!," July 23, 2019, https://www.thirdlove.com/blogs/unhooked/thirdlove-concept-store.

191 the number of shoppers entering its stores: Matthew Boyle, "The iPhone of Toothbrushes to Sell Offline, Too, in Target Push," Bloomberg News, October 1, 2018, https://www.bloomberg.com/news/articles/2018-10-01/the-iphone-of-toothbrushes-to-sell-offline-too-in-target-push.

192 after making an inquiry about buying the company outright: Jason Del Ray, "Target Looked at Buying the Mattress Start-up Casper for $1 Billion but Will Invest Instead," Recode.net, May 19, 2017, https://www.recode.net/2017/5/19/15659562/target-casper-investment-acquisition-talks-foam-mattress.

196 "I was inspired by your creation": Email from Mark Masinter, Open Realty Advisors, to Matt Alexander, February 27, 2017.

198 Less than a year after its first store opened: Matt Alexander, Neighborhood Goods cofounder and CEO, "Announcing Series A and Our Austin Location," September 11, 2019, https://neighborhoodgoods.com/stories/announcing-series-a-our-austin-location.

Chapter 13: Building a Digital Brand Factory

201 with sales of $73.3 million in 2018 and the goal of doubling that in 2019: Author interview with Yaniv Sarig, Mohawk Group cofounder and chief executive, on May 18, 2019.

202 reached nearly $600 million in 2017: Blake Schmidt and Venus Feng, "How to Turn Your Mom's Savings into $1 Billion? Ask This Guy," Bloomberg News, May 20, 2018, https://www.bloomberg.com/news/articles/2018-05-20/amazon-helps-shenzhen-ex-googler-turn-mom-s-money-into-a-billion.

202 "substantial doubt about our ability to continue": Mohawk Group Form S-1 filing with U.S. Securities and Exchange Commission, p. 18, May 10, 2019, https://www.sec.gov/archives/edgar/data/1757715/000119312519144273/d639806ds1.htm.

202 staggering volume of overall sales on Amazon.com: Jeff Bezos, "2018 Letter to Shareholders," April 11, 2019, https://blog.aboutamazon.com/company-news/2018-letter-to-shareholders.

203 they sold Titan to Google for about $150 million: Author interview with Asher Delug, investor and director of Titan Aerospace, April 29, 2019.

204 bringing total investment to $72.6 million: Mohawk Group Form S-1 filing with U.S. Securities and Exchange Commission, p. 66, May 10, 2019, https://www.sec.gov/archives/edgar/data/1757715/000119312519144273/d639806ds1.htm.

204 70 percent of shoppers never go past the first screen: Loren Baker, "Amazon's Search Engine Ranking Algorithm: What Marketers Need to Know," *Search Engine Journal*, August 14, 2018, https://www.searchenginejournal.com/amazon-search-engine-ranking-algorithm-explained/265173/.

205 collecting a fee (typically 15 percent): "Selling on Amazon Fee Schedule," Amazon Seller Central, https://sellercentral.amazon.com/gp/help/external/200336920.

205 search for "teeth whitening": Search performed on June 18, 2019, https://www.amazon.com/s?k=teeth+whitening&ref=nb_sb_noss_1.

205 About 70 percent of the searches: Julie Creswell, "How Amazon Steers Shoppers to Its Own Products," *New York Times*, June 23, 2018, https://www.nytimes.com/2018/06/23/business/amazon-the-brand-buster.html.

208 Of all the reviews for this: Based on reviews on Amazon.com on September 15, 2019. The precise percentages are constantly changing as new reviews are posted by Amazon customers. https://www.amazon.com/Frigidaire-EFIC103-Machine-Icemaker-Stainless/dp/B004VV8GOQ/ref=zg_bs_2399939011_43?_encoding=UTF8&psc=1&refRID=PADTWRA91KFXB010MK5A#customerReviews.

210 It had 1,548 customer reviews: Based on reviews on Amazon.com on April 22, 2019. The precise percentages are constantly changing as new reviews are posted by Amazon customers.

210 The hOmeLabs model would be edged aside: Amazon Best Sellers in Ice Makers, September 15, 2019, https://www.amazon.com/gp/bestsellers/appliances/2399939011/ref=pd_zg_hrsr_appliances. Though the hOmeLabs ice maker was officially ranked as the number five bestseller, one of the products listed ahead of it by Amazon actually was an ice maker water filter. The rankings of top-selling products on Amazon.com can fluctuate depending on customer purchases of different brands and models.

211 "Leaks all over the place": Amazon.com review for Vremi Olive Oil Dispenser Bottle—17 Oz Bottle Glass with No Drip Spout, October 27, 2017.

212 "because Amazon believed they were questionable": Mohawk Group Form S-1 filing with U.S. Securities and Exchange Commission, p. 24, May 10, 2019, https://www.sec.gov/archives/edgar/data/1757715/000119312519144273/d639806ds1.htm.

212 "While the idea of having": "Mohawk Group—Failed IPO," Seeking Alpha, June 13, 2019, https://seekingalpha.com/article/4270193-mohawk-group-failed-ipo.

212 Another company has launched nearly two hundred brands: Amazon.com and TJI Research, https://this.just.in/amazon-brand-database/.

213 "Private Brands is a highly-visible": From Amazon job postings in April 2019, https://www.amazon.jobs/en.

213 it keeps "going and going": Energizer, https://www.energizer.com/energizer-bunny/bunny-timeline.

213 as many as six to eight of the top fifteen brands: "Best Sellers in Household Batteries," Amazon.com, https://www.amazon.com/Best-Sellers-Electronics-Household-Batteries/zgbs/electronics/15745581.

214 *New York* magazine ran a story: Katy Schneider, "The Unlikely Tale of a $140 Amazon Coat That's Taken Over the Upper East Side," *New York*, March

27, 2018, http://nymag.com/strategist/2018/03/the-orolay-amazon-coat-thats
-overtaken-the-upper-east-side.html.

214 Company founder Kevin Chiu: Pei Li and Melissa Fares, "Chinese Firm Behind
the 'Amazon Coat' Hits Jackpot in U.S., Eschews China," Reuters, February 24,
2019, https://www.reuters.com/article/us-china-coat-orolay/chinese-firm-behind
-the-amazon-coat-hits-jackpot-in-u-s-eschews-china-idUSKCN1QD0YD.

215 "are kicking our first party butt": Jeff Bezos, "2018 Letter to Shareholders."

215 Amazon's sales of its own products: "Accelerating Pace of Amazon's Private Label
Launches to Broaden AMZN's Moat," SunTrust Robinson Humphrey, June 4,
2018.

215 new private-label Amazon brands: Even on Amazon.com, it can be difficult to find
all of Amazon's private-label brands. It has a page labeled "Explore Our Brands"
(https://www.amazon.com/b?ie=UTF8&node=17602470011), but a shopper
needs to click through nearly twenty different product categories to see Amazon's
private-label brands in each category.

215 "Look at my listing": Posting on Amazon Services Seller Central forum, August 2018,
https://sellercentral.amazon.com/forums/t/not-very-nice-of-amazon-tagging-on
-my-listing/416713/2.

Chapter 14: The Brand Is Dead, Long Live the Brand

220 By 2018, they together had grabbed: Euromonitor International, a market research
provider, estimates that Dollar Shave Club had a 10.5 percent share and Harry's
had a 3.2 percent share of the U.S. market for men's razors and blades as measured in dollars in 2018. Although Euromonitor doesn't track unit volume, the
two companies' combined market share as measured in the number of razors and
blades sold would be higher, probably approaching around 20 percent, because
their products are less expensive.

220 It is equally hard to imagine Gillette: Euromonitor International estimates that
Gillette had a 52.8 percent share of the U.S. market for men's razors and blades as
measured in dollars in 2018.

220 90 percent had lost market share in recent years: "Catalina Mid-Year Performance
Report Finds Challenging Market for Many of Top 100 CPG Brands," Catalina
Marketing Report, September 30, 2015, https://www.catalina.com/news/press
-releases/catalina-mid-year-performance-report-finds-challenging-market-for
-many-of-top-100-cpg-brands/.

220 more than half of all consumers consider significantly more brands: Accenture,
"U.S. Switching Economy up 29 Percent Since 2010 as Companies Struggle to
Keep Up with the Nonstop Customer, Finds Accenture," news release, January 21,
2015, https://newsroom.accenture.com/subjects/strategy/us-switching-economy
-up-29-percent-since-2010-as-companies-struggle-to-keep-up-with-the-nonstop
-customer-finds-accenture.htm.

220 "Single-brand loyalists are nearing extinction": "Findings from the 10th Annual
Time Inc./YouGov Survey of Affluence and Wealth," YouGov, April 27, 2015,
https://today.yougov.com/topics/lifestyle/articles-reports/2015/04/27/findings-10th
-annual-time-incyougov-survey-affluen.

221 $17 billion in sales shifted from big consumer brands to small brands: "The Next
Frontier: Leveraging Artificial Intelligence and Unstructured Metrics to Identify
CPG Growth Pockets and Outperforming Brands," October 2018 report by

predictive analytics research firm Information Resources Inc., https://www
.iriworldwide.com/IRI/media/Library/pdf/2018_IRI_Demand-Portfolio_2-0_POV
.pdf.

221 small- and medium-size companies sold $160 billion in goods on Amazon: "Small
Business Means Big Opportunity: 2019 Amazon SMB Impact Report," May 7, 2019,
https://d39w7f4ix9f5s9.cloudfront.net/61/3b/1f0c2cd24f37bd0e3794c284cd2f
/2019-amazon-smb-impact-report.pdf.

Acknowledgments

After working for several decades as an editor, I rediscovered the joys of writing again while doing this book—and some of the frustrations, too. Reporting is ultimately about discovery, embarking on a journey that takes you to many different places, some of them that you planned to visit and others that you stumbled upon. It's also about meeting interesting people along the way—in my case, entrepreneurs who were on their own journeys.

It often occurred to me that what I was doing had many things in common with what they were doing. You start with a vision of where you want to end up, but with an otherwise open road ahead, and then you travel all over the map, even as you occasionally ask yourself, When am I going to get there, and will it be the place I want to go?

And then, just when you think that you shouldn't have bothered heading down a particular trail, you meet someone with a compelling story to tell, or you learn about a potentially fascinating factoid that you just have to track down. Slowly, just like an entrepreneur starting a company, you begin to feel that you are on the right path and the journey has been its own reward.

This journalistic excursion now completed, I have many people to thank for helping—some for their advice and counsel on this book, but many who helped me become a better reporter over the years.

I owe so much to my brother, Paul Ingrassia, a celebrated journalist and author of three books, who died in September 2019 as I was finishing this book. He gave me unstinting encouragement throughout my career and instantly told me to go for it when I mentioned that I was thinking about writing a book. Even more, Paul inspired me with the dignity he showed in the face of adversity and tragedy through many bouts with cancer over more than two decades. Everyone should be so lucky to have a brother like Paul.

I have also been lucky to work with some of America's finest reporters, including Ron Suskind, Charles Duhigg, Andrew Ross Sorkin, Helene Cooper, Jenny Anderson, Robert Frank, Diana Henriques, Nick Bilton, Kevin Helliker, Joe Nocera, David Barboza, Bob Hillman, Susanne Craig, David Leonhardt, Nik Deogun, Steve Lipin, and Laura Landro, many of them also authors. Thank you for inspiring me and, even more, for being such great friends. You made it all fun.

I am fortunate, as well, to have worked over the years for so many gifted newspaper editors, who gave me a chance and urged me to think ambitiously, and not to settle for anything but the best: Jill Abramson, Paul Steiger, Bill Keller, John Geddes, and Norman Pearlstine. And with many editing sidekicks: Michael Siconolfi, Adam Bryant, Winnie O'Kelley, Dean Murphy, Paula Dwyer, Bill Grueskin, Susan Chira, John Bussey, Glenn Kramon, Tim O'Brien, Davan Maharaj, Dick Stevenson, Gary Putka, Tom Redburn, Phil Revzin, Joanne Lipman, Alison Mitchell, and Kimi Yoshino.

I'd also like to thank the many entrepreneurs and others who graciously gave me their time, the most precious commodity for anyone trying to build a start-up at breakneck speed. I interviewed nearly two hundred people, a number of them more than once. It takes a leap of faith to do what they did—starting a business (most of all) and then opening up to a writer about the ups and downs along the way.

My talented editor, Paul Golob, provided smart thoughts and guidance throughout ("Stay on point"), from the moment we first chatted about my proposal to the last dangling participle he caught in my manuscript. Also, thanks to my agent, Eric Lupfer, who about midway through the third sentence of my pitch for this book said he totally got the idea and then begin riffing about ways to sharpen the theme and shape the narrative. I'm also grateful to friends who provided me with encouragement (and room and board!): Pat and Susanne Dowdall, Bob and Carlo Prinsky, Glynn and Elizabeth Mapes, and Amy Stillman.

And more than anyone, I want to thank my wife, Vicki, who was at my side, supporting and cheering me at every step along the way, as she has always been. Vicki was my final reader, checking my prose and prompting me to get across the finish line. Many of the people I've thanked will attest to what a special person she is. Thanks also to our children, Nick and Lisa, and their spouses, Sarah and Chris, who shared valuable insights and thoughts about my book, and who have blessed us with their love—and our grandchildren (Charlie, Mason, Nate, Riley, and Georgina). There is no greater joy.

Index

Abercrombie and Fitch, 188
A-B tests, 75
Accenture, 220
accessories, 175–76
acne treatment, 39
acquisitions, 21–22, 25, 121, 124, 127,
    150–51, 168, 170
Active Wow, 206
Advent International, 136, 145,
    150–51
advertising, 13, 18–19, 26, 33–34, 56,
    66–83, 147–50, 160, 178, 186.
    See also marketing
  Amazon and, 209
  Ampush and, 75–76
  Facebook and, 71–72, 74–77
  Google and, 74–75
Aéropostale, 59
affiliate fees, 146–47
AIMEE (Artificial Intelligence Mohawk
    E-commerce Engine), 200–201,
    205–12
Airbnb, 129, 130
airlines, 177
Alba, Jessica, 167

Aldi, 13
Aldo Group, 170
Alexa, 215
Alexander, Matt, 196–97, 199
algorithms, 78, 84–88, 115–16, 126, 187,
    209
Algorithms Tour, 88
Alibaba, 48, 62
Alipay, 49
Allbirds, 79, 183, 217
AllPoints Systems, 117–18
Allswell, 149, 193
Alphabet Inc., 204
Alpha Club, 36
Alston, Bryan, 174, 175, 176, 178
Amazon, 30, 200, 137, 139
  "Best Sellers," 210
  brands created to be sold on,
    200–216
  buyer reviews and, 207–8, 211–12
  data analytics and, 87, 204–8
  free shipping and, 123
  Kiva bought by, 121, 124, 127
  logistics and, 118, 126–27
  prime digital shelf space and, 209

Amazon (*cont'd*)
  private-label brands created by, 149,
    212–17, 220
  Quiet Logistics and, 127–28
  Ring bought by, 168
  small company sales on, 215–16,
    221
  Sponsored ads on, 209
  warehouses and logistics and, 120–22,
    129–30
  working conditions and, 122
AmazonBasics, 213, 215
Amazon Delivery Service Partner, 123
Amazon Flex, 123
Amazon Locker, 122–23
Amazon Marketplace, 204–5, 218
Amazon's Choice label, 210, 214
American Tourister, 166
Ames Research Center, 135
Amos, Chris, 72–73
Ampush, 18, 72–78
Andre, Bret, 50–53
Aniello, Lucia, 6–7
Anker, 202, 211
Apple, 15, 42, 172, 194
Apple Stores, 194–95
appliances, 130, 200–201, 207–11
Arfa Inc., 222
artwork frames, 42
Asian outsourcing companies, 46–47
Audicus, 156
audience platform, 74
audiogram, 154
audiologists, 153, 159
AuraGlow, 206
auto parts and accessories, 42, 142–43
Away, 38, 79, 107, 127, 166–67, 173–80,
    183, 190–91, 217

B8ta, 199
barriers to entry, 27, 103, 134, 168
Bata, Aaron, 105
batteries, 213
Battery Ventures, 16
Bausch & Lomb, 45, 50–51, 54–55, 57
BBC, 120
Beats, 172
BedInABox, 136–37
Belei, 212

Bell, David R., 32–35, 101, 103, 222
Bellantoni, Karen, 188, 190
Berger, Brian, 120
beverage fridges, 201, 210
Bezos, Jeff, 121, 214–15
Bic, 14
bicycles, 42, 48
billboards, 82, 189
Birchbox, 170
Birdies, 38, 217
Bloomberg News, 48–49, 138, 169
Bloomingdale's, 174, 198
Blueprint, 111
Bluesmart, 166–67, 173–74, 176–77,
    179–80
Bluetooth, 165–66, 172
Blumenthal, Neil, 30–31, 38, 97–100,
    103–5, 107–8, 111–13, 190, 221
Blumenthal, Rachel, 38
Boka, 168
Bonobos, 9, 25, 29–30, 35, 104–5,
    114–15, 119, 170, 183, 188, 195–97,
    218, 222
Bosch, 139
braces, 42, 155
BrandBox, 199
Brandless, 79, 217
brassieres, 42, 59–69, 81, 168, 191
Bridgewater Associates, 49
Brin, Sergey, 135
broadcast advertising, 41
Brookfield Place, 185
Brooklinen, 79
Bruush, 168
Buick, Malcolm, 55
Burch, Tory, 167
Burrow, 183
Burst, 168,-69
Businessweek, 120
BuzzFeed News, 180

call centers, 104–7
Camp Moonlight, 214
Canada Goose, 214
Care/of, 88–89
Cargo, 130–31
Casper, 40, 130, 138–41, 144, 146–51,
    169, 180, 183, 191–92, 201, 214,
    218

Cat & Jack, 192
Cavalcade of Sports, 13
Cavitt, Kim, 153
CBD, 149–50
Chanel, 30
check-out experience, 113
Chelsea Market, 199
Cherison, Nisho, 81–82
China, 48, 57, 62, 64–65, 98, 177, 202, 211
Chiu, Kevin, 214
Chunglo, Chris, 140–41
Clairol, 85, 90
Clark, Melissa, 137
cleaning products, 42, 212
clothing and apparel, 9, 28–30, 38–39, 42, 62, 77, 104, 183, 188, 192–93, 211, 213–14
CNBC, 120
Coastal Blue, 217
Cogan, Ben, 44–46, 49–56
Cohen, Ra'el, 60, 62, 69, 191
Colen, Sandy, 37–38
Colgate-Palmolive, 21, 57
Collins, Erin, 108, 110–11
Color&Co, 96
Colson, Eric, 88
computer-vision technology, 61, 88
Consumer Reports, 20
contact lenses, 45, 49–57, 79, 193, 198
contact lens regulations, 53, 55–56
ContactsCart, 57
conversion rate, 80
cookware, 183, 213
CooperVision, 45, 50–51
cosmetics, 38, 79, 101–2
Cotopaxi, 38
Craigslist, 61
Crest Whitestrips, 206
curling irons, 210
Curology, 39
customer acquisition cost (CAC), 6, 68, 86, 186
customer experience (CX), 34, 99–113
customers
    after-sales hand-holding and, 164
    competing for, 168
    connecting or bonding with, 34–35, 39, 41, 98, 101–2, 219–20

cost per order, 176
    physical retail space and, 186, 192
    product promotion by, 71
    soliciting advice from, 101
    targeting, through data, 34–35, 86
Czech manufacturers, 48

Daisy Drive, 214
Dare, Tom, 8
data analysis, 25, 33–35, 61–62, 68, 84–86, 89–96, 107–8, 112, 193, 196–97, 201, 204–12
Davis, Henry, 39–40, 102, 169–70, 185–86, 187, 222
DegreeAmerica.com, 73
dehumidifiers, 201, 210
Delta Airlines, 177
Delug, Asher, 203–4
demand experiment, 52–53
dental insurance, 169
deodorant, 168
department store, reinventing, 193–99
DHL, 126, 127
Diapers.com, 30, 34–35, 212
DiClemente, Gabrielle, 81
direct-mail advertising, 82, 86
direct-to-consumer (DTC) businesses
    advertising and marketing and, 13, 18–19, 26, 33–34, 55–56, 66–83, 138–39, 147–50, 160, 163–64, 167, 175, 178–79, 186
    customer relations and, 34–35, 39, 41, 98–113, 219–20
    funding, 16–17, 33, 36–39 (*see also* venture capital)
    future of, 218–22
    physical retail space and, 104, 182–99
    product sourcing and manufacturing and, 10, 13–14, 45–65, 163, 175, 211
    rise of, 1–22
    warehouse space and, 116–31
discounts, 49, 123, 175
distribution centers, 122
Dollar Shave Club, 2–22, 25, 36, 38–40, 43, 49–52, 57–58, 71, 76–79, 82, 102–3, 137, 139, 168–69, 176, 186–87, 197–98, 200, 214, 217–18, 220

doorbells, 168
Dorco, 10, 12–13, 17–18, 21–22
down jackets, 214
Draper James, 39
drones, 122, 203
Drugstore.com, 118
Dubin, Michael, 1–22, 36, 38–39, 50, 59,
    76, 78, 147, 176, 197–98, 200
Dunn, Andy, 29–30, 188, 196

Eargo, 152–65
eBay, 142, 158, 204
eBay Motors, 142
Echo speaker, 215
Edgewell Personal Care Co., 21, 168, 218
1800contacts.com, 57
electric toothbrushes, 42, 48, 79, 168–69,
    191–92
electronic products, 202, 213
Ella Moon, 214
Ely, Mark, 103
eMusic, 15
energy bars, 168
Enever, Simon, 169, 192
Engadget, 153
eSalon.com, 84–86, 89–96, 108
Estée Lauder, 218
Evans, Chris, 189
Eveready, 118
Everlane, 183, 217
Experian, 89
eyeglasses, 9, 30–33, 58–59, 81, 97–108,
    112, 190, 221
Eyeglasses.Com, 99

Facebook, 2, 9, 18–19, 29, 34, 53, 57,
    67, 71–82, 112, 160, 169, 186–87,
    200, 209
  ad limits and, 81, 187
  Lookalike Audience and, 67–68, 70, 78
  Preferred Marketing Developers, 76
  Strategic Preferred Marketing
    Developer, 76
Farmer's Dog, 39, 88, 183, 217
fashion, 119, 168
Fast Company, 66, 146
Faulk, Rick, 127
Federal Trade Commission (FTC), 57
Federer, Roger, 7

FedEx, 119, 123
Fi GPS Smart Dog Collar, 217
Fire Phone, 215
Fit Finder Quiz, 69, 80
Flexe, 129–31
Flexi Fibers, 159
Food and Drug Administration (FDA),
    45, 50, 52–53, 159
Forbes, 66
Forerunner Ventures, 17, 22–25, 36–40,
    170, 176, 195, 221–22
for-profit colleges, 73, 75–76
Fortune, 15, 139
founders, ownership diluted by VC, 174
Fourpost, 199
FramesDirect, 99
Frederick, Corey, 112
free trials, 66–68, 160
Frigidaire, 208, 210
Frydenlund, Daniel, 180–81
Fulton, Chris, 177
furniture, 42, 119, 183, 212

Gap, 67, 188
General Motors (GM), 143
Gilboa, David, 30, 99
Gillette, 2–3, 5–9, 12–22, 27, 36, 39, 41,
    59, 77, 139, 218–20
Gillette, King C., 3–4
Gilt Groupe, 119
Gimenez, Francisco, 86, 90–91
Ginko International, 57
Giorgio Armani, 30
Gleam, 168
Gleem, 168
globalization, 4, 46–49
Glossier, 38–40, 71, 79, 101–3, 169–70,
    183–86, 188, 193, 200, 218, 222
GlossierBrown, 101
Glow Light, 149
Goby, 168–69
Goggles4u, 99
Goldman Sachs, 72, 75
gold star companies, 48
Goodman, Marla, 101, 185
Google, 9, 41, 59, 62, 71–74, 145, 201,
    203–4, 209
Google Checkout and Shopping, 59
Gordon, Stephen, 194

Gorecki, Ryan, 130–131
Gormsen, Christian, 152–53, 155, 158, 161–65
GQ, 33
Grand Junction, 192
Great Jones, 217
Green, Draymond, 167
Green, Kirsten, 17, 23–25, 27–30, 33, 36–40, 167, 170, 176, 195–97, 221–22
Grobart, Sam, 48–49
groceries, 79
Guess, 188
GV, 204

Hacker News, 139
hair coloring, 78–79, 84, 89–96
hair-loss products for men, 38, 42, 193
Hales, Derek, 145–47
Happy Belly, 212–13
Harrison, Brad, 14
Harry's, 18, 21, 27, 44, 49, 51, 139, 168–69, 191, 198, 218–20
hate list, 134
Hawkins, David, 76, 78
hearing aids, 152–65
HelloBeautiful, 66
Henkel, 96
Henri Bendel, 188
Hill, Ken, 10, 18
Hims, 38, 193
Hinomoto wheels, 173, 175
home décor, 82, 183
hOmeLabs, 130, 200–201, 203, 208–10, 217
Home Try-On, 32, 36, 68, 88, 97–98, 108–10, 112
Honda, 143
Honeywell, 41
Horwitz, Jesse, 44–46, 49–57, 198
HSBC, 56
Hubble, 45–46, 49–57, 58, 71, 78–79, 193, 198, 200, 217
Huffington Post, 100
Huggies, 34
Human Ocean Wing E-commerce, 202
Hybrid Designs, 88
hydrogel, 51, 52, 56

ice makers, 200–201, 207–10
Idea Farm Ventures, 222

iHear Medical, 156
Inc., 66
    5000 list, 78
India, 58, 104
Indochino, 183
influencers, paid, 71
Innovel, 130
Instagram, 9, 29, 40, 71, 79, 82, 101, 167, 184, 186–87, 200
inStyle, 66
intent platform, 74
Interactive Advertising Bureau, 26
Interesting Engineering, 153
International Sleep Products Association, 138
intimate apparel, 183
Into the Gloss blog, 39, 101–2
inventory, 62, 97–99, 117, 167, 174, 176, 179, 191
iPhone, 61–62, 69, 111
IPOs, 168, 202
iTunes, 15

Japan, 10, 51, 54, 124, 143, 173
J. Crew, 188
Jet.com, 25
Jiaxing Zichi Trade Co., 214
Jobs, Steve, 135, 194–95
Johnson, Michael, 117–21, 124–27
Johnson & Johnson, 45, 57
Jones, Michael, 7–10, 17

Kai, 10
Kalvaria, Selena, 175–76
Kangaroo, 130, 218
Kaplan University, 73
Katz-Mayfield, Andy, 219
Kaziukenas, Juozas, 205, 212, 214–15
Kellogg's, 72, 168
Kerouac, Jack, 35
keyword bids, 74–77, 81
Kickstarter, 168
Kim, John Brian, 77–78
kitchenware, 201
Kiva Systems, 118–21, 124–25, 127
Kleiner Perkins, 16
Kmart, 13, 128, 130
Korey, Steph, 107, 175
Koulouris, George, 172–74

Krim, Philip, 138–39
Kumar, Adrian, 127

Lackenby, Steve, 11
Laczay, Tibor, 99, 100
Lai, Patricia, 72, 75
Lane Bryant, 62
Lark & Ro, 214
Laseter, Tim, 123
last-mile problem, 116, 123
laundry detergent, 42
L Brands, 83
lead generation, 73, 76
Le Conte, Thibault, 176, 178–79
Leesa, 146, 183
Lensabl, 221
LensCrafters, 30
Lerer, Ben, 33, 137–38
Lerer Hippeau, 24, 33, 137–38, 170, 180
Levine, Mark, 5, 22
Levi Strauss, 218
Levy, Brian, 50–53
lifestyle branding, 175–76
lifetime guarantee, 175
Lingley, Ann, 95
LinkedIn, 62
Lively, 183
Locus Robotics, 114–17, 125–28, 130
logistics, 115–23
Lola, 217
Lookalike Audience, 78
Lord & Taylor, 182–84, 193–94
L'Oréal, 90, 96
Louis Vuitton, 172
LTV (lifetime value), 77, 86
luggage
    rolling, 171
    smart, 38, 42, 79, 107, 166, 168,
        170–81, 190–91, 213
Lull, 130
Lumi, 39
Luxottica, 30, 36, 108, 219
LVMH, 180
Lyft, 130

machinery, hair coloring production,
    92–93
MacNeil, Thomas, 85, 94–95
Macy's, 174, 188, 198

Made In, 183
Madison Reed, 78–79
Mahoney, Patrick, 106–7
malls, 27, 194–95
Mama Bear, 212, 218
manufacturing, 47–55, 57, 59, 62–65,
    163, 211
Maridou, Evan, 189
Marino, John-Thomas "JT," 133–39,
    145–46, 149–51
marketing, 55, 138–39, 163–64, 167, 175,
    179. See also advertising
    cost per order, 176
    costs of, 212
    data analytics and, 86–87
    discounts and, 175
    physical space as tool for, 189–90
marketing software, 39
Marketplace Pulse, 205
market share, 3, 13, 14, 19, 21, 22, 27,
    36, 45, 54, 59, 83, 96, 165, 209, 211,
    220, 221
Marlboro Man, 101
Masinter, Mark, 193–98
mattresses, 40, 42, 79, 105, 130, 132–51,
    183, 188–89, 191, 193
Mattress Firm, 136, 142
Maveron, 154–55, 157–58, 160–62
May Department Stores, 118
McGhee, Devin, 101–102
McKinsey consulting, 158
MeCommerce Inc., 60
medical devices, 130, 153–54, 158
#MeToo era, 82
MeUndies, 193, 217
Mexican manufacturers, 63–65
M.Gemi, 39
Michael Kors, 188
Michel, Florent, 155–56, 158–59
Michel, Raphael, 156–62, 164–65
Microsoft, 76
Millennials, 16, 28, 40, 55, 100, 167, 172,
    185
minifridges, 130, 201
moats, 103
mobile shopping apps, 39
Mockingbird, 218
ModCloth, 183
Moeller, Jon R., 20

Mohawk Group, 130, 201–13, 215, 221
monocles, 107
Montgomery Securities, 27
Montgomery Ward, 121–22
mountain bikes, 48
Mourad, Omar, 91–92, 94–96
Mourad, Tamim, 85, 89–93
Movado, 168
MultiThreaded blog, 88
Murphy, Bryan, 142–45, 148, 151
Music Parts Plus, 119
MVMT, 79, 168–69, 217
Myspace, 8

NASA, 60, 135
Native, 168, 191, 217
Nau, 28–29
Nectar, 149
Neighborhood Goods, 192–99
Neiman Marcus, 214
Nest Labs, 41–42
Netflix, 87
New Enterprise Associates, 161
New York magazine, 214
New York Times, 22, 57, 83, 138, 171, 174, 183
Nike, 28
Nordstrom, 198, 214
Norton, Mike, 19, 22
nutritional supplements, 212

oligopoly, 153
Olsavsky, Brian, 123
One Kings Lane, 82, 183
One Wipe Charlies, 76
Ong, Jason, 45, 54
"Open Letter to Victoria's Secret, An" (Zak), 83
"Oprah's Favorite Things 2016," 167, 174
optometrists, 46, 52, 54, 56
Orolay Down Jacket, 214
orthodontist, 155
outdoor gear, 38, 130
Outdoor Voices, 39, 183, 217
OWN PWR, 212

Packagd, 39
packaging manufacturers, 39, 120
Painted Heart, 214

Pakistan manufacturers, 48–49
Pakman, David, 14–16, 20, 40–43
Pampers, 34
Panjiva, 47
Park, Daehee, 133–36, 139, 150–51
Patagonia, 28
patents, 4, 14, 20, 61, 127, 140, 171
Pauquet, Jurgen, 164
Payless, 188
PC Magazine, 160
Pearce, Terry, 147
Pearce, Tony, 147
Pearl Automation, 42
Pearle Vision, 30
Pepsi, 72
performance marketing, 71
personal-care products, 222
personal shopping, 87
pet food, 39, 88, 168, 183, 212
Pham, Peter, 9–10, 16–17, 19, 36, 76
Philip Morris, 101
Philippines, 104
Pierce, Eliot, 137
pillows, 149
Pinterest, 88
Pinzon, 212–13
Pixel, 221
Plath, Robert, 171, 179
Playtex, 62
plug-and-play technology, 25
podcasts, 82
Popular Science, 153
pop-up stores, 173–74, 190–91, 193, 195–96
Powell, Veronique, 67–68
Power, Bradley, 126
Prada, 30
predictive analytics, 86–89, 94–95
prescriptions, 55–57
Presto!, 212
Preysman, Michael, 183
PriceGrabber, 89–91
Priceonomics, 137
pricing, 20, 31, 34, 56, 93, 132–33, 136, 138, 173, 175, 177
    testing, 95
print advertising, 77, 82, 83
private equity firms, 27, 136, 145, 150, 180
private labels, 54, 216

Procter & Gamble, 14, 16, 20, 102, 168, 204, 206
products. *See also* manufacturing
   algorithms and, 85. *See also* AIMEE
   designing, 59–61
   sourcing of, 10, 13–14, 45–59, 175
   testing of, 134
profit margins, 41, 54, 149, 191–92
proof-of-concept test, 91
Prose, 39, 79, 89, 217
Pujji, Jesse, 72–75, 77
Purple Innovation, 79, 147–49

quality vs. value, 12–16, 21
Quartz website, 57
Quiet Logistics, 115–16, 119–21, 126–28
Quip, 79, 168–69, 191–92, 218
quizzes, 69, 75, 79–80, 96, 108–10

Raden, 166, 167, 170, 172–81
radio advertising, 13
Raider, Jeffrey, 18, 30, 33, 218–20
Ralph Lauren, 30, 102
Ravenna Home, 212
"Raw Egg Test" video, 148
Ray-Ban, 30
razors and blades, 1–23, 36–37, 44, 49, 51–52, 77, 79, 102, 134, 212, 218–20
Read, Kaki, 113
Red Ventures, 78
Reformation, 38
Reifsnyder, Liz, 25
Related Companies, 127–28
remnant spots, 160
Restoration Hardware, 194
retail stores
   brand-name goods and, 26
   brick-and-mortar, for DTC start-ups, 104, 150, 182–99
   data and, 85
   partnering with, 165
   structural shift from, 33–34
retention rate, 16, 86, 94–95
Retention Science, 39
returns, 117, 160–61, 164, 178
   free, 101
Reuters, 214
reverse logistics, 116–17

review sites, 146
Revlon, 90
Revly, 212
Rimowa, 172, 177, 180
Ring, 168
Ritual, 25, 39, 217
Rivet, 149, 212
robots, 114–16, 119–26
Rockets of Awesome, 38, 192
Rogers, Christopher, 47
Rollaboard, 171, 179
Rothenberg, Randall, 26–27
Rothy's, 79
Rubio, Jen, 107, 175
Rxbar, 168

Sadow, Bernard, 171
salespeople, 133, 134, 164, 189, 198
same-day delivery, 192
Samsonite, 166, 172, 174
Samsung, 72
sandbox entrepreneurship, 73
Sarig, Yaniv, 200–212, 216
Saturn, 143
Schick, 14, 18, 21
Schultz, Howard, 157
Schwab, Charles, 153, 163, 165
Schwarzkopf, 96
Science Inc., 7–9, 11, 16–17, 21–22, 76
Scuba-Track, 59
Sealy, 136, 218
Sears, Roebuck, 121–22, 128, 130
Sebens, David, 172, 177, 180
Securities and Exchange Commission, 202
Seeking Alpha, 212
Seidenfeld, Justin, 167, 173
selfies, 66, 184–85, 214
Sequoia Capital, 59, 60
Serta Simmons Bedding, 133, 136, 139–45, 148, 150–51, 218, 220
7-Eleven, 13
Sewell, Jenny, 95
Shah, Aniket "Nick," 72–74
shampoo, 39, 79, 89, 95
sheets, 149, 212
Shen, Daniel, 156–57, 159
Shenzhen, China, 202, 211

shipping, 12, 32, 114–31, 136, 192
   free, 101
Shipt, 192
shoes, 39, 42, 79, 183
Shopify, 26, 127
Showfields, 183, 199
showroom start-ups, 183, 192–99
Shyn, 168
Siebrecht, Karl, 128–31
Siegel, Eric, 86
Silicon Alley, 24
silicone hydrogel, 51, 52
Silicon Valley, 9, 25, 59, 71
Sit 'n Sleep, 132, 133
6 River Systems, 127
60 Minutes (TV show), 120
"Sleeper Cell" report, 137–38
Sleepopolis, 145–47
Sleepy's, 137
SmileDirectClub, 155
Snapchat, 9
social media, 18, 29, 68–71, 74–75, 81,
   111, 187
SoHo district, 183, 187–91
"Sold Out" message, 99
Solimo, 212, 220
South by Southwest, 11
South Korea, 12–13
Spector, David, 59–67
Sports Illustrated Kids, 1
sportswear, 39
Stage Fund, 180–81
Staples, 119
Starbucks, 157
Stitch Fix, 87–88, 168, 192
Stone & Beam, 212
Strauss, Levi, 3–4
St.Shine Optical, 45, 54–55, 57
StubHub, 78
subscription model, 6, 8, 10, 12, 15–16,
   20–21, 52, 86, 93, 95–96, 102–3,
   168, 170, 192
Sunglass Hut, 30
Sunrise Alarm Clock, 210
Sun Trust Robinson Humphrey, 215
Super Bowl, 13, 19
supply chain, 18, 46, 107, 116, 123
Sussman, Mike, 125
Sylvia, David, 16, 21

tail locations, 34–35
Taiwan, 53–54, 173
tampons, 42
target audience, 74–75, 78–79, 86, 187,
   203–4
Target stores, 123, 191–92, 198
   Store of the Future, 192
Tarlow, Drew, 55–56
Taylor, Jim, 220
TechCrunch, 160
teeth-whitening products, 206
teledentistry, 155
Tempur-Sealy, 133, 135–36
Thermador, 139
thermostats, 41
ThirdLove, 59, 60–71, 79–83, 88, 191,
   200, 217
Thomson, James, 215
Time, 1, 24, 153, 220
Titan Aeropsace, 203
Today (TV show), 83
Tomorrow Sleep, 144–45, 148–51
Topology, 221
Toyota, 143
Toys "R" Us, 118
transgender models, 83
Traub, Michael, 139–44, 148, 150–51
travel magazine, 175
Travelpro, 171, 179
trucking, 116, 122
TrueDepth camera, 111
Try Before Buying campaign, 66–69, 81
Tucker, Colleen, 105–6
Tudor Investment, 28
Tuft & Needle, 105, 127, 134–41, 144–46,
   148–51, 169, 188–91, 195, 217
TulaCo, 11–12
Tumi, 172, 177
TurtleBot, 125
TV advertising, 18, 71, 77, 80, 82, 160
Twitter, 9, 11, 14, 104

Uber, 78, 130
Udashkin, John, 166–67, 170–76, 178–80
Unbranded, 196
underwear, 42, 193
unicorns, 25, 40, 218
Unilever, 21, 25, 57, 168, 204
University of Phoenix, 73

University of Virginia, 123
Upright Citizens Brigade, 2
UPS, 115, 118–19, 122, 131
USA Today, 15
U.S. Postal Service, 32

Valdez, Arthur, 123
Vanity Fair, 24
Venrock Associates, 14–17, 40–42
venture capital (VC), 7–10, 14–17, 23–28,
    33, 36–39, 41–43, 57, 60–61, 76,
    100, 125, 129, 131, 139, 147, 149,
    151, 154, 157, 160–61, 165, 167–70,
    172, 174, 176, 178–80, 204, 221
  self-financing vs., 169–70
Verge, 171
Versace, 30
vertical retailers, 30
Victoria's Secret, 59, 62, 67, 81–83, 188,
    220
videos, 1–3, 6–8, 10–12, 14–19, 76,
    78–81, 147–48, 187
Viking Global Investors, 170
Virtual Try-On, 32, 108, 110–11
VisionSpring, 30
vitamins, 25, 39, 42, 88, 134, 168, 193, 212
Vive, 130–31
Vogue, 33, 39, 83
Vremi, 201, 203, 210–11, 217

Wag, 212
Wall Street Journal, 22
Walmart, 19, 25, 149, 170
  logistics and, 117, 126
Walmart.com, 204
Walton, Chris, 192
Ware2Go, 131
warbybarker.com, 107
Warby Parker, 9, 18, 25, 32–33, 35–38,
    55, 58–60, 71, 88, 97–100, 103–13,
    137, 166, 169, 175, 183, 190, 195,
    197, 200–201, 214, 217–19, 221–22
warehouses, 37
  automated, 116–27

costs of inventory and, 179
  renting space in, 128–31
  vertical, 122, 128
Warner Bros., 164
watches, 79, 168
webfront stores, 28–29
websites, 1–3, 8–9, 11–12, 14, 26, 29,
    32–33, 85
  similar rival, 168–69
Webvan, 119
Weiss, Emily, 39–40, 101–2, 184, 200
Weldon, Mack, 119–20
Welty, Bruce, 117–21, 124–28
WeWork, 23, 183
whales, 77
Wharton Business School, University
    of Pennsylvania, 30, 31–35, 38,
    44, 55, 60, 72, 75, 97, 99, 101, 190,
    222
white label store brands, 13
Wildcat Capital Management, 55
Wilkinson Sword Co., 13–14, 21
Winc, 88
Winfrey, Oprah, 167, 174, 179
Wired, 179
Witherspoon, Reese, 39
World Series, 13, 56
Wu, David, 154–55, 158, 162

Xtava, 201, 203, 210

Yaney, Maximus, 203
Yelp, 185
YKK zippers, 175
Yolles, Ian, 28, 29
YouGov, 220
YouTube, 8–9, 17, 19, 95–96, 138–39

Zak, Heidi, 59–67, 70, 83, 191
Zappos.com, 30
Zenni Optical, 99–100
zero-sum markets, 41
Zinus, 149
Zuckerberg, Mark, 2

About the Author

LAWRENCE INGRASSIA is a former business and economics editor and deputy managing editor at the *New York Times*, having previously spent twenty-five years at the *Wall Street Journal*, as Boston bureau chief, London bureau chief, money and investing editor, and assistant managing editor. He also served as managing editor of the *Los Angeles Times*. The coverage he directed won five Pulitzer Prizes as well as Gerald Loeb Awards and George Polk Awards. He lives in Los Angeles.